Planning and Paying
Your Way to College

by CLODUS R. SMITH

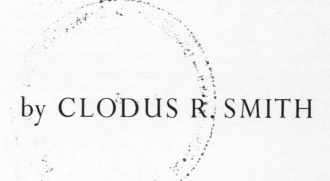

Collier Books, NEW YORK

Collier-Macmillan Ltd., NEW YORK

Grateful acknowledgement is hereby made for permission to reprint the following material:

Summary of the individual admissions policy characterizations given by United States colleges and universities in: Gene R. Hawes, *The New American Guide to Colleges,* Second Edition (New York: The New American Library and Columbia University Press, 1962).

Howard Payne College admissions plans. Reprinted by permission of Guy D. Newman, president, Howard Payne College, Brownwood, Texas.

Excerpts from the 1966–67 University of Maryland Bulletin for University College reprinted by permission of Ray Ehrensberger, dean, University College, University of Maryland, College Park, Maryland.

Excerpts from the University of Missouri General Catalog for 1965–66 by permission of Sam B. Shirky, director, Technical Education Services, University of Missouri, Columbia, Missouri.

Syracuse University Application for Admission and Secondary School Transcript forms reprinted by permission of Lester H. Dye, director, Office of Admissions, Syracuse University, Syracuse, New York.

College Admissions Center student and college transfer registration forms and instruction sheet reprinted by permission of College Admissions Center of the Association of College Admissions Counselors, Evanston, Illinois.

Questions and Answers About College Board Tests reprinted by special permission of Mrs. Shirley Perry of High Point High School, Beltsville, Maryland.

Colorado (statewide) application for admission reprinted by permission of H. Dean Burdick, secretary, Colorado Council on High School-College Relations, Colorado School of Mines, Golden, Colorado.

Montgomery (Maryland) Junior College application for admission reprinted by permission of Bernard Hodinko, dean of students, The Montgomery Junior College, with campuses at Rockville and Takoma Park, Maryland.

Colleges participating in the College Scholarship Service for the 1966–67 academic year; Parents' Confidential Statement (regular and short forms) and instructions and information for parents; Supplement A to be completed by owners of businesses and Supplement B to be completed by farm owners, operators, and tenants. The Parents' Confidential Statement form and material is reproduced with permission from the 1965 edition of the form, published by the College Entrance Examination Board, New York. This form is revised annually by the College Scholarship Service, an activity of the College Entrance Examination Board, and is supplied without cost to high schools for distribution to students who have been advised by colleges or scholarship sponsors to submit the Parents' Confidential Statement. The form may be obtained on request by writing to College Scholarship Service, Box 176, Princeton, New Jersey 08540, or Box 1205, Berkeley, California 94701.

University of Washington Financial Aid Application for entering freshmen reprinted by permission of James F. Bemis, director of student financial aid, University of Washington, Seattle, Washington.

University of Maryland Application for Part-Time Employment reprinted by permission of H. Palmer Hopkins, director, Office of Student Aid, University of Maryland, College Park, Maryland.

Illustration of Insured Tuition Payment Plan is reprinted by permission of Richard C. Knight, Insured Tuition Payment Plan, Boston, Massachusetts.

Sample case study (Norman Olson case) of completed Parents' Confidential Statement from *Manual for Financial Aid Officers,* Appendix A, and Comparison of fifteen state loan plans. Reprinted with permission from the *Manual for Financial Aid Officers,* published in 1967 by the College Entrance Examination Board, New York.

Contents

Illustrations

Foreword

The thesis of this book is that more of today's youth can succeed in college than think they can. It will show that a typical high school student can present a forceful application and be admitted to an accredited institution of higher education.

Just as the world of work demands most of adult energies, and play is the world of children, gaining an education has become the major activity of American youth. Concern for getting into college and earning a degree has become so great that many teen-agers do not have confidence in themselves and question their abilities. The average American youth can achieve far beyond what he thinks his ability is if he plans his effort and follows his plan with discipline. Many students have failed to be admitted to college, not because of their lack of ability or the availability of space in an accredited college, but rather because they did not understand how to take advantage of the opportunities available to them or know how to effectively present their applications to the offices of admissions. There is ample evidence that many can achieve their educational goals if they have a strong desire to do so, plan an effective course of action, and persevere in their efforts.

Many books have been written for the college-bound student of outstanding scholastic ability. Although there is no disagreement with these books, or with the fact that society needs the well-developed talents of our most able persons, it is also a part of the American ideal that each person who can benefit from college should be encouraged to develop his abilities to the fullest extent. It is today's average student who faces frustration in his attempt to be admitted to college, although many colleges do accept students with average scholastic abilities. This book was written for typical teen-agers of average American families who are faced with the problems of planning and paying for college. It is this group of students who will for the most part be served by state colleges and universities, junior and community colleges, and technical training schools. It is for this group that this book was written: the American boys and girls who fill today's high schools and who will improve tomorrow's society after attending college.

Preface

Going to college is an exciting adventure! Going to college is an intellectual endeavor, the learning of new ideas, an adventure of the mind. Going to college is studying with great teachers and leaders and associating with great minds. Going to college is developing yourself mentally, socially, professionally, and economically. Going to college is learning to meet and meeting people from all walks of life, from different cultures, and of different beliefs. College is forming new ideals, making new habits, developing new philosophies, meeting new personalities. College is an ideal place to solidify your aspirations, your way of thinking, your philosophy of life. Whatever the sacrifice, a college education seems to be worth it. However, the potential worth of a college education is only as great as the degree to which your goals and capabilities are in keeping with the general aims of higher education and the purposes of the college you ultimately attend. Colleges offer varied programs. None attempt to be all things for each student. This is why a college may be "right" for one person and "wrong" for another of equal scholastic ability. In the final analysis it is what you put into your studies that determines the value of a college education.

Successful students attend college with a purpose in mind. This purpose often has something to do with a career. "Getting a college degree for the sake of a college degree" is not a very strong reason for going to college. The desire to learn is strongest when a student knows what field he wants to enter. In a professional or vocational sense, education has prime value when applied toward succeeding in a selected career. When college is attended with a future in mind, studies are easier and achievement is higher.

A college education is not a luxury in our society; it is necessary preparation to become a contributing member of it. The primary objective of your higher education is to prepare yourself for the kind of life you want to live.

Chapter One

The College Dilemma

The arrival of a greater number of students on college campuses each fall increases competition among students, increases the pressure on future students and their parents, and challenges the plans and staffs of colleges and universities. The reports about the prestige colleges and universities rejecting five out of seven applications, other selective institutions turning away two out of three, and even some of our large state universities having room for only one-half of the number of students who would like to enter may lead to the erroneous conclusion that there is no place for you at the "educational inn." The facts of the case are that if you are a high school graduate you can go to college. If you go, you can probably succeed if you apply yourself. Although college costs are rising, you can probably afford to go if you explore available sources of financial aid.

It is true that "name" colleges must deny admission to many students who would like to attend them. Competition is keen for a seat in these institutions. It is equally true, however, that space is still available in an accredited college for every high school graduate. It is unfortunate that the myth has arisen that being denied admission to an Ivy League, Big Ten, or Seven Sisters institution indicates that a student is not college material. The idea that all other institutions are second rate is foolish, and the notion that a student not in the top 10 percent of his class can't be admitted to prestige schools is equally untrue. Moreover, highly selective colleges and universities are not the best ones for most students of average ability. They are designed for a particular kind of student. There are dozens of accredited colleges that have seats available for qualified students. Several of these may be equally well suited to satisfy your particular needs. If you are a better-than-average student, there are many institutions that will accept your application.

If you are typical of America's youth, you are probably an average student. Most students are. Now that you are faced with the decision of going to college and enjoying its advantages, or of not going and accepting the consequences, you have a definite problem. You need to know what your chances of being admitted are and what you have to do to improve them.

So you are not in the top 20 percent of your class: does this mean that you can't go to college? What is the average student supposed to do? Doesn't he have a place in the technical and scientific world of tomorrow? Can't he be more than an unskilled laborer? Isn't there some college somewhere that will take the average student? Parents, and some educators, are pointing out that there must remain room for the "middle ground" student, that to eliminate him would be to eliminate future Winston Churchills and Charles Darwins. Many educators feel that too few youths capable of earning a college education continue their studies. Unfortunately, some who can succeed are not encouraged or informed of the possibilities open to them. You can think of other successful persons, perhaps in your hometown, who were near average during their high school days and later "caught fire" in college or in the business world.

If you are an average student who is motivated to work hard in college, you should not be discouraged from applying to college because you fear that your high school studies, your grade average, or your test scores will be viewed unfavorably. Admissions directors know that the best single predictor is your high school grade average and that usually the best combination of predictors is the grade average and your scores on scholastic aptitude tests. But these predictors are limited in ways not yet fully understood by psychologists, admissions counselors, and other personnel interested in why students of average-or-better ability succeed or fail in college. Because prediction for the average student is accurate in only about 40 to 60 percent of the cases, admissions officers study all the available information in making a decision. All of these are factors in the decision to admit or reject you, but no one of them is the deciding factor, because each has only limited value in predicting whether you will or will not succeed in college.

College officials are aware that, at best, admissions policies involve risks and probabilities. Despite the sophisticated techniques, they know better than most laymen and counselors that final judgments are often humble guesses backed by statistics and experience. To be sure, their guesses consider students' high school courses, class rank, test scores, and recommendations. Without doubt these are of outstanding value, but are they enough? In speaking of admissions policies, Louis Benezet, president of Claremont Graduate School and University Center, said: "The judgments have become excruciating, largely because they ask the impossible. Believe me when I say student abilities cannot be so finely predicted at age 17." [1]

That the student of average ability can succeed is shown in figures compiled at the University of Kansas for the classes of 1955 and 1958. Had aptitude tests been used to eliminate applicants in the lower half of the test scores, as is done in many colleges, the loss to the state and nation from the class of 1955 would have been 208 graduates, including forty teachers, twenty-two engineers, seven doctors, seven lawyers, seven pharmacists, five journalists, and ninety-six graduates from the School of Business and the College of Liberal Arts and Sciences. From the class of 1958 the loss would have been sixty teachers, forty engineers, nine pharmacists, seven journalists, six lawyers, four doctors, and more than a hundred graduates in liberal arts and sciences and in business. The dean of the university, in releasing the figures, estimated that in four graduating classes, from 1955 through 1958, more than nine hundred trained graduates would never have been permitted to enroll in the first place had a

cutting score at the fiftieth percentile been used.[2]

Similar research at the University of Wisconsin showed that if admission had been limited to students in the top 30 or 40 percent of their class, approximately 10 to 20 percent of an entire graduating class would have been cut out, including honor students and many heading for occupations with serious manpower shortages. At the University of Toledo, an experiment with "unpromising" students from the bottom third of their class showed that more than half turned out to be normal college students. About a third had no course failures at all.[3]

If you are qualified to enter college, you should seriously consider attending. Deciding whether to go to college is one of the most important decisions that you will make in your life. Deciding to attend college will change the pattern of your life by influencing the kind of work you will do and the type of person you will become. A college education is one of the best kinds of preparation for life, both professionally and culturally. In today's America a premium is placed on creative minds to produce a creative society. Average students become citizens; they become better citizens with a college education.

In general, parents feel quite frustrated about the problem of planning for college, and feel inadequately informed to assist their teen-agers in making decisions about going to college and what they should do when they get there. Planning for college is no small undertaking. Uncertainties, anxieties, concerns, problems, and decisions become your standard "diet" when you begin planning for college. The accuracy of the information you get will influence the decisions you make and will determine how well you solve problems about your future.

When you begin to consider going to college you quickly learn that a number of things are on an increase:

1. Enrollments are increasing at the rate of 10 to 20 percent a year.
2. Entrance requirements are on the rise in an effort to select better qualified students, and to fend off the onslaught of youth eager for a college education.
3. Costs are rising 5 percent a year, and costs are expected to go higher.
4. Academic standards are on the increase in an effort to produce academic excellence.
5. The number of jobs requiring a college degree is increasing each year.
6. The number of concerned parents and students seems to be going up in direct proportion to these increases.

[1] Thomas B. Morgan, "The Class of '68," *Look,* September 22, 1964, p. 33.

[2] George B. Smith, "Who Would Be Eliminated? A Study of Selective Admission to College With an Addendum: The Class of 1958," *Kansas Studies in Education,* December 1956, pp. 1–28.

[3] Sidney Sulkin, *Complete Planning for College* (New York: McGraw-Hill, Inc., 1962).

With the ever-increasing number of students appearing on campuses, policies and standards of admission have also increased out of sheer self-preservation on the part of the colleges and universities. The cost of a college education has risen to take care of part of the selection problem. Parents want their children to get a college education. They have learned to appreciate the value of a college education in providing greater employment opportunities. The cost of education, however, causes parents to be apprehensive about whether their teen-agers should attend college.

As a college-bound teen-ager, you are faced with the frustrating task of selecting a career from an increasing number of alternatives open to you. You must consider your professional career, what course of study to pursue, which colleges offer programs that can prepare you for the career, what high school courses to take to increase your chances of being admitted, when and how to apply, and how best to plan and arrange for paying for college.

Complicating your decision-making is a seemingly endless amount of information and misinformation pointing out the difficulties of gaining admission to college, the courses you need to take in high school, and the high percent of dropouts and failures in college. There is also the pressure of high school counselors, interested teachers, and admissions officers and the not-so-gentle urging and near-frantic insistence of zealous parents. Decisions regarding college have far-reaching effects and too frequently are made under conditions that fall short of ideal because of our having too little of the right kind of information, too much of the wrong kind of information, and because we are hindered by our own ambitions, frustrations, emotions, and preconceived notions.

The stock answer for this problem is to take it to the guidance counselor. Guidance counselors, teachers, and your parents can help you by assisting in securing the information needed to make a choice—such as test results and career opportunities—and by providing mature judgment in helping you to consider all the pertinent facts. If you have a counselor, by all means make the best possible use of him. But for many of you it will be necessary to "go it alone." The U.S. Office of Education reports that only one out of six high schools has a counselor. Even if you are presently attending, or have attended, one of the schools that has a counselor, you may be one of a thousand students placed in his charge. It is obvious that you may have to seek information and make most of the decisions about going to college on your own. It is your future, and most of the decisions about college are yours to make.

College and You

Where else but in college can you "have your cake and eat it too"? Attending college is an enjoyable experience that will enrich your life culturally and socially, as well as financially. Buying professional experience via a college education is a good investment. It is possible that, for each year spent in college, increased earnings accumulated over a professional career of forty years will pay for all college expenses. Few investments pay better dividends, and what you learn can never be taken away. A college education is one of the best kinds of insurance against unemployment. Yet, a college education by itself is not a key to guaranteed success. It can only develop, shape, and mold your potential ability to reap the benefits of living and working in a democratic society.

Without doubt, college admission standards are being raised by many colleges. The publicity this gets usually brings on added concern for interested youth and their parents. If this has been your experience, there is a good chance that much of your concern is unnecessary. Your high school is more capable to prepare you for college than ever before. Also, there is room for every high school graduate interested in attending college. A total of 1,975 institutions were surveyed by the U.S. Office of Education in 1960, of which 1,451 granted degrees. Surely one of these has a place for you. This fact, however, is little reason for not achieving the highest possible marks. Both college applicants and colleges are "graded." A fair student can get in a fair college; a good student can be admitted to a good college; and a better student will be chosen by a selective institution.

Sputnik brought about a clamor for more science and mathematics courses, in particular, and increased academic standards in general. Additional course requirements are being added, and many courses are being updated with new knowledge each year. Increasing entrance requirements and academic standards, the feeling there is no room in college, the fear of not being college material and of risking failure create, rather than lessen, the average student's concern over his chances of success in college.

Not all outstanding high school students go to college, and some not-so-good ones do go. All high school graduates should not attend college, but many more could be successful than is usually thought possible. Many near-average students enroll in college each year, and some succeed. Only slightly more than one-half of the top 10 percent of high school graduates who are encouraged to attend, go to college.

Thinking students look for programs in college that develop cultural understanding and prepare them for professional careers. From your point of view, standards to measure the worth of a college will include accreditation, reputation in the course of study leading to the professional career area you select, requirements for admission and graduation, cost, size, type, and location. Your success in college, and your happiness while there, will depend on making a wise choice. The yardsticks of quality colleges use in selecting students are grades, class rank, test scores, recommendations of the high school, and participation in extracurricular activities. In the simplest terms, students select and apply to colleges they would like to attend, then the colleges select students from the candidates that have made application to them.

Your high school years are a time of preparation for college. High school courses should be selected with an eye to the requirements for entering a particular course in a selected group of colleges. This may or may not include sixteen units of the so-called "solids." How solid a course is will depend on the use you put it to. It is quite possible that you can make equally good or better use of your time in high school in courses other than "solids." Your participation in extracurricular activities may be helpful in being admitted to some colleges, and can open the door to similar participation on the college level after you get there.

It costs a great deal of money to go to college, and college costs continue to rise more than 5 percent a year. It costs about $1,700 a year to attend a state university, and may cost more than twice that amount to attend a privately endowed school. A year's college expenses today is equal to the down payment on a home equal to that from which most students come. By 1970, the cost of a college education will be about the same as the cost of a yacht, from $11,000 to $15,000. Failing to plan to meet college costs is one of the primary reasons that capable students do not attend college.

College is expensive, but there are ways to meet these expenses. You may be surprised to learn of the many sources of financial aid available to interested and qualified students. There are thousands of scholarships available from hundreds of sources. While the average student may not have a good chance of winning a scholarship, he can probably get an educational loan from the federal government, state government, local agencies, and/or other sources. It is still possible to work your way through college at some institutions. This may not be wise in your case, but the chances are good that you can earn a substantial amount of your college expenses. If you are genuinely interested in going to college, can gain admission to an accredited college, and are willing to spend some time and effort exploring the possibilities of financial aid, the chances are good that you can afford to attend college.

Adjustment to college life will require a shift in emphasis for some of you. Attending college is an academic pursuit. Your high school record is the primary factor that gets you into college, but it will be your ability to adjust to college, your initiative, drive, enthusiasm, and perseverance that will keep you there. You can select colleges well and attend one well suited to your needs and interests, but you will be required to prove yourself as a student to remain on campus.

Colleges differ in what they set out to do with and for you, but none aim at making a well-rounded conformist. They want to make you a cooperative individual with initiative, self-directed drive, and purpose, having qualities of leadership, of which knowledge and ability are integral parts. Dr. Robert Hoopes, dean of Michigan State University, stated it well when he said, "We are not interested in producing well-rounded men, but men with sharp, abrasive edges, rebels with clear minds and uncowed consciences, critics of society, not adjusters to it."

A Decade of Records

The demand for a college education is at an all-time high. College and university enrollments reached a new peak in 1965–66 when nearly one-half of the 2,600,000 high school graduates applied for admission to the nation's 2,135 institutions of higher education. A record 1,235,000 freshmen students without prior college experience were admitted. Exceeding the previous year's record enrollment of students by 17 percent, it was the thirteenth consecutive year that enrollment records fell before the tidal wave of students seeking a college education. The total number of students seeking a bachelor or higher degree swelled the college enrollment almost to 5,500,000, breaking all previous records, and more than doubled the 2,469,000 students enrolled ten years earlier. Another 332,400 students attended special terminal programs not leading to a bachelor degree.

Most of the increase has come on the campuses of publicly supported institutions. During the 1950's, public college enrollment increased seven times faster than private college enrollment, probably because private colleges and universities can control their enrollment more easily than can public institutions. Greatest gains in numbers of students have occurred in liberal arts and teachers colleges and universities. From a percentage-increase standpoint, as opposed to the number of students, theological schools and teachers colleges have had the greatest increase during the past fifteen years. In general, the percentage of women students has increased faster than men students during the same period of time.

There appears to be little relief in store for competing students. More students will attend college during the 1960's than during the preceding forty years. A new high will probably be reached by 1970, with 10 to 20 percent more students enrolled each September. Today, two out of five high school graduates attend college, and almost one out of two high school students say they are going to college. This compares with one out of twenty-five in 1900, one out of eight in 1930, and one out of six in 1940.

There has been a shift in the interest and attitude of teen-agers and their parents toward a college education. An increasing number of teen-agers look upon a college degree both as a means to an end — better jobs, more money, and social prestige — and as an end in itself in the form of a richer, fuller life. For a variety of reasons, a greater percentage will continue their education in college. Major reasons for the increased proportion of high school graduates attending college are the increase in the number of employment opportunities that require a college education, the expansion of federal government programs supported by the

National Defense Education Act and the National Science Foundation, and Office of Economic Opportunity programs such as the Work-Study and Upward-Bound that support students from low-income families, and the increase in the sources and amounts of other student aid.

Expected enrollments are based on the historic trend of more college-bound students in each class. However, it is assumed that only 41.2 percent of the pupils who are already in the elementary and secondary schools, and who will be eighteen to twenty-one years of age in 1970, will attend college. Recent predictions on the percentage of high school students who will attend college in 1975 run as high as 65 percent. The projections made by the U.S. Office of Education of population growth and college entrance rates indicate that about 7,950,000 students will attend institutions of higher learning by 1973. And there are more to come: According to the research division of the National Education Association, 43,851,821 children were enrolled in public elementary and secondary schools during the 1966-67 school year.

Your Concerns: Fact or Fantasy?

The question "what about me?" takes into account those of you who decided to go to college late in high school or after graduation, those of you who did not enroll in the college preparatory program or feel that you did not take the right courses in high school, and those of you who are or were average students. Now you want to know about your chances for success in applying for college admission.

The American ideal in education, supported by the land-grant college movement, the National Defense Education Act, the Upward-Bound and other work-study programs, is to provide opportunities in higher education for all individuals capable of benefitting irrespective of the ranks from which they come. The educational policies of the past, based on the presumption that only a small number of persons belong in higher education, are giving way to the American ideal. One only needs to read newspapers, visit a campus, or review the statistics to note the degree to which this past belief has lost its validity. Nor have admissions practices of our institutions reflected the point of view that colleges should be limited to only the intellectually outstanding. Many students who were not fired with enthusiasm for knowledge or who didn't show brilliant scholastic aptitude in their earlier studies have been admitted to college and have earned a degree. Students have been and are still being admitted from all quarters of their high school classes and from nearly all levels of intelligence.[4]

All types of institutions accept students who fall below the published level of acceptance. To substantiate

the hope of the average student, it only needs to be pointed out that average students are admitted to all types of institutions. Although no college has admitted having too many highly qualified students, most colleges do not want all students of one type, and even if they did it would be virtually impossible for them to get such a student body. Yet, it should be remembered that institutions want to admit students who have a good chance of succeeding, and for this reason college admission standards are generally on the rise.

Many, perhaps a majority, of the state colleges and universities admit any graduate of accredited high schools in their respective states. These institutions consider the offering of the opportunity to every high school graduate to earn a college education their responsibility to society. In effect, the result is a self-selection system that places both the initiative and the responsibility for the decision to attend college on the student at the same time that it emphasizes future development of the student's potential rather than his past achievement and test scores. However, fewer land-grant colleges admit all graduates from accredited high schools today then did a decade ago.

More than one-half of the nation's institutions, including outstanding state colleges and universities that use some variation of the open-door policy of admission, recognize that there is hope for students who have not demonstrated outstanding scholastic talent and that they should have the opportunity to prove their merit. Every entering freshman class has a number of students who have not distinguished themselves academically, but who "find themselves" in college and perform outstandingly. Conversely, there are students in every class whose high school record shows they have academic promise but who experience difficulty or failure. Most high school graduates with better than average records will be able to succeed in college if they are highly motivated and apply themselves. They will not have excessive amounts of trouble with most college subjects. Highly motivated students will have little trouble with classes in most state colleges and universities. However, an unmotivated student may have trouble both in a selective institution and at a state college.

Students who have scholastic, financial, or other personal reasons for not attending college full time should consider the possibility of evening college. This is particularly true for the student who finds a new zest for knowledge during his senior year. If he is truly serious about going to college, but finds that time and money are principal obstacles to college attendance, the evening colleges, or colleges of continuing study, may reopen what appeared to be closing doors. Students who earn good grades in courses taken during the evening hours will have a chance to gain admission to a regular day program. In some cases in which evening colleges do not have entrance requirements, a student with an inadequate academic record may attend for college preparatory work leading to full-time college. Without doubt, going to college at night is far better than no college at all.

---

[4] Algo D. Henderson, *Policies and Practices in Higher Education* (New York: Harper & Row, 1960).

Figure 1

GROWTH IN COLLEGE ENROLLMENT

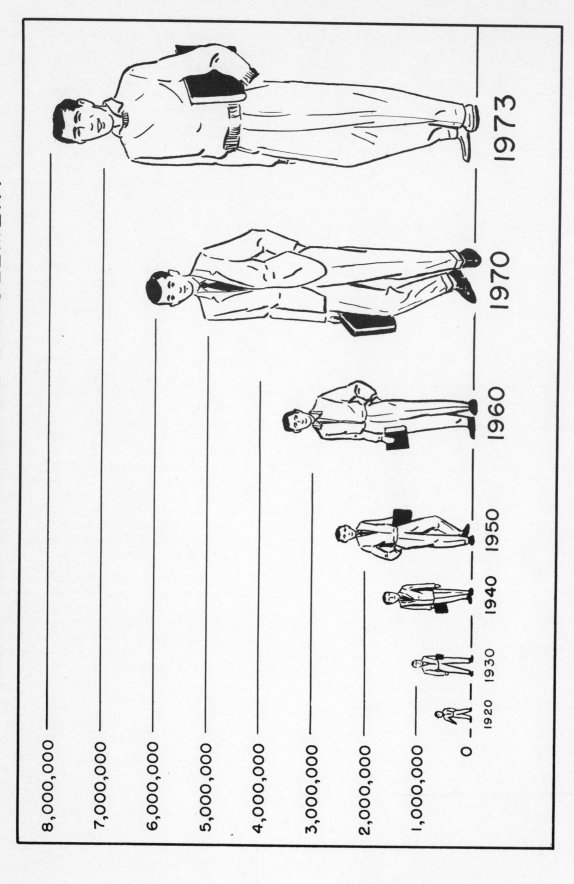

Source of Basic Data: U. S. Office of Education

Maturity deserves special note. As Dean Gardner of the University of Illinois puts it, "Most boys are immature at 18 and some extremely so." [5] He observes that students with poor academic records in college who drop out for one or two semesters and then return usually do better in their studies. The "slow maturers" can usually be spotted when their entrance examination scores are compared with their high school grades. They frequently make better scores on examinations revealing scholastic aptitude than they earn on achievement tests. When this is noted by admissions officers, they consider maturity as a factor and usually react in favor of these students with average high school records. Students who earn high scholastic aptitude scores have a good chance of being admitted, even in selective colleges that are not overcrowded. Most state universities and other publicly supported institutions have policies allowing students who have been in academic difficulty and so were forced to withdraw to re-enter after a stated period of time, usually one year. The lapse of time or experience in the military service, plus the jolt of being dismissed, is sufficient for many students to "find" themselves.

Admissions officers realize that achievement, maturity, and motivation are often related and that academic success is dependent on ability and motivation. For some students, the motivation factor, or the desire to want to learn, changes either because of maturity or changes in life goals. This change affects the achievement level of the student and, in some cases, causes him to succeed in academic areas. Colleges are willing to gamble on some students who have demonstrated through their scholastic aptitude test scores that they have the ability to do college work. They take this gamble simply because they are counting on a change in the student's motivation.

A Solution to the Dilemma

Confusion, misunderstanding, and lack of accurate information are problems compounding the college dilemma. College hopefuls and their parents (because they are so emotionally involved) view admissions procedures as a hazy process, similar to a mysterious ritual, that is foreign to their experience. Many students have been denied college admission, not because of lack of ability to do college work, but rather because they did not know or understand how to take advantage of the opportunities available to them. Identification and analysis of the problems of being admitted to college, and a planned approach for their solution, is one answer to the dilemma.

The best single thought that you can remember about entering the rapidly changing college scene is that the earlier you plan, the better. The earlier in high school you reach the decision to consider going to college, the more time you have to do it. The last two years of your high school record will be reviewed with care. Colleges look most closely for evidence of your scholastic ability. Other things are important, too. You should try to gain valuable experience in extra curricular and leadership activities at school and work experience in your chosen career field.

Planning is the solution to the college dilemma for most students:

- Plan on going to college.
- Plan by reaching the decision as early as possible.
- Plan by sizing up your interests and abilities.
- Plan by tentatively selecting a career field.
- Plan by selecting a group of colleges as possible places for study.
- Plan by taking courses leading to your chosen field of study.
- Plan to earn good grades.
- Plan to get some practical experience in the career area you have tentatively selected.
- Plan how you are to deal with the financing of your college education.

The remaining chapters will provide information that answers questions asked by students interested in going to college. These chapters represent an approach to analyzing the college dilemma as seen through the eyes of high school students. Given at the end of each chapter is a plan designed to serve as a guide in helping you solve that particular problem.

[5] K. E. Gardner, "Too Few Students Finish College," *Illinois Research,* III, No. 4, Agricultural Experiment Station (Urbana: University of Illinois, 1962).

Chapter Two

Meeting College Requirements

If you could believe all that you have read and heard about what you should take in high school to get into college, you would probably enroll only in English, math, and science courses. Many feel these courses prepare students for college more effectively than other courses. On this point, caution is the by-word. There is more to an education and college preparation than a set of specific courses. There has been a good deal of both fact and fantasy on this subject in recent years. It would be very simple if it were possible to say: take two years of math, four years of English, three years of social science, four years of a foreign language, and so on, and this will best prepare you for success in college. If it were such a simple matter to determine which courses contribute most to admission to and completion of college, it would have been done.

Colleges are not satisfied with students' promises and good intentions. They want concrete evidence that you can succeed in college. As colleges and universities become increasingly crowded, they will examine your high school record more carefully. The more selective schools review as many as seven or eight applications for each student admitted. You must prepare the proper kind of evidence to be admitted. Several measures are used to evaluate your scholastic record. Grades in required courses, rank in graduating class, scores on entrance examinations, and other factors are what colleges look for when reviewing applications. These are the factors you must consider when developing your high school program. Any one of these measures may be emphasized more in one college than in another. Your guidance counselor can advise you on which measures are of most value to you in getting into the colleges you are interested in attending.

Your Aptitudes, Interests, and Abilities

Your aptitudes, interests, and abilities are important factors in your preparation for and success in college. Should you attend a college with selective admission standards, all of them may be considered. Your aptitudes, interests, and abilities should be considered so that you may present your best academic achievements, intellectual abilities, and personal qualities to the college you hope to attend. Those that are normally measured by objective tests are discussed in the chapter "Understanding College Entrance Examinations."

Interests and aptitudes have already influenced your life; they will continue to do so. You know that people differ in their aptitudes. You can recognize differences in the abilities and interests of your friends and others around you. Not only are you unlike your brother or sister or classmates in the amount of "mental equipment" you have, but you have different amounts of "brain power" for the various kinds of learning. You may be able to work, or learn to work, rather difficult mathematical problems while your best friend cannot.

Yet most of you will be able to find a place for your talents if time and thought are given to it. This is an area in which your high school counselor can be of valuable service.

Aptitude is the capacity to become proficient in a particular area of learning. You were given aptitude tests in high school that were designed to indicate your potential ability for performance of a certain type of activity in a specialized area. Aptitude indicates the probable degree of successful learning and achievement in a particular field.

No doubt you like some courses more than others because you are interested in what you learn. Your interests are reflected by the things you enjoy doing. The kinds of books you like to read, the hobbies you have, the kinds of experiences you enjoy most reflect your interests. You should be selective in choosing those interests that will help you most effectively prepare for college.

It is important that you choose a curriculum in college that is within the scope of your aptitudes, interests, and abilities. If you are like most students, it is equally important that you choose the "right" career area. Studies show that typical students consider this a part of planning for college. Don't worry too much about a specific job, for it will likely change during your college years. First consideration should be given to the selection of a broad area of interest, an area in which you have some ability or capability of learning, and one in which you would enjoy working. The educational process will broaden your thinking, and you may find new interests and opportunities while you are in college. For example, atomic energy came about while most college students were oriented toward other professions. Chemists and physicists trained for other purposes filled most of the early positions with the Atomic Energy Commission. In the same way, engineers trained to design airliners now work on rockets. Horizons are being pushed back in many fields, and new job requirements are evolving with these developments. Can you really be sure that you want to become a designer of automobile engines? How do you know that gas turbines won't replace them? Or that some other new idea could revolutionize the field? A safe answer is to be an educated engineer who is alert to new possibilities and ready to make necessary adjustments.

Your ability to do "educational work" is of primary importance. Abilities are often reflected in the courses required in high school. It is more accurate to say that required high school courses reflect abilities needed for college. Basically, this is why some courses are referred to as college preparatory courses.

There are other abilities equally important to you individually. The importance of particular abilities will depend on the curriculum and vocation or profession chosen. While ability to use the English language effectively is important to vocations and useful in college courses, it is essential to writers, ministers, teachers, and politicians. Reasoning ability will be important should you desire to become a businessman, army officer, or hold other positions for which judgment is necessary. Mathematical ability is as essential for engineers and space scientists as it is for the businessman and his clerks and accountants.

Are these abilities all that are required? No. Word fluency and an extensive vocabulary are needed by leaders of most publicly oriented professions. Musical aptitudes and abilities are necessary for the musician, and persuasiveness is the "stock in trade" of advertising and sales work. Manual dexterity will be needed by mechanical engineers, but it is equally important to the jet pilot and brain surgeon. Spatial relations, the ability to see the relation of parts to the whole, is an essential ability for the architect and mechanical engineer as well as for the designer of clothes.

There are many abilities associated with performance of certain jobs and vocations. If you have your heart set on a career, you must have an aptitude or capacity for acquiring the necessary skills. Perhaps you may have abilities better suited for another occupational area. Take stock of your abilities and plan accordingly. Seek the advice of your guidance counselor. Take a look at your test results and high school record of achievement. Consider gaining specific extracurricular experiences, such as working on a yearbook or school paper, or seeking opportunities to speak before groups. Since you may have scholastic ability that is not reflected by these measures, further testing may be desirable, particularly tests reflecting native scholastic ability rather than scholastic achievement.

Attending college involves making applications, attending classes, the possibility of failure, and four of the best years of your life. Thus, it is time for absolute honesty with yourself. You must be honest with yourself because any college that receives your application will study your high school record and your test results to determine your abilities for potential success there. The College Entrance Examination Board suggests that your case will be reviewed according to:

1. Your ability to meet the academic demands of a particular program.
2. Industry, willingness to work, determination, perseverance, and persistency — qualities that enable students to work up to their capacity in spite of any obstacles placed in their way.
3. Adaptability, rather than well-roundedness, which enables students to blend into their environment without disturbance; the ability to meet hurdles and disturbing situations.
4. Intellectual curiosity, the ability to get excited about some problem, experiment, line of inquiry, or paper that has been assigned; the desire to read books in seeking additional data and information; and the willingness to ask questions of teachers in an effort to reach decisions.
5. Growability, the ability to grow and develop in intellectual power, self-understanding, and adaptability; growth beyond the student's present level.

Your High School Program and Achievements

High schools in the United States serve all of our youth. To do this, high school subjects provide a common core of knowledge for the potential housewife, mechanic, accountant, newsstand owner, as well as for the potential banker, lawyer, and real estate broker. High school offers general courses that assist everyone in becoming a better citizen. It offers academic courses for future scientists, doctors, college professors, and politicians.

The high school program allows for variation in communities. Programs in high schools meet the differing needs of pupils and the changing desires of parents. Our high schools offer a diversity of subjects that will develop the skills and talents of those who are mechanically minded, mathematically inclined, as well as for those who are academically talented. High school programs in most large high schools are sufficiently flexible to permit a person to elect courses of special interest as well as those required for college.

The factors you should consider when developing your individual high school program are your abilities, interests, and plans, your school's curricula, and the requirements of the colleges to which you plan to apply. Of course, you will want to earn good grades and an acceptable rank in class as well as participate in a planned program of extracurricular activities.

There are several types of curricula offered in American high schools. They may be classified by the kind of programs they offer: trade or vocational curriculum, business or commercial curriculum, college preparatory curriculum, and general academic curriculum. The trade or vocational curriculum provides high school students with an opportunity to take shop subjects and learn specific job skills in addition to acquiring the fundamentals of education. A business or commercial program prepares high school students for a job in business. The general academic curriculum is designed to give a student a broad educational background with the expectation that he will have an opportunity to later specialize in the occupation of his choice, or in college. The college preparatory program includes subjects such as English, math, science, social studies, and foreign language.

Selecting Your High School Program

A well-planned high school program is the primary means by which you can aid your efforts to be admitted to the college of your choice. So you will want to select a curriculum and courses purposefully. These commitments often are made before students and parents are really prepared to make them. When a student elects a curriculum in high school, he may be limiting himself in terms of furthering his education or entering occupations he may be able to follow. But the fact that you have enrolled in a specific curriculum need not hamper you too much in selecting new career choices or new purposes in life. Yet, it is true that the more advanced you become in high school, the less opportunity you have for taking courses outside of the curriculum.

Therefore, identify your vocational interest and its relation to college study at an early date. The longer you wait to decide, the less opportunity you have to prepare for college. The selection of a high school program is ordinarily made at the end of junior high school and at the beginning of senior high school. One of the most important reasons for an early decision is to provide ample time for a suitable program to be initiated. The student who gets to the college doors "first with the most" of what a college wants is the one most likely to be admitted. Some students present too few requirements because they decided too late to take what was recommended. This is a good reason to have specific plans if you are a junior in high school.

The high school program should prepare you for college in the field you plan to study. This does not mean that you necessarily should enroll in the courses suggested for the standard college preparatory curriculum found in many of our larger high schools. There is no "best" program for college-bound students. Choose one that challenges you and that you can master. It may be desirable to take vocational elective subjects, depending on your particular interest, chosen vocation, and the college or university you hope to attend. Also, you may find it desirable to elect courses in art, music, and other cultural-development courses.

No doubt it would alleviate the worry of many high school students and the concern of parents if it could be said: if you take these courses, you can succeed in college. Much of the information appearing in popular magazines leads to this conclusion. Some writers have said that most colleges recommend satisfactory work in sixteen units of the "solids." You can be misled on this point. A careful review of courses listed in several college catalogs will convince you otherwise. Research conducted by professional educators, who face the problem with each new group of college freshmen, cannot substantiate this as being fact. One reason is that "solids" are not always good predictors of college success. If colleges and universities could find a set of courses that would best prepare students for academic success, be assured that they would do so. The purpose of college admission requirements is not merely to determine a student's capacity to achieve academic success in college. There are several other factors to be considered.

Admission requirements at selective private schools are used to choose a uniform student body for their desired purposes. Certain requirements are thought to be of general cultural value. Other requirements are based on the assumption that they require greater scholastic ability and therefore must discriminate against students who may have greater difficulty in college achievement. Harvard wants a sound program with high over-all quality, and M.I.T. does not restrict seven and one-half units of electives. State colleges and junior colleges want their share of "A" and "B" students. In fact, all institutions want to attract outstanding students, but, logically, students planning to attend less selective institutions should have more freedom in choosing their high school courses.

College admissions officers know there are too many variations in students, teachers, courses, and programs to be certain that what is taken will be of equal value to students. Some colleges require students to submit rather specific courses, and others are quite flexible in these requirements. In either case, your record will be reviewed carefully. Generally, the more academic subjects you present with acceptable grades, the more favorably your application will be reviewed. Advanced courses in mathematics, science, and languages are offered to prepare you for college courses in the same or related subjects.

The surest way to plan for college is to obtain and study college catalogs carefully (see chapter IV) and to develop a program according to the requirements. These will vary with the type of institution you select. Although the requirements for college vary, by listing the specific requirements for the colleges you have selected, you will find several courses common to each college's standards. Usually, there are a sufficient number of courses keyed to the requirements of three to five colleges for you to include several electives that are of special interest. It is usually better to choose an academic over a nonacademic course and a college preparatory over a general section. Also, unusual recommended courses may be elected after required courses are taken or planned.

English is the most important high school course you study for college preparation. There is a higher correlation between the number of English courses taken and the grades made in them and academic success in college than there is in any other subject taken in high school. Mastery of the English language — reading skill and comprehension, as well as vocabulary and English usage — is necessary for high achievement in college. If you are an average student, the key to being admitted to college and succeeding after you get there may depend on your willingness and effort in a remedial program. Your guidance counselor and teachers, particularly your English teacher, can help you plan a program that will sharpen your reading, writing, and spelling skills. They will ask you to do drills in spelling, syntax, and grammar. They will want you to read a variety of material to increase your reading skill and your comprehension of what you read. They will have you write, rewrite, and write again. They will insist that you know why you use words as you do. Just using them will not be enough to succeed in college.

What can you do to improve in this area while you are still in high school? First of all, take renewed interest in your English courses. The next suggestion is to read a variety of material — fiction, poetry, philosophy, history, magazines. Read widely, but above all, read!

The scope of your studies will normally be limited by the scope of your school's offerings. Not all schools offer recommended courses such as foreign languages. Few students have the resources or make the effort to take courses outside their regular high school. Students attending large high schools usually have the best opportunity to develop a broad academic background. The responsibility of knowing what courses are available and for making the greatest possible use of them rests with you.

What About Foreign Languages?   Why take a foreign language in high school? The political and economic role of the United States has tended to clarify the importance of foreign languages in our high schools. It is doubtful that the English-speaking nations can require all other nations to speak English to trade or communicate with them. Leaders of tomorrow will have to learn to communicate with others in their languages. It seems almost certain that proficiency in a foreign language will be a valuable asset to have in your professional tool kit. Many suggest that it will be of value to our nation, as well as for our leaders of the future, to be able to speak more than one language. With jet travel, foreigners and natives have more contact than ever before, and this trend will continue. It is not possible to predict in which country you will be living ten or twenty years from now.

The study of a foreign language has been thought to yield general cultural value that gives students a broad outlook on life. There was a time when having studied a foreign language was the difference between the educated elite and the educated. Languages were treated as a subject for the "better students." In keeping with the ideals of our present-day schools, every student with aptitude for the study of foreign languages should have an opportunity to study them. When average students study foreign languages, they usually succeed in relation to their desire and effort.

The U.S. Office of Education reports in "Modern Foreign Language — A Counselor's Guide" that the number of institutions requiring and recommending foreign languages is increasing. In Pennsylvania, reports from fifty-three institutions offering the B.A. degree showed that forty of them require a foreign language for entrance and that fifty-one have a requirement for graduation. Coe College, Hood College, Yankton College, Rice Institute, Southern Methodist University, and Texas Christian University are among the institutions that have recently strengthened their foreign language degree requirements.

The important question is: will a high school foreign language course help you get into and complete college? There are two considerations. First, if what you learn in a course is necessary to the career you plan to enter, you should take it. Equally important to college-bound students is the consideration of college entrance requirements. If a college or university recommends a foreign language, or if the college you hope to attend is highly selective, take it.

What About Vocational Courses?   The value of vocational courses for students who plan to attend college is a subject of controversy in higher education. The usual recommendation for such students is to spend their time on academic rather than vocational courses. Although admission requirements indicate that students who elect vocational subjects may be at a disadvantage on being admitted, these courses are not an obstacle to their academic success.

The purpose of taking vocational and technical courses is not usually to prepare for college. In the defense of courses that are not college preparatory, many students who have begun a vocational curriculum have become interested in professional opportunities that require a college education. For some, these vocational courses were the most important factor in stimulating their interest in going to college to pursue a professional career in areas related to the vocational areas studied earlier.

Many students presently enrolled in vocational and general courses may be considering college. If you are one of these, you may find yourself in the position that Billy C. was in when a college dean visited his high school on a "career day" visit.

Billy C., an above-average student, was concerned about his chances of being admitted to the state university because he was enrolled in a vocational curriculum. He was a junior and had recently decided to enter the university, following graduation, to become an industrial arts teacher. Through contact with his shop teacher, whom he admired, he had become interested in teaching as a career. Although he had an obvious aptitude for work with his hands, he was only slightly above average in the academic subjects he had taken. Now that he was interested in attending college, Billy felt that he would have difficulty passing the required English and science courses at the university because he had taken vocational subjects. His greatest concern was that college courses would be too difficult for him. However, he knew that he would not be interested in college had it not been for his experience in the vocational course.

There are implications in Billy's plight that reflect the concern of many typical students who are enrolled in vocational courses in high school. Are the assumptions underlying these implications true? Does the election of vocational courses in high school lessen a student's chances for completion of English and science courses in college?

Vocational courses do not contribute to college failure. Many research studies agree that vocational courses make a contribution to college work equal to that of other courses. If Billy fails to succeed in college English and science courses, it will not be because he has taken vocational courses in high school. It will probably be due to the quality of English,

mathematics, and science taken in high school. Too often, perhaps, students in vocational courses are placed in sections of English and science other than those designed to prepare students for college work.

Vocational courses may help prepare a person for college in the event that the student plans to enroll in a related field in college. For example, mechanical drawing would be a good course to take in preparing to be a mechanical engineer. Yet, in many high schools, mechanical drawing may be offered only in a vocational curriculum. Placement of students in various curricula in high school is an efficiency plan in the operation of a school. It is up to the student and his parents to perceive when to cross the line between vocational and academic subjects in an effort to best prepare for college study in the field he plans to enter.

High school students can solve this problem by seeking vocational and educational guidance from counselors and teachers in the courses related to those in which they plan to enroll in college. This should be done early in the high school program. If you reach the decision to study a college field related to a vocational course, you should request to be placed in college preparatory English, math, and science courses. You will not be doing yourself a favor by enrolling in "easy" courses.

Here is a high school program that will provide the recommended courses to meet requirements for admission to liberal arts colleges, selective entrance institutions, and state universities.

Units	Subjects	Units	Subjects
1	Social Sciences	4	English
4	Foreign Languages	3	Mathematics
3	Electives	1	Natural Sciences

But suppose that you are an engineering prospect. Using the same information, a program can be developed that meets the recommendations of the Universities of California, University of Pennsylvania, M.I.T., and state universities.

Units	Subjects	Units	Subjects
4	English	2	Social Sciences
2	Algebra	2	Physics and Physical Sciences
1	Geometry		
2	Foreign Languages	½	Trigonometry
		2½	Electives

For the purpose of further clarifying the procedure, two programs are presented. One program is for those students choosing foreign languages, and one is for those electing courses other than foreign languages. We will assume that other requirements are the same.

A high school program leading to college admission with a foreign language required or recommended should include four years of study in one language. In this way, study will continue through the twelfth grade and is aimed toward mastery of a single language rather than exposure to two or more languages.

Courses Required for an Academic High School Diploma

Units	Subjects	Units	Subjects
4	English	1	Natural Science
4	Foreign Language	1	Social Sciences
3	Mathematics	3	Electives

With only slight modification, in mathematics and physical and social science areas, it will meet the requirements for the college of engineering also.

The general academic program may use the additional units freed by omitting language for mathematics, science courses, or for courses of special interest to you. Such courses may include vocational or technical studies, or other courses of value to you in your chosen career.

Courses Required for a General Academic Diploma

Units	Subjects	Units	Subjects
4	English	2	Social Sciences
2	Mathematics	6	Electives
2	Natural Sciences		

There is room for flexibility in this program. Write for the list of required and recommended courses at the college you hope to attend. Make a composite list. See where you stand. Do it now, while you have time for changes, if you are still in high school.

Let's plan a program starting from where you are.

Step 1. List all the courses you have had or in which you are now enrolled.

_____ _____
_____ _____
_____ _____
_____ _____

Step 2. List courses required for high school graduation.

_____ _____
_____ _____
_____ _____
_____ _____

Step 3. Make a composite list of the courses required for admission at the colleges and universities you would like to attend. Omit the courses you have listed in step 1.

_____ _____
_____ _____
_____ _____
_____ _____

Step 4. List the courses in which you have a special interest or ability that you would like to take in high school.

_____ _____
_____ _____
_____ _____
_____ _____

With the information gained from the above process, you can now plan your high school program to meet the admission requirements in the college that you hope to attend. The steps are listed in the order of suggested priority. Step 1 is what you have to work with at the present time. If you are a senior, you have less opportunity and flexibility in your program to take courses of special interest. Courses you list in step 3 must necessarily be given priority over courses listed in step 4 if college admission is your aim.

High School Grades: Are They Important?

There should be no misunderstanding about it: selective institutions use grades as a basic tool for determining whether you will be admitted or rejected. Most colleges, even ones with open-door policies, use high school grades as the first consideration in determining students' probable success in colleges. Grades are important.

To the extent that all those who take a course cannot excel, grades are competitive. Grades are used for the selection of people for future careers, for the professions, for skilled labor positions, for semiskilled, and unskilled work. Society demands that the educational system perform this function. It is a part of our value system that the better trained, the academically able students in high school, should have first choice of colleges. The use of grades is a built-in mechanism to see that this happens. You don't have to make all "A's," but "C's" won't be too impressive to selection committees.

Grades are of more value in gaining entrance to college than having had specific courses, although you will want to have the basic courses required by the institution that you plan to attend. There are two reasons why grades are of more value than high school courses in gaining admission. In the first place, grades show how you "stack up" against others in meeting the standards for a class. They show evidence of your academic achievement and ability. Secondly, your grades indicate how well you are motivated to do scholastic work. Naturally, colleges and universities are looking for students with the greatest chance of success. The better your grades, the better your chances are for gaining admission to the college of your choice.

You should understand, however, that grades from different high schools have different values. In one school in a suburban area in the East, roughly 80 percent of the graduates go to college. In this school, competition for good grades is high. Classes are highly competitive for college-bound students, and they are aware of the pressures of getting into a desirable college. By contrast, in some schools only 10 or 15 percent of each graduating class plan to go to college. The academic atmosphere is not likely to be as competitive in the second school as in the first. Three-fourths of the class are not competing with those planning to attend college, and elements of challenge are missing for the limited number that hope to attend college.

Grades in different courses have different values for you, too. Grades in "solids" carry more weight than grades in elective courses. This is true whether the grades are good or poor. An average grade in a solid course and an "A" in an elective course will indicate to a college admissions officer that you may be an average student with an outstanding aptitude for a specific field of study. Your chances of being admitted may depend on the curriculum that you are planning to take in college and the course you elect in high school. The value of a course is partially determined by the use you make of it. For example, grades in industrial arts in high school may be of weight equal to grades in a solid if you plan to become a high school teacher of industrial arts upon graduation from college.

One thing you should remember is that all of your grades are used to determine your grade point average and your rank in class. Do not say, "This is an elective, so it does not matter." It may very well matter if it pulls your grade point average down. To an admissions officer, this may say something about your maturity, purposefulness, and perseverance. When you elect a course, you have exercised a free choice to study something of value and interest to you. The selection carries with it an obligation. Your interest and purposefulness are factors that can be of immeasurable value to you.

All is not lost, however, if you have not responded to the increased competitive spirit. Many state universities have policies that make it difficult for them not to admit in-state high school graduates with nominal qualifications. But this is no reason for taking the matter of grades lightly. They do not have to keep you long. Some state colleges and universities are just as "tough" to stay in as the more selective private schools. The "flunk-out" rate is higher in state universities and in city colleges where "anyone can get in" than it is in more selective institutions.

Publicly supported institutions are dedicated to the cause of creating every opportunity for you to develop your abilities to the fullest potential, but they are also trying to build a desirable reputation to attract better students. This reputation must be built on quality — quality of instruction, quality of work carried out at the institution, and the quality and performance of their graduates. These measures of quality are most often reflected in academic standards.

In some schools concerned with preparing students specifically for college, students secure an evaluation of their work periodically. Approximately once each month students are asked, or permitted, to have a "progress report" completed by teachers. Usually these are returned to the counselor. After evaluating the progress reports the counselor has more information, more evidence, to use when counseling the students.

If your school does not follow such a program, you may still have the benefit of a progress report on how well you are progressing toward satisfactory achievement. The following progress report was prepared for use by teachers and counselors, but will serve as a guide should you want to initiate the use of such a report.

Progress Report

Student's Name_____ Section_____ Return by_____
Subject_____ Teacher_____
Please comment on any of the following items so we may see how this student is doing at this time:
Homework _____
Classwork _____
Attitude _____
Participation _____
Tests and Quizzes (list letter grades) _____
Conduct _____
Comment _____
Return this form to Miss Doe, Guidance Counselor

There are other forms that may be used to find out how well you are progressing. The "student check list" is a teacher evaluation of how well a student is doing in relation to other class members and how well he could do in the opinion of the teacher. Such a check list is of value in getting teachers to offer suggestions for improvement. You can prepare a form similar to the one shown below to fit your individual purpose.

STUDENT CHECK LIST

Name_____ Date_____ Subject_____ Section_____

| | | | Above | Excel- | |
Poor	Fair	Average	Average	lent	Comments
Homework					
Classwork					
Grades					
Tests					
Quizzes					
Attitude					
Behavior					

Grades in high school should show consistent improvement, particularly during the last two years. Identify areas of weakness and work toward improvement. Getting into college may be an end for high school students, but getting the best job in your chosen vocation or profession is an end sought by many college students. Persons who succeed in college will get the best jobs. Continually improve your grades and study habits while you are in high school. Your effort will pay handsome dividends in college!

Class Rank: What Does It Mean?

In an effort to select students with a good chance for academic success, colleges and universities look deeper than grades. They look at your standing in comparison with other students in your school. What was your rank in your graduating class? The answer to this question concerns you because it is important to the office of admissions at the college you are seeking to attend. Your high school rank is a part of your scholastic record in high school.

Class rank is a relative score. It compares your academic achievement with others in your graduating class. For example, class rank in the seventieth percentile means that you have succeeded better than 70 percent of those in your class. Class rank is a more meaningful indicator of relative achievement than grades in courses or grade averages, and college admissions officers have learned that rank in the high school graduating class is one of the more reliable measures used in deciding the probable success of students. Because of their confidence in it, class rank is being used by an increasing number of colleges as a basic tool to determine those who are risks. It does not, however, show either your strong points or your weak areas of study. It shows how well you fared in all courses taken with other students, regardless of what courses they took within the same curriculum.

About one-half of the students who graduate in the upper 50 percent of their high school graduating classes continue their education in college on a full-time basis. Of this group, about three out of four will receive a degree. Let's take a total graduating class in America and see how high school standing related to college graduation. The following information is from the U.S. Office of Education.

High School Rank	College Graduates per 1000 High School Graduates
Top tenth	406
2nd tenth	332
3rd tenth	169
4th tenth	162
5th tenth	92
6th tenth	70
7th tenth	40
8th tenth	31
9th tenth	13
Lowest	7

Another way to look at it is to consider all students graduating from high school in the same year who continued their education in the fall semester. About 32 percent of the graduates in the nation that year entered college in the fall. Another 11 percent continued on a part-time basis. In a comparison of the students in the upper half of the class with all the students, 50 percent of those in the upper half continued their education on a full-time basis and 16 percent did so on a part-time basis.

In considering your rank, college admissions officers realize that the grades you make in high school are dependent on the quality of your high school. Likewise, the rank you achieve is dependent on the school's standards. All high schools do not have the same standards or send an equal percentage of students to college. Therefore, your rank is not necessarily of equal value to the same rank of a person from another school. Your standing in a class from a school that traditionally sends 75 percent of its graduates to college is likely to be viewed more favorably than a similar rank of a student graduating from a school that only sends 20 percent of its students to college. Admissions personnel, who review thousands of applications each year, recognize that some schools offer better college preparation than others.

Rank in high school is just one measure of your ability; it is not foolproof. If your rank is high, don't be overelated. If it is lower than you think it should be, don't be too dejected. If a student is in the upper one-fourth of the class, his chances of being admitted to most colleges are excellent. Chances for success in college are also good. A rank falling in the third or fourth quarter will be viewed as a risk by admissions officers in selective institutions. Students who graduate in the top half of their graduating class have a good chance of completing college. But remember, the more selective the institution is, the higher the marks you need; therefore, the higher your rank is, the greater are your chances of being admitted, according to studies made in this field.

How should you rank? The safest answer is at the head of the class, but this will sound a bit "ivory towered" to most typical students. It is a good goal, though. In general, you should be in the top 25 percent of your graduating class to be a good prospect for a selective or semiselective college. It is true that institutions having open-door policies will admit you with a lower rank, some regardless of your rank. Staying in college may be another matter. You will need to be in the top half of your class if you are to maintain the pace in most accredited colleges. Most of you will not attend a highly selective institution, but there is a place for you in one of the many other good, accredited institutions. A rank in the third quarter will not keep you out of college if your high school record shows improvement in the last two years, particularly if the improvement is in the areas of English and mathematics.

The Value of Extracurricular Activities

The extracurricular activities you participate in are part of your high school record reviewed for college admission. You should consider these activities when preparing for college. Participation in extracurricular activities demonstrates an active, inquiring mind and can support and further develop interests and abilities that contribute to college admission. However, scholastic achievement and academic potential are given priority by admissions officers.

Colleges know there is more to education and learning than books and classes. Grades and class rank do not necessarily reflect leadership qualities, interests in areas other than courses, and nonscholastic aptitudes. Extracurricular activities add depth and breadth to students' intellectual, social, and physical experiences. Your record of participation in these activities provides admissions officers with an insight into qualities of your personality not otherwise shown on your application.

Most institutions prefer a well-rounded student body, but they also want to have students with individuality. Selective colleges are interested in having a cosmopolitan student group and will admit students of modest ability if their extracurricular records are outstanding. They recognize the contribution of learning experiences gained through participation in a wide range of extracurricular activities. Students exercise free choice in the selection of extracurricular activities, which indicates to admissions officers their interest and, to a degree, their aptitude for the field in which the activity is associated. Their record will be an indication of their motivation and drive in these activities. These activities are a measure of students' interests and special talents, which add to the environment of the college campus they attend.

Most high schools have a comprehensive extracurricular program to meet the interests and needs of all their students. Consider activities that have meaning to you. Make full use of those that contribute to your social and intellectual development. You should be selective in choosing from the many worthwhile activities, but do not choose too many. Your studies come first. Unless you have outstanding ability in an activity in demand by colleges, you should not sacrifice grades for extracurricular activities. It is better to achieve satisfaction and excel in a few activities than to be a "joiner." The number you choose should be determined by the amount of time you can give them.

Major and minor sports, drama, art, music, special-interest clubs, and school publications have their value in producing social and intellectual growth. Debating, leadership activities, religious programs, and experience in summer camps may be of equal value. In choosing activities, consider the interests and qualities you do not have that may be needed in your chosen field and helpful in college admission. There are few better opportunities to develop interests than in the school's planned extracurricular program.

A Planned College Admissions Program

Your high school record is the single most important factor received by the admissions offices. It is what you can do, as evidenced by what you have done on an everyday basis in your academic studies. Start with a strong, sincere desire to go to college. Stick with your conviction that there will be a place for you in college if you prepare while in high school. Plan a broad program, including recommended and required courses for the curriculum you will take in college. Enroll in high school electives in which you have an interest, and for which you have an aptitude. Include four years of college preparatory English.

In planning for college, you must meet two standards. Your high school offers you practical and cultural education as well as preparation for college. Courses required for high school graduation and those recommended for college admission are not necessarily the same, but a common ground can usually be reached in planning your high school program. Your objective is to. meet college requirements and recommendations. To do so you must choose certain courses in addition to the basic courses in high school. You can elect courses that are recommended by several institutions if they all interest you for the same reason. For example, if you plan to become a chemist you cannot expect recommendations to be the same for all institutions, because they do not serve the same purposes or enjoy equal reputations.

It has been plain from the start that no one set of courses meets the needs of all college-bound students. There is only one safe decision that will get you into college: take those courses required by the college you plan to attend and earn the best possible grades. Only in a systematic manner can you plan a program to assure college admittance. Cooperate with your guidance counselor, but don't leave all the planning up to him. You have more at stake than anyone else. It is your future.

High school counselors stress the importance of students planning to meet specific admissions standards. The following statement of a counselor in an average-size Iowa high school denotes the anxiety, concerns, and apprehensions of students during the period of planning and applying for college.

Mike S., a rural student of average scholastic ability and having ambition and desire to go to college, is typical of many students who hope to attend college. Mike's family has an average income. Mike received encouragement from his parents during his elementary school years, which is so necessary for a future decision regarding college. Mike, like others, has taken the achievement, aptitude and interest tests and inventories throughout his school program to help determine his scholastic status and potential. The results showed him to be average or slightly above. He has a weakness in English and some strength in science and math. He was above 70 percent of his class. He was urged, as most students are, to take a foreign language, but he felt that a language was not necessary for him.

Mike had vocational plans typical of ninth and tenth grade students. He developed interest in first one area and then another; for example, veterinary medicine, and engineering. In his junior year Mike found it more difficult to decide on a career as he became aware of the greater choice of subjects in the school curriculum. Concern for better grades, the demand to do better in subject matter, and the urging of his family to work toward the top of the class now had its affect on Mike. For the first time the need to earn high grades and test scores became quite real, a compulsion.

Mike struggled under the need to do well on the Preliminary Scholastic Aptitude Test and the qualifying scholarship test during his junior year. His standard scores on the PSAT were 38 verbal and 49 mathematics, which placed him at the 70th and 82nd percentiles respectively on national norms. On the National Merit his standard scores and placement norms were: English usage, 24 (92nd percentile); math usage, 23 (86th percentile); social studies reading, 21 (73rd percentile); natural science reading 21 (73rd percentile); and word usage, 16 (44th percentile).

It was necessary to help Mike see himself as an average student in relation to others he would compete with, especially in his freshman year at college. Additional courses in math, science, and especially in English were discussed, which would give additional background and ease in the competitive pressure at college. Informative tools included interpreting Mike's test scores in ranges rather than absolute scores, and comparing entering college freshmen profile scores with those of Mike's: his grade average of 3.42 out of 4.00 and rank in class of 5th out of 76, as well as other factors of college success. As the test results were interpreted, Mike seemed both elated and deflated when he compared his scores with those of students with similar plans. It was in these sessions that he changed his plans and decided to begin career planning for a science teacher.

Mike showed apprehensive attitudes toward "career night" and "college day," when he had to decide which group he should meet with or which representative he should visit. He would have liked to attend all sessions of the sophomore career night, when occupational information was given by successful representatives of various working fields. Mike's choice of sessions were veterinary medicine, teaching, and engineering. Topics covered by the speakers were the nature of the occupation, the training needed, qualifications and advancement, employment, future job outlook, expected earnings and working conditions, and fringe benefits. These sessions gave Mike insight into career possibilities in relation to courses needed to reach the various occupational goals.

"College day" programs provided Mike with an opportunity to question representatives of the colleges in which he was especially interested and to gain additional firsthand information with which to narrow his choice of prospective schools. Here, choice revolved about availability of the programs of study in which he was interested, costs, course requirements, housing, scholarship, and loans. Later, actual visits would be made to the campuses of his choice.

During the demanding period of making a choice, Mike was assisted by his parents and by the individual attention given him by his teachers, counselor, and principal. The interpretation of his rank in class and the test results seemed to relieve him of his tension and give him the self-confidence in considering career and college alternatives.

Mike's period of decision and choice stretched over several school years and was a necessary preliminary to attending college. In his senior year he had required courses to complete and he used his elective units to enroll in additional courses in English and an extra course in math and science with other college preparatory students. He took the required Scholastic Aptitude Test of the College Entrance Examination Board and tried to do his very best, especially in order to show scholastic promise and to qualify for scholarship and loan programs. His high school credits met the minimum admission requirements of the colleges in which he was interested, and he now narrowed his choice of schools and visited the campuses. In some cases, he had scheduled interviews with the admissions and financial aid offices. Mike was careful to learn well in advance what was needed and to follow exactly the detailed admissions procedures in obtaining, filling out, and returning applications for admission and housing. He also completed an application for a scholarship. He arranged to have transcripts of credits, college entrance examination scores, and letters of recommendation from the principal and guidance officers sent to the colleges. He sent necessary matriculation fees and room deposits before any notification of acceptance. It may mean applying for summer employment to supplement Mike's savings for college.

For Mike, the preparation was accomplished, but the period of waiting had just begun. For his future was indefinite; he must await the decision of the colleges. Again his emotions were in a turmoil, and at the back of his mind he was continually asking himself, "Am I doing the right thing?"

In March, after weeks of impatient waiting, Mike finally received a letter from the admissions office at the state university affirming his acceptance.

It is apparent that college-bound students should do certain things to get the most out of their high school education. The following is a suggested guide that will help you choose the right high school courses.

1. Plan your high school program early. Time is golden. The earlier you plan, the greater will be your opportunity to take courses required and recommended by the college you hope to attend.
2. Review the catalogs from the colleges you hope to attend. Prepare a list of courses required for admission to each of the institutions. There will be several duplications. Most of the courses required by publicly supported state colleges will be required for high school graduation also.

3. Prepare a list of courses required for high school graduation. Your student handbook will provide this information. This list can be secured from the guidance counselor's or principal's office.

4. Select courses in high school that develop understandings and abilities that will be of value in college courses you plan to take. Many of these will be required in high school.

5. Continue to take courses within your vocational interest. Research does not indicate these courses to be hindrances, and in many instances they may prove to be of value in your career. The fact that you are taking a course in which you are genuinely interested usually means that you will apply yourself more and, therefore, will derive more value from it.

6. Plan a well-integrated, balanced but flexible program. Elect as many courses as you can adequately handle. Include courses of special interest and cultural value. Your high school education is your foundation for future educational and cultural development.

7. Plan your program into a time sequence study schedule for the remaining years in high school, including those courses required for both high school graduation and college admission. Take college preparatory sections when available. This is especially important in the case of English, math, and sciences. This is your blueprint for college admission.

8. Plan and participate in extracurricular activities that will contribute to your program.

By following this procedure you should be able to plan a program that will meet the requirements and recommendations of all the colleges you are considering. Now that you know the courses you must take, your task is to make your grades and class rank good enough to keep the door to the college of your choice open to you. Strive for excellence and it will pay off. If you are typical, you can do much better than you think.

Chapter Three

Which College Should I Attend?

Two things are important in selecting a college: your needs and abilities, and your pocketbook. You are more important than money. That's what makes choosing a college a very serious business. The one you choose will have an effect on your personality, your potential success in the career world you choose, and your future. It is not a question to be solved by the simple process of elimination, either. There are many colleges — more than two thousand in fact, and new ones are being formed. Your choice will come from institutions of varying sizes, programs, locations, and admission requirements.

The variety of colleges and universities in the United States is far greater than in any other country of the world. The admission requirements of any two colleges or universities are not exactly alike. Some offer only one field of study, some offer other fields of study, and still others offer several fields of study. Some colleges are traditional, some are reserved and dignified, and some are progressive. Some are accredited, and some are not. Some are large; some are small. All of these differences create a perplexing situation for prospective college students and their parents that makes choosing a college more difficult.

You have developed some kind of an impression or opinion of colleges and college life. Probably you think of "name" colleges first, even if you don't plan to go there. The prestige colleges, such as Columbia and Cornell, Harvard and Haverford, M.I.T. and Mount Holyoke, Stanford and Swarthmore, have served a useful purpose by creating in the minds of parents and college-bound students an image of "ideal" colleges and universities. They have given many undecided students a target at which to aim. For some this image of perfection, this goal in life, may have meant the difference between attending or not attending college, even though they attended a state college much closer to home. However, each year many times the number of students attending "name" colleges attend state-supported institutions that are operated according to the belief that each American boy and girl should be given an opportunity to get all the education he or she can.

Sizing Up Admissions Standards

Only a small percentage of our institutions have really "tough" policies. Some colleges, well known and well respected, are dedicated to the idea that average students should have the right to enter. To put it another way, these colleges have a "right to fail" policy. You may have the right to enter, but you also have the opportunity to fail. It will remain with the student to prove himself worthy of a degree. There are about eight hundred and fifty colleges in this group that will accept students ranked in the top half of their high school classes. Perhaps you will find your place in one of these colleges. Some of them offer excellent curricula in liberal arts and some special fields. Many state colleges and teachers colleges, and some state universities, fall into this group.

The average American student has the opportunity to attend an accredited college because of the great variation in admissions standards, which reflect the different purposes of the individual institutions. The easiest colleges to get into are junior and teachers colleges. State colleges and universities are usually of average difficulty to enter. Prestige colleges and universities and institites of technology are the most difficult to enter.

The vast majority, about 80 percent, of the nation's institutions of higher education are not highly competitive. That admissions standards vary and that there is ample opportunity for high school graduates to be admitted to college is clearly shown in the findings of a recent survey. The results of the survey revealed that far more colleges and universities admitted high school graduates with a "C" average than the number that did not. The survey showed that, for the nation as a whole, students may attend colleges with the following admissions policies:[1]

Policy	Percent of Institutions
Accept all or almost all high school graduates	33.5
Accept all "C" average high school graduates	19.3
Accept all "B" average high school graduates	26.2
Highly competitive or competitive policy	21.0

So that students throughout the nation may size up the situation in their respective areas, admission patterns by region are presented.[2]

WEST SOUTH CENTRAL STATES (Louisiana, Texas, Arkansas, Oklahoma), 230 colleges—8.9 percent of all the colleges in the United States

Highly competitive or competitive	3.1%
Accepts all B-average high school graduates	9.6%
Accepts all C-average high school graduates	21.7%
Accepts all, or almost all, high school graduates	65.6%

WEST NORTH CENTRAL STATES (Iowa, Kansas, Missouri, Nebraska, Minnesota, North Dakota, South Dakota), 279 colleges—10.8 percent of all the colleges in the United States

Highly competitive or competitive	9.4%
Accepts all B-average high school graduates	29.4%
Accepts all C-average high school graduates	9.8%
Accepts all, or almost all, high school graduates	51.4%

MOUNTAIN STATES (Idaho, Montana, Nevada, Utah, Wyoming, Colorado, Arizona, New Mexico), 118 colleges—4.5 percent of all the colleges in the United States

Highly competitive or competitive	2.8%
Accepts all B-average high school graduates	5.6%
Accepts all C-average high school graduates	40.2%
Accepts all, or almost all, high school graduates	51.4%

[1] Summary of the individual admissions policy characterizations given by U. S. colleges and universities in: Gene R. Hawes, *The New American Guide to Colleges,* Second Edition (New York: The New American Library and Columbia University Press, 1962).

[2] Gene R. Hawes, *The New American Guide to Colleges,* Second Edition (New York: The New American Library and Columbia University Press, 1962).

EAST SOUTH CENTRAL STATES (Alabama, Mississippi, Kentucky, Tennessee), 191 colleges—7.4 percent of all the colleges in the United States

Highly competitive or competitive	7.0%
Accepts all B-average high school graduates	21.0%
Accepts all C-average high school graduates	25.2%
Accepts all, or almost all, high school graduates	46.8%

PACIFIC STATES (California, Oregon, Washington, Alaska, Hawaii), 267 colleges—9.7 percent of all the colleges in the United States

Highly competitive or competitive	7.9%
Accepts all B-average high school graduates	28.1%
Accepts all C-average high school graduates	20.1%
Accepts all, or almost all, high school graduates	43.9%

SOUTH ATLANTIC STATES (Delaware, Maryland, Washington, D.C., Virginia, West Virginia, North Carolina, South Carolina, Georgia, Florida), 370 colleges—14.3 percent of all the colleges in the United States

Highly competitive or competitive	26.9%
Accepts all B-average (top ½) high school graduates	21.8%
Accepts all C-average (top ¾) high school graduates	20.7%
Accepts all, or almost all, high school graduates	30.6%

EAST NORTH CENTRAL STATES (Illinois, Indiana, Michigan, Ohio, Wisconsin), 470 colleges—18.1 percent of all the colleges in the United States

Highly competitive or competitive	13.8%
Accepts all B-average (top ½) high school graduates	33.6%
Accepts all C-average (top ¾) high school graduates	25.3%
Accepts all, or almost all, high school graduates	27.3%

NEW ENGLAND (Maine, New Hampshire, Vermont, Massachusetts, Rhode Island, Connecticut), 217 colleges—8 percent of all the colleges in the United States

Highly competitive or competitive	50.8%
Accepts all B-average (top ½) high school graduates	32.8%
Accepts all C-average (top ¾) high school graduates	7.9%
Accepts all, or almost all, high school graduates	8.5%

MIDDLE ATLANTIC STATES (New York, New Jersey, Pennsylvania), 434 colleges—16.7 percent of all the colleges in the United States

Highly competitive or competitive	50.0%
Accepts all B-average (top ½) high school graduates	33.8%
Accepts all C-average (top ¾) high school graduates	9.2%
Accepts all, or almost all, high school graduates	7.0%

When interpreting these policies it should be remembered that competitive institutions have no available space and offer only limited opportunity for the typical student. However, institutions in each group are known to make exceptions to their printed admissions policies. Further, you should keep in mind that admissions policies are not devised to select all students of the same intellectual and scholastic ability. Outstanding students are found in all colleges with open-door policies, and students who have limited capacity for distinguished achievement are found in institutions that have selective admissions policies.

Understanding Colleges and Universities

You have read more about the eight Ivy League schools — Brown, Columbia, Cornell, Dartmouth, Harvard, Princeton, Yale, and the University of Pennslyvania, which enroll only about 1 percent of the nation's freshman class — than you have about the sixty-eight fine land-grant colleges and universities that educate 20 percent of our undergraduates. Land-grant colleges, located in each state, are dedicated to the higher education of all who are interested, and have a near-open-door policy as enrollments and available space will permit. Many of the "middle fifth" students acquire their college education in these institutions.

There is no "magic" in a particular school. Any "magic" that exists comes from within the individual; it can only be stimulated by experience, of which education is one kind. The Ivy League has produced some failures, and some outstanding persons began their studies in little-known and infrequently mentioned institutions. No college or university can force a student to attain understanding, knowledge, skill, and wisdom, or guarantee him future success, although authoritative sources agree that many colleges meet the academic and career needs of most students. Your appreciation of and attitude toward a college education is much more important than the selection of a particular college. There are several colleges that are just as "right" for you as any one institution. Students frequently consider too few colleges in making a choice. Likewise, too much emphasis is placed on the first choice. In the final analysis, your selection can be made among several colleges on a personal-preference basis, if you are genuinely interested in attending college, willing to put out the necessary effort to locate college vacancies, and have average scholastic aptitude and ability.

The word *college* has taken on several meanings. Frequently, it is used to mean any formal education received after high school graduation. When students say they are going to college, they may actually be attending a university, junior college, or technical institute, accounting night school, or barber's college. Technically speaking, *college* refers to an institution of higher learning offering a curriculum leading to a degree. A *university* usually has a college of liberal arts, offers a program of graduate study, and has two or more other colleges or professional schools that grant degrees in several fields of study.

Some state colleges have "schools" of agriculture, education, and arts and sciences and are much like a university. *Teachers colleges,* as the name suggests, are designed to prepare students for teaching careers. Because of the importance our society has placed on education, states have seen fit to provide one or more teachers colleges. They may be a part of a university, as in the case of the College of Teacher Education, New Mexico State University, or may not be associated with a college or university, such as Appalachian State Teachers College in North Carolina.

The fields of study offered differ among colleges. This will likely be an important consideration for students who have tentatively selected a career field. You can find the fields of study, or majors, that you can study by reviewing college catalogs. If a degree is necessary for your career, you should select a college that offers a curriculum that can prepare you in the chosen career field. The catalog will also tell you how many years — two, four, or more — of study will be necessary for success in the field you plan to enter.

The most familiar college program is liberal arts. A *liberal arts college* is one with a curriculum leading to a broad academic education, as contrasted with vocational education leading to a specialized career. Many students are encouraged to study in liberal arts colleges because the learning acquired there will either specifically or generally apply to almost any field one may enter. In addition, there are many career fields that are specialized to varying degrees in the so-called liberal arts.

Public Institutions. An educational institution is public if its financial support is derived from tax sources and it is controlled by the state. Each state provides money for the support of one or more state college, colleges, or universities. Each state has a land-grant college or university. There are also community and city colleges, such as Frederick Community College in Maryland and City College of New York. About three-fifths of America's college students attend public colleges and universities. It is estimated that these institutions will enroll most of the increase in students in the next decade, when about three-fourths of all college students will attend public colleges and universities. Certainly, most students of average ability will find their places in public institutions.

Public institutions, like private institutions, vary in terms of admissions standards. A distinction should be noted between the public institutions that are required by law to admit all applicants and those that have an option. It is common practice of public junior and community colleges to admit any student with a high school diploma. Many state colleges and universities with available space use this practice, particularly with resident students. Some public institutions that have the right to be selective do not exercise it, but may as they become more crowded. Other institutions, such as the state-supported colleges in Michigan, New York, and California, have the right of selective admission and do refuse a large number of applicants. Students of average ability living in these states may find their place in colleges in other states.

Independent and Private Institutions. Private and independent institutions are those under the control of governing boards that are free of public control on academic matters. These colleges and universities may receive financial support from endowed funds and other sources, such as trust funds and investments. Since private and independent colleges must look to sources other than taxation to keep their doors open, their tuition rates and fixed fees are usually relatively high.

Some of the outstanding colleges and universities of traditional character fall into this category. The Ivy League is composed of private institutions that are independent of standards imposed by state authority, except those colleges within the institutions receiving state support.

Independent and private institutions may be supported by religious denominations or groups. Church-supported colleges emphasize spiritual and moral, as well as intellectual, aspects of student development. Some institutions started by churches are essentially independent now. The University of Denver, which has a relation with the Methodist church, is an institution in this group. Many of these colleges and universities enjoy reputations of high quality in many selected fields. There are large church-supported schools, like the University of Notre Dame and Boston University, and small ones, such as Midland College in Nebraska.

A college's name is not an indication of its means of support. For example, Syracuse University is classified as private, while New York Community College is supported and controlled by the City of New York. A helpful guide is the *College Facts Chart*, published by the National Beta Club, Spartanburg, South Carolina. It costs only 50 cents. Ask your counselor or librarian; they may have a copy.

Types of Institutions and Their Requirements

Colleges and universities have expanded their fields so much that you can't always tell the original purpose of an institution. There was a time when liberal arts colleges taught the arts and technical institutions taught specific skills. This is no longer true. A student can major in the fine arts in most state colleges or universities and possibly room with a student majoring in engineering or agriculture. Teachers colleges have become state colleges and offer programs in liberal arts. Liberal arts colleges offer occupationally oriented programs, and technical institutes have grown into colleges that train teachers, engineers, and farmers, and many offer a liberal arts program, too. In recent years there has been an increasing tendency for colleges to follow the footsteps of the university by offering a wide choice of fields of study.

Institutions of higher education differ widely in purposes and programs. This variation offers students of modest ability a measure of assurance that they have an opportunity for a place in college. In addition to accreditation, institutions may be classified by the kind and amount of education offered, and the source of financial support, but the bases for classifying colleges are not mutually exclusive. A college of one type may have certain characteristics, usually associated with other classifications. For example, a private church-related institution, such as Southern Methodist University, may offer a wide variety of fields of study for persons desiring two, four, or more years of education. Also, colleges stress different scholastic qualifications.

Some schools place first priority on grades in high school or grades in academic courses; others place an emphasis on class rank; still others emphasize "college board" scores; and some colleges allow admission to any graduate of an accredited high school.

A variety of institutions — selective, public, private,

and state college and universities — have been selected to show the variation in requirements for admission. You need to review the catalogs published by the colleges and universities that you are considering attending, but these examples will be helpful in orienting you to the situation. These selected institutions offer educational opportunities to those who have not yet distinguished themselves as outstanding scholars, but they do not cater to the mediocre student, and they certainly are not "degree mills." They have a commitment to education that is different from highly selective institutions. Many have outstanding programs in areas of specialization. Admittedly, other examples of only "A" and "B" students who rank in the top one-fourth of their respective classes could be given in each type. The following institutions were selected so that you may gain greater understanding of the opportunities open to the typical student. They include universities and colleges, teachers colleges, junior and community colleges and technical institutes, and evening colleges and colleges of general studies.

Universities and Colleges.   A university is a complex of several colleges or schools empowered to confer degrees in their respective fields. The college of arts and sciences usually offers the general-education courses for all students in addition to the specialized courses for its majors. Other colleges within a typical university include education, business and public administration, health and physical education, agriculture, fine arts, etc. Some institutions called colleges are in fact universities and have schools that are the equivalent to colleges of other universities.

There are about one hundred and fifty universities. They tend to be quite large because they enroll students in the several colleges that comprise the institution. Some public universities enroll more than thirty thousand students, of which about one-half are undergraduates. Independent and private universities tend to be one-half that size, and some are much smaller. Both private and public universities may vary in programs offered and in admissions standards. In addition to undergraduate courses, graduate work through the master's degree is offered in most areas, with work toward the doctorate offered in the stronger areas of the university.

Long Island University serves well as an example of an independent nonsectarian coeducational institution. Although no high school grades were reported in its 1965 bulletin, the specific requirements varied with each college. The admissions requirements for the College of Business Administration at L.I.U. are fulfilled by most high school graduates:

English	4 units
Social Studies	3 units
Algebra	1 unit

A student may present four free elective units and four units of modern language, social studies, math, or social sciences.

Most college-minded students of modest academic achievement in high school will find their place in a state college or university. Auburn University was selected because it is an example of a land-grant institution. There is a land-grant college located in your state. Auburn University's 1964 bulletin states:

Admission to Auburn University, in keeping with the land-grant tradition, is open to the men and women in all economic stations, giving them the benefits of higher education formerly reserved to the few. . . .

The requirements for admission shall be graduation from an approved secondary school with the minimum of 15 units (or 12 units from a three-year senior high school) or the equivalent of this requirement as shown by examination.

Graduates of accredited Alabama secondary schools who attain composite scores of 16 or above on the American College Test and who present satisfactory grades in college preparatory courses are academically eligible for admission.

Nonresident students must have graduated from an accredited high school with an over-all average of "C" and have attained an acceptable score on the ACT or Scholastic Aptitude Test (SAT). Nonresident students may be admitted by satisfactory test scores, also.

To point out opportunity and availability of space for average students you need only to read the following sample of Oklahoma State University's requirements as they appeared in its 1965 bulletin.

A. Residents of Oklahoma

Any resident of Oklahoma who (a) is a graduate of an accredited high school, (b) has participated in the American College Testing Program and, (c) meets at least one of the following requirements is eligible for admission to Oklahoma State University.

  1. Maintained an average of C or above in the 4 years of his high school study.
  2. Ranked scholastically among the upper three-fourths of the members of his high school graduating class.
  3. Attained a composite score on the American College Testing Program which would place him among the upper three-fourths of all high school seniors, based on twelfth-grade national norms.

An individual not eligible for admission as stated above may, if he is a high school graduate and has participated in the ACTP, be admitted on probation for study in the second semester of the academic year following high school graduation or in any term thereafter.

B. Non-residents of Oklahoma

A non-resident of Oklahoma in order to be eligible for admission to study as a first-time entering freshmen at OSU must (a) be a graduate of a high school accredited by the regional association or by an appropriate accrediting agency of his home state, (b) have earned not less than a C average over all high school work attempted and, (c) have participated in the ACTP or a similar acceptable battery of tests. In addition, he must meet one of the following requirements.

  1. Rank among the upper one-half of the members of his graduating class.
  2. Attain a composite score on the ACTP or a similar acceptable battery of tests which would place him among the upper one-half of all high school seniors, based on twelfth-grade national norms.

In addition to the above, resident students may be admitted on a probational basis if he or she is 21 years of age or over and has not graduated from high school. A student admitted under this regulation must make a "C" average over his first semester's work to be eligible to return for the second semester.

Another example of the admissions requirements at state colleges and universities is South Dakota State University. To gain admission to South Dakota State, resident students must present four specific academic units in college preparatory courses to meet the general requirements. These are three units of English and one unit of algebra. Resident students presenting fifteen units including these requirements will be admitted. Some schools within the university require additional units of math. Out-of-state students who are in the upper 50 percent of their class are normally eligible for unconditional admission, and those in the lower half may be admitted on probation.

The usual requirement of most state colleges and universities for out-of-state students as compared to resident students is that out-of-state students be in the top one-half of their graduating class and resident students be in the top two-thirds. Requirements for both groups vary among institutions.

Many students will attend church-supported universities, either because they are interested in the religious denomination, a field of study offered, or because it is located close to home or in a city where they would prefer to live. Although many Methodist students attend American University in Washington, D.C., which is supported by the central body of the Methodist church, the largest number of students who attend are Jewish.

Admission to Brigham Young University is granted on the basis of an official application received from the office of admissions and records. It is not necessary to pass an entrance examination in order to be admitted to Brigham Young. Students who apply for admission and who are accepted by Brigham Young University are required to maintain ideals and standards in harmony with those of the Church of Jesus Christ of Latter-Day Saints. High standards of honor, integrity and morality, graciousness in personal behavior, application of Christian ideals in everyday living, and abstinence from alcohol and tobacco are required of students. To be admitted, students must be graduates of an approved high school with a total of nine credits in English, science, social sciences, mathematics, and a foreign language.

Bob Jones University, an orthodox Christian-supported college located in Greenville, South Carolina, lists its essential admissions requirements as graduation from high school with sixteen credits of which ten should be in English, mathematics, natural sciences, social studies, and a foreign language, or by any of the following:

1. High school equivalency
2. Satisfactory USAFI General Education Development Test scores, with or without a diploma
3. Satisfactory scores achieved on the Bob Jones University Entrance Examination, or
4. Satisfactory scores on a similar examination of the College Entrance Examination Board or similar recognized organization

The admissions requirements to Howard Payne College, Brownsville, Texas, are similar to those of other church-related universities. Howard Payne, a liberal arts college that offers other programs such as teacher education, is supported by the Baptist church. Interested students may be admitted to Howard Payne by examination did not graduate from an accredited high school, or earned a class rank in the lower fourth. Also, students from other institutions may transfer credit for degree purposes to Howard Payne in courses in which they earned a "D" if such grades are compensated by other grades of "B" or better. A "C" is required to graduate.

The three plans under which a student may be admitted to Howard Payne College are described below.

I. *By Graduation from an Accredited High School.* Graduates of high schools affiliated with the Texas Education Agency or standard classification agencies of other states must present at least 15 accredited units, eight of which are prescribed as follows:

English (preferably 4)	3 units
Social Sciences	2 units
Mathematics	2 units
Natural Sciences (laboratory)	1 unit

The other seven units may be selected from the list of subjects accepted by the Texas Education Agency. Not more than four can be accepted from any group.

The student must also be in the upper three-fourths of the graduating class to be accepted for unconditional academic admission.

II. *By Examination.* Applicants who have been graduated from unaffiliated schools or those who do not have 15 affiliated units to their credit even though they were graduated from affiliated schools, or those who ranked in the lower one-fourth of graduating class, may be admitted by examination. Only veterans 18 years of age and other persons over 21 years of age who have not been graduated from high school will be permitted to enter by examination without being graduated from a secondary school. The General Education Development test designed by the USAFI is used. The examination can be taken at Howard Payne College before registration day. Please allow at least two days to complete the test.

III. *By Transfer from Another College or University.* Students who wish to transfer from other institutions of higher learning are required to submit transcripts from the school previously attended. Credit toward a degree at Howard Payne College will be granted on courses in which the grade is "D", only when such grades are compensated by other grades or "B" or better. The overall average must be "C", as this is the average grade required for graduation.

The maximum number of hours that can be transferred from a junior college is 64. This includes four hours of physical training. No advanced hours can be transferred from a junior college.

No student who is under suspension at another institution will be considered for admission to Howard Payne College until he is eligible for readmission to the former institution and presents grades equivalent to those necessary to remain in Howard Payne.

Teachers Colleges — Colleges of Education. These institutions offer specific programs for students who wish to become teachers. There are about two hundred teachers colleges found throughout the country. The program of studies offered is specialized to enable the future teacher to meet state requirements for certification. Of course, state colleges and universities and many independent and private institutions have colleges of education. Therefore, it is not necessary for a future teacher to attend a teachers college if it is to his or her advantage to attend another institution because of location, finances, or other reasons.

In addition to the possibility of preparing for a teaching career, there are three reasons why the typical student may wish to consider attending a teachers college. These are admissions standards, costs and proximity, and transferability of credits.

1. Admissions standards are often quite liberal. Of the four-year publicly controlled institutions, it is generally accepted that teachers colleges are the easiest to get into. No doubt some have higher requirements, but the two examples of admissions standards at teachers colleges given below are typical.
2. It generally costs students less to attend teachers colleges than any other type of four-year college. Because of the demand for public school teachers, the state often subsidizes the cost of preparing teachers. The subsidy is passed on to the student as a saving in the form of reduced costs for tuition, room, and board. In some states tuition is free to students who become teachers for a designated period of time.

3. An increasing number of state teachers colleges are becoming state colleges and universities by broadening their liberal arts and science programs. With this change comes opportunity for attendance by students who live within commuting distances and who might otherwise be unable to attend. For many students who are not interested in a teaching career, these institutions, with their liberal admissions standards, offer an opportunity to "try" college with a low investment in time and money. You may wish to attend a nearby teachers college and later transfer to the college of your choice to complete degree requirements.

The primary purpose of Illinois State University at Normal, Illinois, is the preparation of teachers. The 1965 bulletin states the requirements for beginning freshmen:

1. An applicant must be a graduate of a recognized or accredited high school.
2. An applicant should rank in the upper two-thirds of his graduating class. An out-of-state applicant must rank in the upper one-half.
3. An applicant must submit scores on the American College Testing Program before he is permitted to enter. An applicant who ranks in the lower one-half of his high school class must submit these scores before he can be considered for admission.
4. An applicant who ranks in the lowest one-third of his graduating class may be considered on the basis of his scores on the American College Testing Program. If these scores are satisfactory, the Committee on Admissions will consider the application.
5. The applicant's own physician must give him a physical examination and a vaccination against smallpox during the 60 days preceding registration. The report of this examination must include evidence that the applicant for admission has had a chest X-ray or skin test for tuberculosis within the preceding year. Hearing and speech tests are parts of the registration procedure.

Located in the District of Columbia, the D.C. Teachers College is another example of this type of institution. The requirements for entering freshmen are listed below:

a. *Graduation from an approved senior high school*
Applicants for admission must have completed 16 Carnegie units accepted for graduation which must include as a minimum the following college preparatory courses as prescribed by the Board of Education of the District of Columbia:

Subject	Units
English	4
Foreign Language	2
Mathematics	2
Science (laboratory science)	1
Social Studies	1½
Specified academic units	5½
(Or the equivalent)	
	16

Where a student changes his general English to college preparatory level and keeps it on the college preparatory level with success, such English may be considered as college preparatory for college entrance even though it may not have begun as such.

Courses in biology, physics, chemistry, algebra, geometry (plane, solid and analytical), trigonometry, calculus, foreign languages, and the social studies are set up at the college preparatory level and will be counted as college preparatory credits whether they are taken by regular college preparatory or general students.

An official transcript of the high school work is required.

b. *Expressed intention to teach*
Applicants for admission shall state their intention to become teachers.

c. *Recommendation from high school official*
Each candidate for admission must be recommended by the high school principal or by some other high school official certifying that he possesses moral and physical fitness, emotional stability, and qualities of scholarship deemed necessary for success in college courses.

d. *Physical examination*
A physical examination by the college physician is required of all students. There must be no irremediable physical defects which would interfere with successful performance of the duties of a teacher.

e. *Entrance examinations*
Applicants for admission to the freshman class are required to take entrance examinations administered by the College or the Scholastic Aptitude Test of the College Entrance Examination Board. These examinations aid in determining academic ability.

f. *Personal interview*
All applicants, except pre-accepted students from foreign countries, are required to have a personal interview with the Director of Admissions or with a member of the Committee on Admissions. Attention is given to the applicant's personality, voice and speech pattern, special interests, and promise of professional development.

If you plan to pursue a course other than teaching, it will be necessary to be selective in the courses you take. Keep your professional objectives in mind. Courses taken for transfer should be identified from the catalog of the institution where you plan to complete your program requirements.

Liberal Arts Colleges.   The more than seven hundred liberal arts colleges deserve special explanation. Some of the older institutions with long-standing reputations began as excellent liberal arts colleges and are among the most difficult institutions to which to gain admission. There are, however, many liberal arts colleges that maintain standards that are no more difficult to meet than those of state colleges and universities. Also, you should remember that a liberal arts education can be acquired in universities and in some colleges that serve other purposes. Nearly all of the nation's liberal arts colleges are independently and privately supported. They enroll about one-fourth of the persons attending college.

The primary objective of liberal arts colleges is to give the student an education rich and broad in the basic academic and cultural areas rather than to train for a career area. The programs offered in liberal arts colleges allow students to concentrate their studies in art, English, math, science, music, language, and so forth. Most liberal arts colleges offer programs in preparation for professional areas requiring more than a four-year education, such as pre-law, pre-medicine, and pre-dentistry. Some offer areas of specialization.

Although there are opportunities for the "middle fifth" student in many liberal arts colleges, including some that enjoy outstanding reputations, the students who attend them tend to be more cosmopolitan than on other campuses. Some liberal arts colleges attempt to attract out-of-state students. As indicated, persons preparing for professional careers find liberal arts colleges a desirable place to continue their studies. Outstanding students frequently choose this type of education. Persons who elect to study areas such as English and history should and do choose these colleges. Also, many persons who have no clear-cut career choice or who are undecided attend liberal arts colleges.

The requirements of the University of Chattanooga, a private liberal arts university, are as follows:

> Freshmen — Applicants must be graduates of accredited high schools. Those who are not graduates of accredited high schools will be considered for admission if appropriate evidence of their attainment of the educational level of an accredited high school graduate can be given. Such applicants should consult the director of admissions for assistance in determining the necessary procedure.
>
> It is recommended that applicants have at least 12 academic (non-vocational) high school units of which four should be English, two foreign language, and the remainder in mathematics, natural sciences and social sciences.

Like many liberal arts colleges. Centre College of Kentucky was founded under Presbyterian auspices in 1819. In addition to "college board" examinations and character references. the 1965 catalog for Centre College states:

> Centre is concerned with the soundness of a student's

whole program and the quality of his performance in school. Although the college does not prescribe rigidly the units to be presented, a minimum of twelve academic units is required. The college strongly recommends a program including four units of English literature and composition; three or more units in mathematics; three or more units of one foreign language (no credit allowed for less than two years in one language); three or more units in history and other social studies; and two or more units in laboratory science.

The "College Preparatory Course" in most secondary schools will ordinarily contain all or most of this suggested program. Unless an applicant's program differs radically from that here recommended, he will not be at a disadvantage when his record is evaluated. Graduation from an accredited secondary school, with a program including fifteen units of acceptable work, is required. Centre does not accept courses of less than one-half unit toward the required total of fifteen units. The college also requires an affirmative recommendation from the applicant's secondary school.

Saint Norbert College, a small Catholic coeducation independent liberal arts college, located in West De Pere, Wisconsin, welcomes students of all faiths. It admits students whose scholastic backgrounds, aptitudes, and personal characteristics indicate a fitness to undertake and to benefit from the kind of education that Saint Norbert offers. To be admitted students should be in the upper half of their graduating classes. "College board" examinations are required, and personal interviews are recommended.

Evening Colleges and Colleges of General Studies

Not everyone can have a full-time college education. Persons with families, limited incomes, or with other responsibilities may want to go to college over an extended period of time. If you cannot attend college full time because of work, or if you wish to "try" college to test your abilities, there may be opportunity to attend college in the evening. As an extra benefit, you will save the cost of room and board because you can live at home.

Many institutions have well-developed programs that extend the campus in time, space, and scope for qualified students. They are usually referred to as the college of general studies, university college, university evening college, or the college of continuing education. They provide a realistic opportunity for many students who otherwise might not be able to continue their education after high school. According to the joint report of the Association of University Evening Colleges and the National University Extension Association, there were more than 2,600,000 enrollments in both credit and noncredit courses offered in 1966 in extension programs.

The NUEA states that university evening colleges are usually located in metropolitan areas and offer credit and noncredit college courses in liberal arts, sciences, and the professions. Centers located in most states offer several courses for students who can begin and later transfer for the completion of a degree or certification. Many evening college centers have complete degree and certificate curricula. University extension programs frequently transport instructors and materials to small communities and educationally isolated industrial communities in addition to providing numerous offerings in metropolitan and suburban areas. This practice is in use at the University of Nevada, where instructors are flown by university planes to remote cities of the state for classes twice each week.

Most high school graduates can qualify and continue their education through colleges of general studies and university extension. The University of Maryland's University College is an outstanding example of this type of program. It offers degree and nondegree programs in the late afternoon and evening throughout the State of Maryland, the District of Columbia, and in dozens of centers located in twenty-four foreign countries and four continents. The overseas programs are offered for U. S. military and civilian personnel and their dependents. Through University College the university grants a bachelor of arts degree and an Associate in Arts certificate to students who complete the first two years of an established curriculum. The final fifteen semester hours for the certificate must be earned in residence with a minimum of a "C" average. Part-time students studying in the college may study other university degree programs under the supervision of the specific degree-granting college.

The following appears in the 1966–67 University of Maryland bulletin for the University College:

REQUIREMENTS FOR UNDERGRADUATES:

I. The minimum admission requirements for *all adult* (married, military, or over 21) University College Students are:

A. For High School Graduates or Equivalent: Graduation from an approved high school or the high school GED equivalent (a minimum standard score of 45 on each of the five tests or an average of 50 with no score below 40 on any of the five parts).
B. Former College Students: An acceptable college record from the last institution attended on a full-time basis (or if part-time, a minimum of 12 semester hours) showing good standing and not on academic or disciplinary probation.
  1. In the event the student has had previous academic difficulty, he may be permitted to enroll as a "Special Student" provided that two years have elapsed since his last full-time enrollment (or part-time equivalent). A student in this category with previous academic difficulties may become a "Regular Student" pursuing a degree program with the University of Maryland after he has com-

pleted at least 15 semester hours with a minimum grade average of "C" at this institution.
  2. A student who has completed less than 12 semester hours will have his overall record, college and high school, evaluated to determine admissibility to this institution.
  3. In the event that a student does not fit any of the above categories, he should request the review of his record by the appropriate admissions office prior to registration.

Adult students enrolling for their first Maryland course may be permitted to register pending receipt of the documentation confirming high school graduation or the equivalent, or good standing with the last college attended. It is the student's responsibility to see that official documents are mailed directly to the appropriate University of Maryland Admissions Office from the issuing institution by not later than one month prior to the end of the initial term of enrollment.

PROCEDURES FOR ADMISSION:

While filing their Application for Admission, students must immediately request that the records indicated below be sent *directly from* the institution(s) attended *to* the Admissions Office and address indicated on the Application for Admission form submitted.

HIGH SCHOOL GRADUATES: high school transcript.
HIGH SCHOOL EQUIVALENT: copy of student's GED test report (Request this report from USAFI, Madison 3, Wisconsin. It is recommended that the student, when requesting the forwarding of this test report, give full name, military serial number, and the place and approximate date the GED tests were taken.)
COLLEGE TRANSFER STUDENTS: high school transcript and transcripts from all colleges attended.
STUDENTS WISHING POSSIBLE CREDIT FOR MILITARY SERVICE: DD Form 295 in duplicate and official certificates of completion from military service schools when applicable.

OFFICIAL EVALUATION (STATEMENT OF ADVANCED STANDING):

An Official Evaluation, or Statement of Advanced Standing, will be prepared by the *Director of Admissions* when the following conditions have been fulfilled:

1. The Admission "Procedures for Undergraduates" . . . have been satisfactorily followed;
2. Completion of twelve (12) semester hours of University of Maryland course work with a minimum grade average of "C". In certain cases, completion of fifteen (15) semester hours is required; and
3. Receipt of a written request from the student indicating the degree program to be followed, the field of primary concentration, field (or fields) of

secondary concentration and your present address. Students are encouraged to have an appointment with an official University College representative, especially if there are questions regarding this written request or the concentrations being selected.

UNOFFICIAL EVALUATIONS: A tentative and unofficial evaluation may be requested at any time by consulting an *official University College representative.*

Tentative evaluations are possible only when a student presents records (preferably but not necessarily transcripts) of courses and grades from other institutions attended, a record of the college-level GED test scores (if such tests have been taken), and a list of the advanced military service schools which he has successfully completed. With such records a University College counselor can give a reasonable *estimate* of the student's requirements in relation to the degree administered by University College.

Establishment of Credit

CORRESPONDENCE COURSES: For the degree administered by University College, a maximum of 12 semester hours of correspondence credit may be accepted provided: (1) the minimum grade earned is at least the equivalent of a Maryland "C"; (2) the course was administered by an accredited institution; and (3) the credit is acceptable by the institution conducting the correspondence course toward one of its own baccalaureate degrees. The University of Maryland does not offer correspondence courses of any kind. Certain United States Armed Forces Institute (USAFI) college-level correspondence courses at the freshman and sophomore levels only may also be accepted for credit if the work is of acceptable quality. Credit will be granted provided *all lessons have been completed, submitted,* and the work has been validated by successful completion of the appropriate end-of-course examination. No credit is allowed for USAFI self-study or group-study courses, nor will credit be given for correspondence courses in public speaking or foreign languages.

A student planning to enroll in correspondence study, either with USAFI or another institution, must first check with the Dean of University College concerning acceptability of the course(s) in the curriculum being pursued. It is the student's responsibility to obtain the Dean's approval.

CREDIT BY USAFI GED TESTS: To be eligible for college-level GED credit, a student must have completed the tests with acceptable scores *prior to September, 1, 1963, and* his first enrollment with Maryland must have taken *place prior to that date.* A student who first enrolls with Maryland after *September 1, 1963,* or, if already enrolled, takes GED college-level tests after that date will not receive credit based on the tests.

OTHER CREDIT BY EXAMINATION: Under limited circumstances, credit toward a baccalaureate degree may be established by examination provided the individual can exhibit an area of competence. A request to establish credit by examination must be approved by the head of the academic department, the dean of the academic college in which the examination is offered, and by the dean of the college in which the student is enrolled. Not all academic departments permit credit by examination. A student may not establish foreign language credit by examination in freshman or sophomore courses of his native language, the one which he first learned to read and write as a child through regular schooling. It is not necessarily the language of his parents or of the country in which he was born. With the exception of the USAFI GED tests, no more than twenty (20) semester credits can be granted by examination. The fee for establishing credit by examination is $5.00 per semester hour of credit. Applicants must have completed at least 12 semester credits with the University of Maryland with a minimum average grade of "C" and have the status of "Regular Student" before making application for an examination to establish credit. Credit by examination will not normally be accepted for any of the final 30 semester credits leading to graduation. The maximum of GED and other examination credit is 24 semester hours.

TRANSFER CREDIT FOR FORMAL CLASSROOM COURSES: The University of Maryland will accept transfer credit for courses taken with other accredited colleges and universities under the following conditions:

a. The courses for which transfer credit is sought must be applicable to the student's curriculum.

b. Each grade received must be a "C" or higher under a marking system equivalent to that of the University of Maryland.

c. The institution must grant credit for the courses toward one of its own baccalaureate degrees.

d. A properly certified transcript must be sent by the institution directly to the appropriate office of the Director of Admissions, University of Maryland.

e. Written approval of the Dean of University College must be obtained prior to taking any course within the last 30 semester hours of the student's degree requirements.

f. A student with junior standing (56 hours of academic credit) will not receive transfer credit for *elective* courses taken at a junior college. To be eligible for transfer credit from an *accredited* junior college, a course must be one that is required by the student's curriculum in University College.

The Evening Divisions of Northwestern University has similar requirements. Its 1964–65 bulletin states:

Undergraduate students: The Evening Division of Northwestern University admits those students who can benefit from and contribute to its educational program. The minimum requirement for admission is graduation from an accredited high school. An applicant who does not meet this requirement, but who is over twenty-one years of age, may be permitted to register if, in the opinion of a faculty adviser, he is qualified to pursue the work.

Junior Colleges, Community Colleges, and Technical Institutes

A junior college, community college, or technical institute may be the best possible place for you, particularly if space in college, pace of studies, and money are your concerns. Many students have a more satisfying experience in a two-year institution than they would have in a four-year one. The completion of a certificate or Associate in Arts program will enable you to identify with a college and possibly will have more lasting value than an unsuccessful experience in a four-year college. Another factor in favor of junior colleges is the slower adjustment to college life they offer students, particularly those from small high schools who may find the step up to a large college too great for easy social adjustment. Junior colleges have outstanding counseling available for students who have not decided on a career or are not sure that they want to take a full four-year course. As the pressure for advanced education increases, more and more persons will find two-year colleges a desirable place to study. These institutions provide the average student an excellent chance to prove himself.

There are more than seven hundred two-year colleges and technical institutes. More are being developed each year; fifty new ones opened their doors in 1966. More than a million students are enrolled in two-year institutions, including one-fourth of all new students. It is predicted that almost 50 percent of all high school graduates expect to attend them in the future. To keep space open in these colleges, the federal government, under the Higher Education Facilities Act of 1963, is spending $50 million a year to build and expand public junior and community colleges. Instruction in some of them is equal to or better than that offered during the first two years in some large universities, and, in nearly all cases, the relationship between professors and students and among students are more informal. Many students save money because a junior college, community college, or technical institute is located within driving distance of their home, and tuition is free or much less than in other types of institutions.

One of the basic reasons these institutions have experienced dramatic growth development is that they offer students a variety of choices. They are of three basic types:

1. The two-year extension of a four-year college or university through off-campus centers, as developed in Pennsylvania, Indiana, and Wisconsin

2. Regional institutions maintained by the state, as found in Oklahoma, Utah, Georgia, and New York

3. Local public community colleges maintained and financed through local school districts, as typified in California [3]

Programs offered by junior and community colleges and technical institutes are of two kinds: transfer programs for students planning to continue their education at four-year colleges, and terminal programs in vocational, technical, and pre- or sub-professional areas. The transfer program is an equivalent of the first two years' work at liberal arts colleges.

The admissions standards are often quite liberal. It is a common practice to admit any student with a high school diploma. Students usually come from a geographical area such as a school district, a municipality, or region within a state. However, out-of-state students are welcomed. Many of these colleges and institutes offer associate degrees to students who complete their programs. Some are being elevated into four-year baccalaureate degree-granting institutions.

At the more than sixty-five public supported junior colleges in California, resident students can attend without paying tuition. Transfer programs include liberal arts, business, medicine, engineering, and many other fields. Terminal programs include such fields as auto and aviation mechanics, journalism, art, and general education for those who do not plan to attend for longer periods. New technical programs will be offered as facilities permit. The junior colleges in California grant the Associate in Arts certificate to students who complete program requirements.

A system of technical colleges is being developed in many states, such as North Carolina and Virginia. In Virginia, students who are high school graduates and eighteen or older will be admitted. The curriculum includes a wide variety of courses and programs in business, industry, agriculture, medicine, and other areas. Both short-term and associate degree programs are offered.

In a strict definition of the word, institutes are devoted to research and specialized education, usually in some field of technology. Some offer training for short periods of time. New York State has developed several technical institutes that offer a variety of training programs of two years or less. Other institutes offer training at undergraduate and graduate levels. Cal. Tech. and V.P.I. are examples of this type of institution.

You have read much about the need for persons in the professions. There is an even greater need for persons in technical and vocational fields. A study of 1,091 sample industries in New York State found that there is opportunity for about six people with some technological or other specialized training at the college level for each opening on the professional level.

[3] Chris A. DeYoung and Richard Wynn, *American Education,* Fifth Edition (New York: McGraw-Hill, Inc., 1964).

The outlook is bright for the technical institutes and their graduates.

With the present emphasis on the thirteenth and fourteenth years of education and on recent state and federal legislation, junior colleges are expected to continue to grow. Many students will find it advantageous to start their studies in junior colleges. For additional information about junior colleges, community colleges, and technical institutes, write to:

The American Association of Junior Colleges
1785 Massachusetts Avenue, N.W.
Washington, D.C. 20036

Engineers' Council for Professional Development
345 East 47th Street
New York, New York 10017

National Council of Technical Schools
Room 103, M. Street, N.W.
Washington, D.C. 20005

For other books emphasizing two-year institutions, review:

American Junior Colleges, by Jesse P. Bogue
American Council on Education
1785 Massachusetts Avenue, N.W.
Washington, D.C. 20036

The Junior College Directory
American Association of Junior Colleges
1315 16th Street
N.W. Washington, D.C. 20036

Lovejoy's Vocational School Guide, by Clarence E.
  Lovejoy
Simon and Schuster, Inc.
630 Fifth Avenue
New York, New York 10020

*Sargent's Junior College and Specialized Schools and
  Colleges,* by F. Porter Sargent
Porter Sargent (publisher), third edition, 1959
11 Beacon Street
Boston, Massachusetts 02108

Barron's Guide to the Two-Year Colleges, by Seymour Eskow
Barron's Educational Series, Inc.
343 Great Neck Road
Great Neck, New York 11021

Accreditation and What It Means

To say that an institution is accredited means that it has met required standards of quality established by a competent agency. High schools are accredited by state departments of education and regional agencies. Colleges may be accredited by one or more agencies.

A college or university is accredited only after careful evaluation by the regional association. State, municipal, and incorporated private institutions offering two or more years of higher education at the undergraduate level or one year at the graduate level may be accredited. In addition, their enrollment must be sufficiently large to continue a well-planned program for a period of years, and must operate under legal authority granted by the state or national government. College accreditation means that a certifying agency has confidence in the institution's purposes, that the college has found the necessary resources to achieve these purposes, and that its purposes are being met and will continue to be met for a reasonable time.

It is very important that you select a college or university that is accredited. Should you want to transfer to another institution, credits earned at an accredited college or university will usually be accepted at face value by the new institution. This is not necessarily the case if the college first attended was not accredited. Thus, when a student enters an unaccredited institution he should have an especially good reason for doing so since other schools may not accept his credits should he transfer.

Colleges and universities that most of you will be interested in are accredited by one of six regional accrediting associations. These six independent, voluntary, regional associations are the nation's highest general accrediting authority. Their requirements are similar but not identical. They are:

1. Middle States Association of Colleges and Secondary Schools
2. New England Association of Colleges and Secondary Schools
3. North Central Association of Colleges and Secondary Schools
4. Northwest Association of Secondary and Higher Education
5. Southern Association of Colleges and Secondary Schools
6. Western College Association

A list of institutions accredited by these associations is published annually by the U.S. Office of Education[4] and by other organizations.[5]

Certain areas of specialization have their own accrediting agencies. Many groups, such as the National League for Nursing, the American Council on Pharmaceutical Education, the American Chemical Society, and others, examine the college department of their field at the request of the college. These agencies, in turn, publish lists of certified and accredited institutions. Should you have an interest in a particular school, ask for information regarding its accreditation.

Factors in the Selection of a College

There are some time-proven guides that will help you in reaching a sound decision.

[4] U.S. Department of Health, Education, and Welfare, *Education Directory, Part III, Higher Education,* annual edition (Washington, D.C.: U.S. Government Printing Office).

[5] American Association of Collegiate Registrars and Admissions Officers, *Credit Given,* annual edition (Washington, D.C.: American Council on Education, 1785 Massachusetts Avenue, N.W.).

Let's start with a question or two. Why do you want to go to college? What do you expect a college education to do for you? What things are important to you and your career plans? Does the college have a placement bureau? Will financing an education be a problem?

Your career plans will likely enter into the selection of a college, for college prepares you for your career. To a large extent, it is the college's reputation in the particular field you enter that helps you get your first job after graduation. The quality of professional education found at a college or university can be measured by the success of its graduates, and employers know it. You will want to select a college on the basis of your intellectual development and potential, and personality, also. Colleges are different just as high schools are different and people are different. There are other deciding factors as well. The amount of money available to you as compared to college costs is a consideration. Family preferences are acceptable considerations, but the other points should be considered first. Get all available information on the colleges you are interested in attending. Make good use of your counselor, for he can be of valuable assistance. He has information and college catalogs from several institutions and can get others. But remember: No one can make this decision but you. The responsibility for making the final selection is yours.

Philosophy and Standards. The aims and purposes of the college you select should mesh with your set of objectives in life. The philosophy and standards of the college can influence and change your life. If your outlook on life is too different from that of the college, or if the standards that you are willing to accept and be happy with are much higher or lower than that of the college, you very likely will not feel comfortable or be able to apply yourself in a satisfactory manner.

You should inquire about the social standards of the colleges you are considering. You are expected to obey the rules and regulations when you enroll. If you can't live up to the expectations of the institution, then you should consider another one.

Field of Study. It should be crystal-clear that college attendance is not an end in itself; it is a means to an end. For a majority of typical students from middle-class families, college is preparation for some career or profession. You can't make a sound selection without giving primary consideration to this factor. In a recent survey it was found that many high school students had applied for admission to colleges that did not offer programs of study in the fields in which they had planned to major. This suggests that little attention was paid to preparing for a career in the selection of a college to attend. A college's reputation in the particular field of study is of vital importance to you in terms of placement and advancement in a profession or career.

Whether you should enter a liberal arts college depends on your abilities, career aspirations, and personal preferences. If you are pretty sure of what you wish to do in life and it requires specialized training, then a liberal arts college is not for you. If you are not sure, liberal arts may be the place for you. Other things being equal, a liberal arts education will provide you with knowledge useable in a variety of career opportunities. This is worth considering, for after college you must "merchandise" your education to your employer.

There is another factor worth considering by those of you who are undecided about a career. Unless you are quite sure you are going to enter a particular career field, you should choose a large university. Of course, you should enroll in the college within the university that you think will best prepare you for a particular field, if you have any preference of a career. The reasoning behind this advice is that by attending a large institution you can transfer to other departments or colleges within the same university with little or no loss of credits. There can be a considerable loss in transferring credits from one institution to another, depending on accreditation and other factors.

Cost. For some students, college costs will be a primary consideration. You may ask, when considering a college, "Can I afford it?" Do so only incomparing it to the cost of other schools. If the question means considering not attending college at all, a more logical question may be, "Can I afford not to go to college?"

A college education is expensive. College expenses may vary by as much as $3,000 a year. The major cost items are tuition, room, and board. Don't forget to include fees, books, travel to and from college, and other incidental expenses. The other side of the cost "coin" is financial aid. Some schools offer part-time work, loans, grants in aid, and other special programs. A letter of inquiry can be an inexpensive lead to financial assistance. For additional information on college costs and how to meet them, see chapters VIII and IX.

Requirements for Admission and Graduation. When you consider which college to attend, admission requirements are one factor. There is an overwhelming amount of evidence indicating that there is a place for you in college. The typical admissions standards shown in this chapter under "Types of Institutions and Their Requirements" clearly shows you can be admitted to college. Because of the advantages a college education offers you, it will be worth your time and effort to select one in which you can succeed. You should also consider the requirements for graduation, because they vary among institutions.

Location. The distance from home is usually considered both by parents and students in selecting a college, but there is usually little agreement on how close or far away from home a college should be. There are no sure answers on location and distance. Attending college away from your home town or a long distance from home usually requires a degree of maturity. Some boys and girls need to be placed on their own; some are not ready. To others, attending college away from home would make little difference because they are socially mature. Independence, an indicator of maturity, is often realized by attending college some distance from home.

Living away from the college you hope to attend may actually increase your chances of being admitted to that college. This is not a good single reason for selecting a college, but neither is distance, nor a belief that being an out-of-stater will hinder your chances of being admitted, a reason for not applying. In some colleges, as much as 20 percent of total enrollment may be from out of state. Some colleges, particularly "name" colleges and liberal arts colleges, attempt to attract students from all parts of the country to provide a national atmosphere about the campus. It is felt that associating with students from other parts of the country will broaden one's understanding of people and their culture, which is a part of a good education.

Location will determine to some extent what type of recreation you may enjoy. Some campuses are close to cultural centers. Also, you may wish to inquire about the religious facilities of your faith.

Size. Some students are sensitive to the bigness and littleness of colleges. Actually, there is no clear line between a large and a small college: how large is large and how small is small? Some institutions are small by choice and have no desire to become larger. The trend is for large colleges and universities to become larger and small ones to remain small, relatively speaking.

Small colleges offer a closer relationship between faculty and students than do larger institutions. Larger colleges and universities, however, offer a wider choice of courses and a greater opportunity for meeting diversified people. Many feel that small colleges are less formal, offer fewer educational opportunities, have fewer facilities such as libraries and laboratories, and have fewer and less-qualified professors. Persons who believe this say that larger institutions have higher standards and more and better facilities and faculties. This may be true in general, but there are some notable exceptions. Most small colleges do not limit enrollment to only honor students, but some do. Regardless of your choice, you should inquire about the facilities, standards, etc., in the particular field you plan to study.

Without question, there are some small colleges that enjoy a reputation of having high standards. For example, Hope College in Holland, Michigan, a small church-supported college, has standards acceptable to most graduate schools and professional fields of specialization. Hope College students earn as many of the preferred graduate fellowships as do students of any other college in the country. Many of its graduates have achieved positions of authority in several fields outside the influence of the church denomination that supports it. There are many other outstanding small colleges.

There is little question that junior colleges are going to grow in number and in enrollment in the years to come, but most will enroll comparatively few students. Many will be accredited and some will become accepted branches of colleges and universities. This is a fact in several states, with California being outstanding.

Co-ed vs. Non-coed. Whether the institution you choose is coeducational is a factor to be considered. You may not think this is important, but some students do. The large number of girls who fail to complete their education because of marriage is sufficient evidence that many do consider this factor in selecting a college. A vast majority of the colleges and universities in our nation are coeducational. The effectiveness of an institution is not greatly influenced by either arrangement.

There are advantages to both kinds. In institutions not coeducational, the distractions of social life are not so pressing. From the point of view of social development, social skills are likely to be developed more easily and fully by students enrolled in coeducational institutions. For most persons, this is personal preference.

Personal Preference. In selecting a college, much depends on you — your personal wishes, your likes and dislikes, and your individual academic and personality development. Don't try to measure a college by someone else's standards. It is your life; make it fit your needs. When you realize there is no one best college for you, that regardless of the factors you consider with an open mind, several colleges could probably meet your educational and personal needs, then it is up to you to choose from the group for which you feel you are best suited.

Without considering other factors, you may think that Dartmouth or Radcliffe, for example, is *the* one for you. Both are very outstanding and highly selective, if not exclusive, colleges. But for you and your particular needs, Arizona State or the University of Illinois may be a much better choice. You may place high priority on location. Some prefer smaller and less rigorous colleges where they can feel closer to the faculty and find more opportunity for self-expression. You may be a person who prefers a junior college or a small college so that you "can get to know everyone." On the other hand, you may prefer a large college or one with reputation, prestige, cultural advantages, and, yes, the glamor of an outstanding football team and other athletic events. There is no hard and fast rule for the selection of a college, even when personal preference gets into the picture. So we come down to it again: it depends on you, your objectives for going to college, your personal aspirations. It always depends on *you*.

Additional Information. There is no shortage of sources from which you can get other valuable information about colleges. Several college directories are on the market. All of them contain information useful to you in deciding on the group of colleges best suited to your specific needs. They do not provide the same information, and you may wish to review two or three of them. Ask your counselor or librarian for the following directories:

American Universities and Colleges (ninth edition, 1964)

American Council on Education
1785 Massachusetts Avenue, N.W.
Washington, D.C. 20036

College Facts Chart
National Beta Club
Spartanburg, South Carolina 29301

Directory of Small Colleges
Council for the Advancement of Small Colleges
1818 R Street, N.W.
Washington, D.C. 20009

Lovejoy's College Guide
Simon and Schuster, Inc.
630 Fifth Avenue
New York, New York 10020

New American Guide to Colleges
by Gene R. Hawes
The New American Library
1301 Avenue of the Americas
New York, New York 10019

The College Blue Book
Christian E. Burchel, publisher
P. O. Box 311
Yonkers, New York 10702

The College Handbook
College Entrance Examination Board
P. O. Box 592
Princeton, New Jersey 08540, or
P. O. Box 1025
Berkeley, California 94701

Junior College Directory (issued annually)
American Association of Junior Colleges
1785 Massachusetts Avenue, N.W.
Washington, D.C. 20036

Making a Selection

Most people agree that the selection of a college warrants considerable study by students, their parents, and their counselors. It should not be a snap judgment. Obviously, if you decide while still in high school, you will be able to take courses recommended as background for your major field in college. Before making application, and with the aid of the counselor and your parents, you should select three or four colleges offering your chosen program. At least one college selected should be within your financial means and be very likely to accept you. The many facts about colleges that make them good or poor choices must be reviewed in light of your individual situation. It is not wrong to let personal preference guide your choice at this point; only then can you make a valid selection. If you have followed this plan, all the selected institutions should suit your purposes. Making this selection during the second semester of the junior year should be near the right time for most students. This is only a rule of thumb, however, and can be varied without too much confusion.

Take Stock of Yourself. Begin with yourself — your interests, personality, personal and professional aspirations, your need for social contact, and other needs. You should know why you want to go to college, the extent of your ability to work independently and make decisions, and how well you accept responsibility. Colleges vary in what they expect of students. The level of success you hope to attain will have something to do with the school you select. If you merely want to "get a college education," then probably you will not be motivated to enroll in a better college. On the other hand, if you aspire to great success in life, you will want to enroll in a college with a desirable reputation in the area in which you hope to specialize.

Be realistic in your tentative choices. You know how well you ranked in class, what courses you took in high school, and the grades you made. Don't underrate your abilities, but don't overrate your chances of being admitted to highly selective schools. Consult with your guidance counselor on your potential success. Colleges admit students who have a reasonable chance of succeeding. You should consider this a wise policy and choose a college from which you will have a reasonable chance of graduating.

Collect Information. Among other things, colleges and universities are composed of people, classrooms, and other facilities. It is important that you know something of these in the college you are considering. It is highly recommended that you survey the requirements and recommendations of colleges. Make a composite list and compare the requirements found in bulletins from several institutions. This will help you decide the purpose of your study. Pay particular attention to courses recommended within your study area, for it may be assumed that you will have had certain courses or experiences before entering college. A college's reputation is usually based on the quality of its program as shown by the success of its graduates. This is a sound basis for deciding which institution to attend.

Information can be obtained from many sources. Most of you will know someone who has attended one of the colleges you may be considering. Talk with graduates to get information that is not in the catalogs and brochures. Have them relate to you their college experiences. You must remember, however, they will give you only their impressions, which may be somewhat biased.

With the assistance of the guidance counselor and your parents, review the information you have collected, and choose several colleges and universities that meet your demands based on the factors mentioned previously in this chapter. You will want to collect specific information on some colleges. One very good and inexpensive way to secure additional information is to write directly to the office of admissions and ask for a general catalog, application forms, and other information prepared for prospective students (see "Interpreting a College Catalog" in chapter IV). The following may serve as a guide for a letter or postal card:

Dean of Admissions
(Name of college or university)
(City and State)

Dear Sir:

I am a (*junior or senior*) in (*name of high school*) and will be graduate in (*month and year*). I am considering attending (*name of college or university*) to study (*department*). Would you please send a bulletin, application forms, and other information regarding (*name of college or university*).

Thank you for your assistance.

Yours truly,

(*Your signature*)

Visiting Campuses.   Visits to campuses and interviews with admissions officers and others are usually conducted on the same trip to the campus, but they serve different purposes. The interview is primarily to the advantage of the institution in deciding if you are the type of student they would like to have study there. Of course, what you learn during an interview will be of value to you, too. The visit to the campus is of most use to you, the prospective student, in deciding if the institution is where you wish to study. Colleges and universities are alike in some ways, and very much different in other ways. While some information may be obtained from guidance counselors, from alumni, and from college catalogs, one of the best ways to get to know the general atmosphere of the campus and interest and spirit of the student body is to visit the campuses of those colleges you are seriously considering. All the secondhand information is not as valuable as a few minutes of walking across the campus, strolling through dorms, and visiting informally with students.

A visit to college campuses will dispel much of the mystery of colleges and admissions procedures that, in the minds of prospective students and their parents, shrouds the campus. A visit gives teen-agers a "feel" for campus life that will lessen their uncertainty, anxiety, and hesitation. Teen-agers seem to be able to "size up" the campus faster than their parents. Before making the visit, you, your parents, and counselor should agree on a limited number of accredited colleges that will meet your needs. These should be ranked in a 1, 2, 3 order. You will probably apply for admission at each. Now you are ready to visit the campuses.

To be of most value, a campus visit should be made during the academic year while classes are in session. Of course, you will want to arrange for a conference with admissions personnel, but get a student perspective while you are there by sitting in on classes, talking with professors, having lunch in the dining hall, and looking over "college town." After looking over each campus, you will have clearly in mind what you are looking for in a college, and probably will have found it. Many students have indicated that it was the visit on campus that was most helpful in reaching a final decision.

When you are on the campus, give your attention to things of particular importance to you. Where will you stay? How do students "see" and respect the professors? How high is student interest? How good is the food? What is "college town" like? There are some campus visits "do not's." Visiting a college on a Saturday morning preceding a football game is hardly the appropriate time to see a true picture of college life in action. Don't rush through a visit; make the most of your visit. You should not schedule your visit near the beginning or end of a semester. During these times admissions and registrar personnel are literally swamped with records to be posted, applications to be processed, and so on. Plan your visit at a more appropriate time.

The National Vocational Guidance Association has prepared and published a small guide on "How to Visit Colleges." If you are interested, write to the association at 1605 New Hampshire Avenue, Washington, D.C. 20009.

Ten-Point Selection Guide

Here is a ten-point plan that will serve as a guide in making a final selection.

1. Meet with your counselor and identify career fields for which you have an aptitude.
2. Consider all the factors important to your individual situation.
3. Consider only those colleges offering programs that will prepare you for your chosen career field.
4. Select a group of colleges that interest you from the list of accredited institutions to which you think you can be admitted.
5. Collect information by writing for specifics, reviewing catalogs, discussing colleges with your counselor, and listening and raising important questions.
6. Narrow the field to the three to five colleges most nearly meeting your needs.
7. Place colleges in a tentative 1, 2, 3 preference rank.
8. Arrange for interviews and visit all the colleges on the most-likely-to-be-selected list.
9. Make a final choice by ranking colleges based on your visit. If undecided, reconsider liberal arts in a large institution, junior or community college, or evening college with plans to transfer at a later date.
10. Apply for admission to the colleges you have selected. Be certain of deadlines, etc. (see chapter IV, "When and How Should I Apply?").

Chapter Four

When and How Should I Apply?

The process of gaining admission to a college is not as simple as you may think, and often is not fully understood by students when applying. Many, if not most, students and their parents find college admission procedures baffling. College admissions offices seem mysterious to students and their parents because the practices used are foreign to their experience. Now that you have reached the decision to attend college, you must know when and how you can apply to your best advantage.

It was suggested earlier that you should select three to five accredited colleges by considering their philosophy and standards, the kind and amount of education offered in the field of study you plan to pursue, the amount of money it will cost, requirements for admission and graduation, distance from home, and size and type of college. Presuming you have selected several colleges, you are ready to apply.

Dr. Frank Bowles, president of the College Entrance Examination Board, states that application and admission to college is a three-step process.[1]

1. The candidate and his school supply the college with the necessary information for it to determine the academic potential of the student.
2. The college considers the information it has received and decides to admit or reject the student.
3. Admitted students decide whether to accept admissions offered by institutions.

From the institution's point of view, your application and other necessary information must be collected and filed so that an admissions committee can act on your application. From your position, you must do those things necessary to reach your immediate objective of being admitted to college. You must contact the college and let the office of admissions know that you are interested in attending, complete the forms required for admission, pay $5 to $25 application fee, and collect and send, or arrange to have sent, your high school records and other information needed by the college to consider your application. Colleges have learned that approximately 35 percent of the students admitted do not enroll. The small application fee is charged to pay part of the cost of processing your application and to discourage students from "shopping around" for a college education unless they are really interested in attending.

The process of gaining admission involves many details that must be handled with care. Each of the several forms, records, and test scores have rigid time schedules, thus failure to answer letters or file completed forms on time may result in being denied admission to the college you hope to attend. So that students may know specifically what is expected of them, colleges attempt to present their admissions procedures in an understandable manner.

In this section, the mechanics of making application

[1] Frank H. Bowles, *How To Get Into College* (New York: E. P. Dutton & Co., Inc., 1960).

35

are presented. To increase your chances of being selected; you will want to know when and how to apply. Your objective is to present your application as forcefully as possible. If your choices are realistic and you plan well and follow your plan, you will probably be admitted to a college that will meet your particular needs. If you are not successful, you will have the satisfaction of knowing you have made an organized and diligent effort and will then wish to consider the other alternatives open to you.

Interpreting a College Catalog

In planning to meet college requirements and in making application, there is no better single source of information about a college than its bulletin. The main function of a college catalog is to provide information for current use, and to serve as an official and legal document. It is through the catalog that the college relates itself to students and their parents, because it gives a full and detailed account of what courses and programs of study the college offers. If you do not have catalogs for the colleges you are considering, check with your high school counselor or principal. It is a good idea to review several catalogs to get the college "picture" in mind before considering the selection of specific colleges. When you are ready to consider specific institutions, you will want to to request catalogs from them. The sample letter of request found on page 34 will guide you in writing for catalogs.

The college catalog will give you the most complete, reliable, and accurate information available. Since it contains information on fees, dates, requirements, and courses, it is written for a specific purpose and with care. It will be up to you to interpret it. Be certain that you have the most recent one.

Terminology and Definitions. College catalogs are technical publications. One of the chief problems faced by college personnel in preparing catalogs is to make certain that the terminology used will be understood by the readers. Some catalogs use the practice of adding a section on terms and their definitions. Excerpts from the Iowa State Teachers College Bulletin provide an example:

Adviser, advisee	Your adviser or counselor is the instructor assigned by the college to help you with your problems. You are called his advisee.
Course	A particular subject being studied—thus a course in English.
Curriculum	The whole body of courses required for a degree.
Department	A division of the college which offers instruction in a particular branch of knowledge: The Department of Music.
Elective	A subject or course which you may choose to study as distinguished from required courses which you are asked to take.
Matriculation	The act of enrolling for the first time as a student at the college.
Prerequisite	The preliminary requirement which must be met before a certain course can be taken. Thus, English I is a prerequisite to all other courses in English and must be successfully completed before other English courses are taken.
Registration	The act of enrolling in classes, usually at the beginning of a semester. This involves choosing your classes with the help of your counselor.
Schedule	A list of the courses you are taking each quarter. Your schedule is your program of studies.
Undergraduate	A student who has not yet obtained the bachelor's degree.

Finding Desired Information. No two colleges are alike. For this reason, no two colleges or universities include the same items of information in their catalogs, nor do they list items in the same order. As an example, some institutions prefer to present information concerning admissions, costs, financial aids, and student services before presenting general information.

So that you may become familiar with the contents of a college catalog, examine the following example, used by the Committee on Catalogues of the American Association of Collegiate Registrars and Admissions Officers and prepared by its members.

BULLETIN OF THE UNIVERSITY OF THE UNITED NATIONS
New York, New York

1. Date of Publication.
2. Second class mailing privilege.
3. Table of Contents.
4. College or university calendar of information and events.
5. Calendar for the years(s) during which the catalog is effective.
6. Names of governing board members.
7. Names of administrative officers.
8. Names of teaching faculty.
9. Location of school and availability of transportation facilities.
10. History of the school.
11. Organization.
12. Accreditation.
13. Description of buildings and grounds.
14. Library facilities.
15. Degrees offered.

16. Entrance requirements clearly and briefly stated for:
    Freshmen.
    Transfer students.
    Graduate students.
    Special or unclassified students.
    Students from other countries.
17. Costs:
    Tuition and other fees.
    Housing accommodations.
    Boarding accommodations.
    Books and supplies.
18. Financial aids:
    Assistantships, fellowships and scholarships.
    Student employment opportunities.
    Awards.
    Loans.
    Aids for veterans.
19. Student services:
    Health service.
    Testing.
    Advising and counseling.
    Placement upon graduation.
20. Organizations:
    Honor.
    Recognition.
    Fraternal.
    Professional.
21. Regulations and requirements for degrees:
    Definition of unit of credit.
    Student load requirements and limits.
    Marking system.
    Academic disqualification and condition for re-instatement.
    Conditions for good standing.
    Requirements for graduation with honors.
    Class attendance.
    Course requirements by level as indicated by numbering system.
22. Intercollegiate athletic policy.
23. Student activities:
    Publications.
    Organizations.
    Councils.
    Religious activities.
24. Course offerings:
    Numbers.
    Titles.
    Descriptions.
    Units of credit.
25. Tabulation of enrollment.
26. Index.

Using the Catalog. The value of some of the information will depend on your stage of planning for college. The general information section of the catalog will contain the purpose and history of the institution, including specifics, such as whether it is a liberal arts, coeducational, and land-grant school. Location may be given and may be of importance to you.

You will want to study carefully the information on admission requirements and procedures. From the statements on admission requirements you should be able to determine if you qualify. Should you consider applying, review the specific application procedures, noting dates of examinations and deadlines for receiving application forms. Should you be uncertain on important points, write the admissions office for clarification. You will want to review the requirements for graduation, also.

Other important areas of the catalog relate to costs, which include tuition and other fees, housing accommodations, boarding accomodations, and books and supplies, but do not include incidental and other living expenses. For a review of college costs and how to meet them, see chapters VIII and IX.

College catalogs contain program and curriculum requirements and other policies of interest to students. Should you need help in interpreting them, consult your counselor, principal, or teachers. If you visit the campus of colleges you are considering, feel free to raise unanswered questions with appropriate persons.

So that you may understand more fully the meaning of college catalogs, an explanation of the two important areas of admission for new and transfer students is provided and departmental course descriptions are presented and explained in detail.

* SPEECH AND DRAMATIC ART

CHARLOTTE GERTRUDE WELLES, Ph.D., *Chairman,* Prof. of Speech
ROBERT PHILLIP FRIEDMAN, Ph.D., Prof. of Speech
BARTON LOVEWELL GRIFFITH, Ph.D., Assoc. Prof. of **1.** Speech
ROBIN HUMPHREY, M.A., Asst. Prof. of Speech
FRANCES LEA MCCURDY, Ph.D., Assoc. Prof. of Speech
LOREN DUDLEY REID, Ph.D., Prof. of Speech
HENRY DONOVAN RHYNSBURGER, M.F.A., Prof. of Speech
MAURICE EARL SHELBY, JR., Ph.D., Asst. Prof. of Speech
LEWIS WALDO STOERKER, M.F.A., Assoc. Prof. of Speech

THELMA WOODHOUSE TROMBLY, Ph.D., Assoc. Prof. of Speech
DONALD GRAY WILLIAMSON, Ph.D., Asst. Prof. of Speech

Instructors: Milton Eugene Bierbaum, M.A.; Robert Lee Dillard, M.A.; Leila Okino Kanno, M.A.; Ronald Joseph Koperski, M.A.; John Bertram Long, M.A.; Donald Wallace MacLennan, M.A.; Jimmie Lonnie Meese, M.A.; Leonard Bernard Wurthman, M.A.

* Reprinted by permission of Mr. Sam B. Shirky, director, Technical Education Services, University of Missouri, Columbia, Missouri.

Assistant Instructors: Mary Eleanor Anderson, M.A.; Barry Jay Cronin, M.A.; Alice Donaldson, M.A.; Donna Russell Fox, M.A.; Russell Malloy Keeling, M.A.; Charles Russell McNames, M.A.; Frank William Oglesbee, M.A.; Doyle Glynn Ward, M.A.

Graduate Assistants: Howard Edward Headrick, B.Sc.; Melvin Jay Marshall, B.A.

Speech Test. Students entering the University with fewer than 24 hours of credit are required to take a speech test. Those classified as "Excused" in this test have fulfilled prerequisite for courses 2, 7, 172, and have met one prerequisite for 175. Those advised to enroll for 1 must complete 1 if they wish to enroll in 2, 7, 172, or 175. **2.**

Speech and Hearing Clinic. Any student enrolled in the University may be admitted to the Speech and Hearing Clinic at the discretion of the Director. Residents of Missouri may be admitted, whenever facilities permit, by complying with regulations governing the Clinic. FOX, HEADRICK, KANNO, LONG, TROMBLY, WARD, WELLS, WILLIAMSON. **3.**

1. Oral Communication (2) f, w. **4.**
   No credit toward degree in Arts & Science or Engr. Principles of adequate speech production, platform behavior. Special help for those needing a remedial course. WARD.

2. Voice and Articulation (2) f, w, s.
   Prerequisite: 1 (if recommended). Techniques for improving speaking voice, theories underlying techniques. Attention to student's articulation, pronunciation, voice quality, general expressiveness. FOX, HUMPHREY, KANNO, WARD.

6. Introduction to the Theatre (2) f, w.
   Contributions to modern dramatic production by directors, actors, designers, playwrights. Appreciation of contemporary theatre. Recordings giving the development of musical comedy. RHYNSBURGER.

7. Beginning Collegiate Debate (1) f, w.
   Prerequisites: 1 (if recommended) & consent of instr. Procedures, practice in collegiate debating for students with limited or no experience in competitive debating. FRIEDMAN.

Departmental Descriptions in College Catalogs

[*1.*] The department chairman is listed first. The chairmanship may be a regular administrative appointment, may be rotated systematically at regular intervals, or may be departmentally decided, depending on the college or university. The abbreviations represent earned degrees, from highest to lowest: doctor of philosophy, master of fine arts and master of arts, bachelor of science, and bachelor of arts. Professorial rank is based on a number of things, including degrees, length of time at the college, academic activities such as publication and outstanding teaching, and available openings in departmental ranks.

[2.] Most colleges require at least one course in speech of all degree candidates. If the transferring student has not fulfilled the requirement elsewhere, he is expected to do so at the new college. "Prerequisites" for enrolling in a course are other courses and requirements that must precede enrollment.

[3.] Speech and hearing clinics are used to assist students with hearing and speech difficulties, to train speech students, and, when staff permits, to assist the public, especially if the college is publically supported.

[4.] The first figure is the course number and would be written Sp. 1 or Sh. 1, depending on the college's system of abbreviations, usually explained in the annual catalog. Each college also has its own course-numbering system, which indicates the relative rank of courses—freshman, sophomore, and so forth—by the number preceding the course title.

The parenthetical number following the course title indicates the semester (or other) hours of credit for successful completion of the course. For each class hour per week of attendance for approximately sixteen weeks (in colleges on the semester system) one hour of credit is earned. Laboratory courses in science and physical education, for example, require more hours of attendance than the hours in earned credit.

The small letters indicate the semester when the course is given—fall, winter, summer. In trimester-system or quarter-system schools the letter *s* may mean spring.

Specific speech requirements for the Colleges of Engineering and Arts and Sciences must be learned from the catalog material on those particular parts of the university.

ADMISSION

Inquiries regarding entrance to all divisions of the University of Missouri, Columbia, should be addressed to the Director of Admissions, 130 Jesse Hall. Information concerning the University of Missouri at Rolla; University of Missouri at St. Louis; and the University of Missouri at Kansas City may be obtained by writing to the Director of Admissions at the campus concerned. **1.**

Directions to New Students
New students must submit credentials before August 1 for the fall semester, January 1 for the winter se- **2.**

mester, and May 1 for the summer session. Admission can be determined only after all credentials are on file. All new students are required to submit application blanks which may be obtained from the Director of Admissions, 130 Jesse Hall. Out-of-state undergraduate students are required to submit a non-refundable application evaluation fee of $10 *with* the application for admission. In addition the following credentials are required.

Entering Freshmen. The entering freshman must submit a high school transcript certified by the proper official of the school in which the credits were earned, and reports of medical history and physical examination forms completed by the applicant's personal physician.

Transfer Students. An undergraduate student who has attended college elsewhere must submit an official high school transcript, official college transcripts from *each college* attended including statements of honorable dismissal. Reports of medical history and physical examination forms must be submitted by the applicant's personal physician.

Graduate Students. A graduate student must have a transcript sent from the institution conferring his bachelor's degree and from each graduate school attended. Reports of medical history and physical examination forms must be submitted by the applicant's personal physician.

Advance Payment on Fees. All new students upon notification of acceptance to the Fall or Winter semester will be requested to submit a non-refundable advance payment of $20 on his registration fee. This amount is credited to the student's incidental fee when he enrolls in the University. **3.**

Veterans. In addition to official school records, a veteran who wishes credit for service experience, or excuse from physical education, must submit a photostatic copy of his separation papers (Form DD-214) and official USAFI reports, Madison, Wisconsin 53703, if applicable. **4.**

Admission Requirements for a Typical State University

[*1.*] Requests for application forms and catalogs may be sent on postal cards. Be sure to give your return address on both sides of the postal card and to allow at least two weeks for the catalog to reach you, since second-class mail of this type need not move rapidly.

Address your requests to the Director of Admissions. Addressing the president of the university or college only causes a delay in responding to your request.

[*2.*] "Credentials" is a term covering all required materials — application form and fee in check or money order, high school and college transcripts, medical examination form, photograph, and any other requested items, all properly and fully completed and signed. Because many high schools and colleges have little or no summer clerical staff or have staff on vacation, requests

for transcripts should be made no later than May 1. If transcripts were requested at the end of the fall semester and follow-up transcripts are needed in June, be sure to make both requests. The follow-up transcripts *are not* sent automatically by most high schools and colleges. Requests for medical appointments must also be made as early as possible, for in May and June medical doctors are busy with pre-school children and youngsters being readied for summer camp.

[*3.*] Advance payments on fees are normally non-refundable and serve to compensate the college to some extent for the work done in good faith for an applicant. The applicant who changes his mind and decides not to attend or to attend another college does not always realize that the college he will not attend has arranged for faculty to teach, custodians to keep the grounds and buildings, and space for sleeping and eating. When large numbers of students "shop around" and apply to several colleges, as has become the American custom, they force institutions to prepare for more students than actually register, and these contracts for personnel and equipment cannot be canceled.

[*4.*] Veterans who do not comply with these requests at the time of application or first registration are penalized by many colleges with the loss of possible elective or required course credit and/or credit for basic military training in lieu of required physical education. It is the student's responsibility to procure photostatic copies of his military papers prior to registration.

FRESHMAN STUDENTS

Admission

It is the policy of the University of Missouri to admit into regular standing all high school graduates *with satisfactory records.* **5.**

The Colleges of Agriculture, Arts and Science, Education, Engineering, and the Schools of Home Economics and Forestry and Nursing* at Columbia, the University of Missouri at Rolla, the University of Missouri at St. Louis, and the University of Missouri at Kansas City are regularly open to freshmen. Students may be admitted to the freshman class by:

Plan A — Graduates of fully accredited high schools may be admitted by certificate or transcript of record without examination. Applicants must have passed their high school courses with satisfactory marks. Admission by certificate is restricted to graduates of schools accredited by the University of Missouri, by other state universities of similar rank, by the North Central Association, or by other recognized accrediting agencies. **6.**

Plan B — A student who is not a graduate of a

* Freshman enrollment is limited.

four-year high school and who is at least 18 years of age may qualify for admission to the freshman class by examination. The examination will presume training and experience compensating for the lack of formal training to be had in an accredited high school. Adults, military personnel and veterans may qualify for admission by satisfactorily passing the high school level General Educational Development tests prepared for the **7.** United States Armed Forces Institute.

Missouri Freshmen

Top Third: Applicants will be accepted and admission granted at any time during the senior high school year to students who ranked in the top third of the class at the end of the first six semesters.

Middle Third: Applications will be accepted and admission granted at any time during the final semester of the senior high school year to students who ranked in the middle of the class at the end of the seventh semester.

Lowest Third: Students who rank in the lowest third of the high school graduating class may submit applications during the final semester of the senior year. Before admission can be considered Placement Tests and, **8.** in some cases, additional tests are required. Some students are required to qualify through summer work. Students in this group, *if admitted,* will be on scholastic **9.** probation. Applicants will be notified concerning their admission status upon receipt of their final eighth semester high school transcript.   **10.**

[5.] "Satisfactory records" is explained under the headings, "Missouri Freshmen," catalog page 25, and "Out-of-State Freshmen," page 26. The requirements are somewhat higher for the out-of-state student, since a public institution has no obligation to accept a nonresident who does not appear to be capable of successful college work.

[6.] "Admission by certificate" is admission on the basis of the high school record. The exact requirements for out-of-state students are given at the top of page 26 of the catalog.

A college may or may not supply a standard form upon which the secondary school record is to be transmitted. This or a photostatic copy of the school record is the "transcript of record," and must be sent by the high school directly to the college admissions office.

[7.] The General Educational Development Tests were originally used in World War II by the military services to determine the educational attainment of men who had not finished high school. They are now used by many state departments of education for adults who wish to qualify for high school diplomas by examination. Successful candidates receive equivalency certificates that may be used for entrance to many colleges, but particularly to community or junior colleges.

[8.] Placement tests determine the individual's skill in such areas as reading, English, and algebra, especially the skills of the student with a poor high school record or of the student who has been out of school for a number of years. Remedial work may be recommended on the basis of these tests.

[9.] The terms of scholastic probation vary from college to college. Generally, however, the student accepted "on probation" must have no mark below "D" and an over-all average of "C" or higher during any semester, trimester, quarter, or term he is on probation. A student who has not met all the entrance requirements may be placed on probation or "on condition" until he has met these requirements. Again, the grade penalty usually applies, his continuance in college depending on a "C" average or better.

[10.] Students in the lower rank of the high school class are denied admission to many institutions. In cases when their admission is pending on final high school grades, admission will be denied if these grades do not show marked improvement.

Out-of-State Freshmen

Out-of-State students must rank in the upper half **11.** of their high school graduating classes in order to be eligible for admission by certificate.

The requirement for admission by certificate to the Colleges of Agriculture, Arts and Science, Education, Engineering, and the Schools of Forestry, Home Economics, and Nursing, at Columbia, the School of Mines and Metallurgy at the University of Missouri at Rolla, the University of Missouri at St. Louis, and the University of Missouri at Kansas City, is the satisfactory completion of a four-year high school course, including 15 acceptable units. All courses, with the exception of physical education and military science, offered by an accredited high school for its diploma may be accepted toward entrance. However, no more than two units in diversified occupations will be accepted. Specific units required by each of the colleges and schools are included in the section on each division.

Freshman Placement Tests   **12.**

Freshman placement tests are required of all students enrolling in the University with fewer than 24 hours of college credit. The results of these tests are of benefit to both the student and his adviser in planning the student's program and in considering his educational and professional objective. Freshman placement tests are administered during the preregistration period, during new student orientation, and during the spring.

Careful correlation of data reveals that the student **13.** who ranks in the lowest fourth of his high school graduating class or who scores below the 20 percentile on the placement tests given to entering freshmen will find college work quite difficult. Rarely does a student with

low scholastic standing in high school complete a four-year college program. The student who has had little success or aptitude as a scholar is advised not to attempt college. If he should choose to come to the University, however, he should be aware that his chances for completing a four-year program are small. There-
38–MacMillan Co.– Planning and Paying Your Way
fore, he should plan his course of study toward securing the maximum advantage from a program of fewer than four years. The student should contact his high school principal or guidance counselor for advice concerning his probable success in college.

Advanced Standing Tests for Freshmen   14.

The University of Missouri grants advanced standing to entering freshmen who, on the basis of performance on comprehensive examinations, demonstrate proficiency in certain college-level courses such as English, mathematics, history, botany, zoology, chemistry, accounting, political science, and foreign languages. Students should consult their high school principals or counselors for information concerning the advanced standing program. Entering freshmen desiring to take the examinations should write to the Director of Admissions, 130 Jesse Hall.

[*11.*] For college admission purposes most high schools determine rank in class on the basis of seven semesters of marks or at the end of the first semester of the senior year. The ranking may or may not be adjusted at the end of the senior year, depending on the policy of the individual high school. College admission granted on the basis of seven or fewer semesters of work is tentative until the student satisfactorily completes the final semester.

[*12.*] If placement tests are given, the student may be required to succeed in noncredit remedial work before he is admitted to certain of the required credit courses, such as English, speech, and mathematics. Students who miss placement tests may be barred from registering until the tests have been completed, may be required to pay late-registration fees, or may be delayed a semester in registering, depending on college policy. Dates of placement tests and similar events are given in the annual college calendar published in the catalog, or on information sheets sent to the student with his application material.

[*13.*] Because a small number of students in the lower third or fourth of their high school class will succeed in college, some public four-year colleges and universities admit such students "on probation." (See explanation 9.) However, in states supporting a junior college system, these students are usually required to complete a year or more of work successfully in the two-year college before requesting admission to the four-year college.

[*14.*] "Advanced standing" is the opportunity to enter

areas of study at a point somewhere above the first college-level course. Placement tests often provide such opportunity. The student who wishes advanced placement may submit scores on a nationally administered test, such as the specialized tests given by the College Entrance Examination Board and described in various annual publications of the board, especially *Advanced Placement Program: Course Descriptions*. High school counselors usually have the college board publications available for examination by students, or a price list may be requested by writing to the board at Box 592, Princeton, N. J. 08540, or at Box 1025, Berkeley, Calif. 94701.

TRANSFER STUDENTS

Admission

A student who has been enrolled in another college or university may be admitted to the University of Mis- **15.** souri provided his scholastic record has been satisfactory. A student whose record is unsatisfactory, is not eligible for admission. A student, however, who is a Missouri resident and whose record is not satisfactory may be requested to take a battery of tests and have his application and credentials reviewed by the Committee on Entrance.

Official transcripts from each college attended and **16.** a high school transcript should be filed with the Director of Admissions at least eight weeks prior to registration. All credentials submitted for admission become the property of the University of Missouri and are permanently filed.

The University may not admit any student who is **17.** under suspension or dismissal, or whose previous record shows work of an inferior or unsatisfactory quality.

Advanced Standing

Credit hours in the form of advanced standing may be allowed for work satisfactorily completed in another college or university of recognized standing insofar as such work satisfies the requirements of the division of the University in which the student registers. Courses with grades of "D" are not accepted. Advanced standing **18.** for the work of the senior year will not be granted. Claims for advanced standing, in order to receive rec- **19.** ognition, must be made by the student within one semester after entrance.

Graduates of accredited junior colleges will be admitted without examination to junior standing in the colleges of the University, provided, upon examination of official transcripts, they have satisfied the entrance requirements and have paralleled the work of the first two years of the particular college.

Admission to Undergraduate Schools

The Schools of Business and Public Administration, Journalism, Law, Medicine, and Veterinary Medicine re- **20.**

quire for admission two years or more of college work including certain specific subjects. College subjects required for admission are designated in terms of semester hours. An hour is defined as a college subject pursued one period a week for a semester of at least sixteen weeks or for a minimum of sixteen periods for one term.

[15.] A satisfactory record entitles the student to a statement that he is "in good standing," that he is eligible to continue or to transfer elsewhere. However, because of variations in academic standards among colleges, a satisfactory record at one may not be acceptable at another, especially a record containing several hours of "D" marks.

[16.] Always ask every college attended to forward a transcript of records directly to the admissions office. Women who have high school or college records under maiden and married names must remember to clarify transcript requests with maiden and married names, years of attendance, and year of birth. It is important to give one's current address, also, in order that the bill for sending a record may be forwarded. Most colleges give the first transcript without charge. One dollar is the general fee for each additional transcript, but this charge varies. Even some high schools now charge for transcripts. Transcripts brought by hand must be in a sealed official envelope of the high school or college and may even then be acceptable only for preliminary evaluation. Two to six weeks should be allowed for transmittal of records, especially from May 1 to October 1 and from December 1 to March 1 each year, when the college registrars are extremely busy with current admissions and registrations or with commencement and record transmittal for new graduates.

[17.] Suspension for academic or disciplinary reasons involves a fixed time after which a student may apply for readmission. Transfer to another college should not be attempted until a student can produce a letter readmitting him to the last college attended.
Dismissal does not involve a fixed time when a student may return. If readmission is granted it is usually after a period of a year or more. Students dismissed at one college are almost never accepted at another reputable college unless they have obtained permission to re-enter the last college attended.

[18.] A transfer student is usually asked to complete the last year or a minimum of thirty semester hours at the college from which he seeks the baccalaureate degree.

[19.] Difficulty is avoided if all transcripts or other sources of credit, such as military training certificates, have been supplied to the admissions office prior to their final evaluation of applications.

[20.] Faculty members normally serve as student advisors, often reluctantly. They are far from infallible concerning course requirements, and it is the student's responsibility to know all regulations and course requirements for professional schools and for degrees. These requirements should be learned by careful study of the catalogs.

When to Apply

The time to make application depends on when the institutions you select will accept application forms. The specific dates for receiving your formal application will vary from institution to institution. You will want to apply for admission by the date designated in the catalogs of institutions you have selected. Institutions must receive your application in ample time to assemble your records, test results, and other information to be reviewed by the admissions committee and to let you know its decision by an early date. Review college catalogs carefully and comply with the instructions.

Regular Admissions. Most colleges want students to apply during the fall semester of their senior year. This gives admissions committees a chance to evaluate applications early in the second semester. Students usually are admitted during the last semester of their senior year in high school. State universities that are obligated to admit state-resident students who have graduated with a satisfactory high school record usually prefer that students not make application until spring of their graduating year. Junior colleges request applications to be filed as far as possible in advance of the desired registration date, and some state colleges will admit students during the summer for fall registration. Selective institutions request students to indicate their interest by letter at an early date, with formal application to be made during the senior year.

When you return your application to a college, applications for housing, scholarship, loan, or part-time work should be included. If you are admitted, you will receive information regarding these applications by mail.

Candidates usually receive decisions from colleges during April, May, and June, with the exception of institutions participating in "early admission" plans. If you have been accepted, your letter from the office of admissions will indicate that you have been accepted pending your continued success in your high school program. When you have been accepted by one of the institutions to which you have applied you should accept, unless there is a good reason for not doing so. Most selection and semi-selective colleges will give you a date by which you must commit your intention. This practice allows the college to select another student should you not plan to attend. It is foolish to run the risk of not attending a good school by trying to "wait out" the approval of your application at another school of near-equal standing. "One in the hand is better than two in the bush" when the average student is gaining admission to college.

Early Admissions. About two hundred colleges and universities, primarily selective ones in which competition is keen, want applicants to make preliminary application during their junior year. This practice was developed to encourage outstanding students to make an early decision about which college to attend. Students are considered on the basis of three years' work. Successful students are notified by December of their senior year.

A majority of institutions follow a system of observing a specific date for all applications to be filed. Institutions that are considered semiselective prefer to have students state their interest in attending early, but do not require a preliminary application to be filed. Institutions accepting most high school graduates may require no advance notice of a student's desire to enroll. In short, the greater the competition for a seat in a particular college, the earlier you should apply.

Early admission is given only to outstanding students. Generally, the average student will not have an advantage by applying by this procedure, because only a small number of candidates are admitted in this manner to any one college. If the institution you wish to attend has an early admissions policy, and you are encouraged to try by your counselor, little will be lost by applying. Your application will be considered with others applying for the first time. If you are unsuccessful, there is no adverse effect and you are free to apply to the same institution or elsewhere the following year.

Typical Application Dates. A review of dates that colleges want students to meet will help you understand the "when" of making application. At the University of Pennsylvania and Cornell University, formal applications should be received by January 1 of the year of enrollment. Officials at the University of Southern California request that applications be made as early as possible and that all material be supplied to the office of admissions so that a decision can be reached at an early date. A recent bulletin states that applications received at the University of Southern California after August 15 for the fall semester and January 1 for the spring semester cannot be assured consideration for admission, but will be reviewed if time permits and space is available. Applicants seeking September admission to New York University should file before March 1; those seeking February admission should file before November 1. Applications submitted after these dates are considered in the order received as long as space is available.

How to Apply

Admission to college is determined by the office of admissions and a selection committee appointed for the purpose of screening applicants. The office receives and processes all applications, evaluates records, and issues permits to register to students that the selection committee approves. Your first step is to write the office of admissions indicating your interest and requesting an application blank. A form postal card requesting a catalog and application forms is shown in chapter III, page 34.

Colleges tell students what information to send. An application for college admission is more than a completed application form; it is all the information the college uses in making a decision whether to admit a student. Included with the application forms will be requests for the specific records, test results, letters of recommendation, and other information needed by the college. Health forms are requested by some colleges; others request these after students are admitted. If an autobiographical letter is requested, be sure to provide any information specifically requested, and pay close attention to organization, sentence structure, grammar, and spelling. A letter regarding your character and potential as a student is usually requested from your high school principal or guidance counselor.

The more competitive the institution, the more selective admissions officers can be, but they can only select from the students with whom they come in contact. Selective colleges may require personal interviews and letters of recommendation in addition to high school records and personal application.

Colleges and universities with an open-door policy require only your high school record and completed application. All colleges have the same objective — they want the best qualified students that they can attract, and many colleges select such students only on the basis of the completed application forms they receive through the mail.

Preparing a Forceful Application. College admissions personnel can only evaluate what you send. All the information you present to a college is important, but, to many institutions, the most important item is your application form. When distance makes a personal interview on the campus impractical for an applicant, the college will often arrange for a visiting representative or an alumnus to conduct an interview in the student's home. Figure 5 (pp. 69-70) illustrates the report form used by one well-known university for securing interview results from alumni representatives. A study of this form will give you an idea of what personal characteristics the colleges are concerned about when representatives talk with you, whether off-campus or on. A neat, well-prepared application form will make a more favorable impression on the evaluator than a messy one.

The following suggestions are offered on how to present an application for admission:

1. Before completing application forms, read the instructions carefully. Follow instructions and

Figure 2

SYRACUSE UNIVERSITY

APPLICATION FOR ADMISSION

This form is to be completed and returned to the Office of Admissions, Syracuse University, Syracuse 10, N. Y., together with an application fee of $10.00, the Index Card, and the Information Card. The application fee is not refundable. Please make check or money order payable to Syracuse University.

Date_____

1. Type or print legal name in full.
   Miss ☐
   Mrs. ☐
   Mr. ☐ _____
          (Last Name)   (First Name)   (Middle Name)   Space above reserved for photograph.

2. Permanent residence
   address _____
      (Number & Street) (City) (Zone) (State) (County) (Telephone No.)

3. Mailing address_____
      (Number & Street) (City) (Zone) (State) (Telephone No.)

4. Underscore the course, school, or college you wish to enter:

Architecture (5 years)
Architecture, Landscape Architecture

Art
Design, Illustration, Industrial Design, Interior Decoration, Painting, Sculpture, Art Education

Business Administration
Accounting (C.P.A.)
Business Education
Combination Business Administration-Law (6 years)
General Business
Journalism
Program for Women
Secretarial Science
Two-Year Program (A.A.S.)

Education
Early Childhood Education, Elementary Education, Special Education
Library Science

Engineering
Chemical
Metallurgical Engineering Option
Civil
Photogrammetry
Electrical
Industrial
Mechanical
Aeronautical Engineering Option

Home Economics
Applied Arts and Fashion Merchandising
Family Relations and Child Development
Foods and Nutrition
Cooperative programs with:
Broadcasting (Radio and Television)
Journalism
Education

Journalism
Newspaper, Magazine, Advertising, News, Radio-Television, Public Relations, Publishing
Combined programs with: Business Administration, Home Economics, Liberal Arts, Speech and Dramatic Art

Liberal Arts
A.B.
B.S. (Bacteriology, Botany, Geology, Mathematics, Physics, Zoology)
B.S. in Chemistry
Combination Liberal Arts-Architecture (6 years)
Combination Liberal Arts-Engineering (5 years)
Combination Liberal Arts-Law (6 years)
Fine Arts Concentration
Journalism
Laboratory Technician
Library Science
Physical Education
Professional Option (Dentistry, Medicine)
Teacher Preparation

Music
Bachelor of Music Degree
Music Education, Organ, Percussion, Piano, a String or Wind Instrument, Theory and Composition, Voice
Bachelor of Arts Degree
Music (dual enrollment in the College of Liberal Arts)

Nursing
Baccalaureate Basic Program
General Nursing Program (for Graduate Nurses)

Public Health Nursing

Speech and Dramatic Art
Audiology and Speech Pathology
Combination Speech-Law
Drama
Interpretation
Journalism
Public Address
Radio and Television
Speech Education

NOTE: Do **not** use this application form if you wish to apply for admission to the New York State College of FORESTRY or any of the GRADUATE divisions of the University; application blanks for such purpose may be obtained from the particular school or college concerned. If you wish to be considered for admission to UNIVERSITY COLLEGE (evening division), you should obtain a special application form for University College entrance from the Office of Admissions.

5. Underscore the date you wish to enter: February, 196_____; June / July 196_____; September, 196_____.

6. Indicate the high schools or preparatory schools you have attended.
   (Give name and location of each, inclusive dates of attendance, and date of graduation. Request the Principal or Headmaster of each school to send an official transcript directly to the Office of Admissions, Syracuse University.)

   _____

   _____

7. (a) Have you attended any school, college, or university on any basis since graduation from high school? _____ Name each and give inclusive dates. _____

   _____

   (IMPORTANT: If you have attended any institution on any basis, for any period of time, since graduation from high school, you are required to have **TWO** official transcripts of your record sent directly from **EACH** institution attended to the Office of Admissions, Syracuse University, with a statement to the effect that you are eligible to return in good standing. This must be done whether or not you intend to ask for transfer credit.)

(Form 106-11 Rev.) SU 25M 8-61—40749 (26-30b)

- 2 -

(b) If you have served in the armed forces, list attendance at colleges or universities while in the service. Indicate names and addresses of institutions and inclusive dates.

----

8. Have you taken the Scholastic Aptitude Test of the College Entrance Examination Board for college entrance purposes? _____ If so, give date _____

   If not, when do you plan to take it? _____

   (Please request the College Entrance Examination Board, P. O. Box 592, Princeton, N. J., to send a report of your scores to Office of Admissions, Syracuse University.)

9. Have you had any military service? _____ If so, give inclusive dates _____

10. Have you applied before for admission to Syracuse University? _____ If so, give date_____

11. Have you attended University College or Summer School of Syracuse University?_____

12. Date of birth_____
                 (Year)   (Month)   (Day)

13. Give as references the names and addresses of three responsible citizens:

----

14. Are you a citizen of the U. S.? _____ If not, of what country are you a citizen? _____

15. Father's full name_____

    It is understood that the registration of all students admitted to Syracuse University is subject to the following conditions:

    Attendance at the University is a privilege and not a right. The University reserves the right to require the withdrawal of any student at any time for any reason which it deems sufficient, and no reason for requiring such withdrawal need be given. All students are required to live in houses approved by the University. The University reserves the right to cancel any course the registration for which is too small to warrant its being given. The University reserves the right to make any changes which are deemed advisable in the rules and regulations and also in the fees. A candidate who, in the judgment of the health authorities of the University, is physically or mentally unfit for University work, will not be regarded as fully admitted to any department of the University and may be rejected.

    Refusal of admission or cancellation of registration will result from any attempt at misrepresentation in any portion of this six-page application form.

    We, the undersigned, make application for admission of _____
                                                                (Name of Applicant)
    as a student to the underscored course at Syracuse University, subject to all terms and conditions herein mentioned, and agree to pay all tuition, dues, fees, and charges of Syracuse University to the student for his/her entire attendance at Syracuse University.

Signature _____ (Applicant)

Signature _____(Parent or Guardian)

Address (Parent or Guardian)_____

NOTE: Each of the questions on this application must be answered and the application signed by the applicant and parent or guardian before action can be taken on this application.

-3-

INFORMATION FOR PERSONNEL DIVISION

Date_____

1. Miss ☐
    Mrs. ☐
    Mr. ☐ _____
    PLEASE PRINT (Last Name)   (First Name)   (Middle Name)

2. Permanent residence address:_____
                                   (Number and Street)   (City)   (Zone) (State) (County) (Telephone No.)

3. Applying to the College of_____
                                (e.g., Business Administration, Liberal Arts, etc.)

4. Name and address of high school attended_____

    _____

    Number in graduating class_____ Your rank: (Please underscore)

    Highest quarter, Second quarter, Third quarter, Lowest quarter.

5. Have you attended any school, college, or university on any basis

    since graduation from high school?_____ Name each and give

    inclusive dates _____

    _____

6. Have you had any military service?_____

    If so, give inclusive dates _____   Space above reserved
                                                                      for photograph.

7. Date of birth _____8. Height _____ Weight _____
                  (Year)   (Month)   (Day)

9. Are you a citizen of the U. S.? _____ If not, of what country are you a citizen?_____

10. Are you married?_____ If so, have you any children? _____

11. Spouse's full name_____

12. Do you have any physical handicaps? (If so, state nature) _____

    _____

13. Father's full name _____ If deceased, state year _____

14. Father's home address _____

15. Father's business address _____

16. Father's occupation _____ 17. Did he attend college? _____

18. What college? _____ 19. Did he graduate?_____

20. Mother's full name _____ If deceased, state year _____

21. Mother's home address _____

22. Is she employed at present? _____ If so, state occupation _____

23. Did she attend college? _____ 24. What college? _____

25. Did she graduate? _____ 26. If parents are not college graduates indicate any training beyond

    grades _____

27.

Names of Brothers and Sisters	Sex	Age	Marital Status	Extent of Education	Occupation

-4-

28. List major school and/or community activities in which you have participated. Indicate offices held.

----

29. What high school subjects did you like the most? ----------------- The least? -----------------

30. What high school subjects did you find the easiest? ------------- The most difficult? -------------

31. Name in order of preference the three occupations in which you would most prefer to be employed. After each, give the reason for your choice.

a. --   --

    ----

b. --   --

    ----

c. --   --

    ----

32. If more than six months have elapsed since your high school graduation, indicate what you have

been doing. (If working, state types of jobs.) ---

----

33. If you are a transfer applicant, indicate your reasons for transferring. ---------------------------

----

----

34. Are you personally acquainted with any faculty members in the University? Give names.

----

35. Name three alumni or students of Syracuse whom you know. -----------------------------------

----

-5-

36. Give the names of all relatives who have attended Syracuse University and state their relationship to you _____

_____

37. Name and address of person responsible for your expenses _____

_____

38. Do you plan to apply for financial aid (scholarship, loan, or part-time work) from Syracuse University? _____ If so, have you received the leaflet entitled, "Financial Aid Opportunities at Syracuse University"?_____

39. On this and the next page write an autobiography which includes additional information about yourself. We want you to give us an idea of the experiences and opportunities which have had the most to do with making you the type of person you believe you are. Please conclude this statement with your reasons for wanting a college education at Syracuse. **This autobiography must be in your own handwriting.**

I assume complete responsibility for the completeness and accuracy of this information.

                                                       Signature of Applicant

note all deadlines that apply. Seek advice from your counselor and parents as needed.

2. Prepare a draft of each form.
3. Answer all questions carefully. Make certain your spelling and grammar are correct.
4. Use as references people who know you well and who will give honest and objective opinions of your abilities. You should ask their permission to use their names. At a later time, ask them if they have sent letters to the admissions office.
5. Have the drafts reviewed by the counselor, a teacher, or your parents.
6. Complete all official forms requested by using a typewriter, if acceptable. Enter on the official forms requested information after you are satisfied with your application. Send in before deadline date.
7. Arrange to take any required tests.
8. Check to see that the school has forwarded all necessary information to the college.
9. Should you earn any awards or there be any change in your situation that affects your plans or would make your application more forceful, notify the college at your earliest opportunity.

Obtaining Letters of Recommendation. Although not required by all institutions, two types of letters of recommendation may be requested: confidential letters from the guidance counselor and principal, and letters from persons not related to the student or the school. Of the two types, the letters from the counselor and the principal are the most important. To have uniform information for all students, a form providing the principal's estimate of student's success may be provided for completion.

The confidential letter from your counselor or principal is valued by the colleges because it provides an appraisal of your achievements based on the reactions of your teachers and other school personnel. It usually reveals something of your experiences and your likely academic success in college. The school is the most informed source to which the college can turn for this kind of information.

Other letters of recommendation indicate your out-of-school interests and abilities. Persons who can best speak objectively about your specific activities and academic abilities and who know you well should be selected. Former employers, clergymen, and professional people are usually preferred. Letters from alumni are of limited value unless they can meet the above qualifications. It is usually a mistake to have unsolicited letters sent to the admissions office in your behalf. Admissions officers may question the ethics of students who have influential people write unnecessary letters supporting them. Asking for these letters not only wastes several people's time, but may unintentionally reveal things about you that will damage your chances of being admitted.

Preparing Your Autobiography. The autobiography is used by the admissions office as another source of information. The purpose of it is to gain a knowledge of your background and experience, and to provide a basis of evaluating your ability to express your thoughts and feelings about college. It is doubtful that students are approved or deprived of admission on the

Figure 3

IMPORTANT

1. TO THE STUDENT:

Do NOT give this Secondary School Transcript Form to your Guidance Counselor for completion until after you have mailed your formal application for admission to the Director of Admissions, Syracuse University.

IF YOUR TRANSCRIPT IS RECEIVED BY THE ADMISSIONS OFFICE BEFORE YOUR FORMAL APPLICATION, IT WILL BE PLACED IN AN INACTIVE FILE.

Please complete the following note to the Guidance Counselor before giving the Secondary School Transcript Form to him/her for completion.

2. TO THE GUIDANCE COUNSELOR:

This is to inform you that I mailed my formal application for admission to the Director of Admissions, Syracuse University, on _____.
                    Date

_____
Signature of Student

SYRACUSE UNIVERSITY
SYRACUSE, N. Y.

SECONDARY SCHOOL TRANSCRIPT

NAME, IN FULL_____ SEX_____

LAST NAME   FIRST NAME   MIDDLE NAME   M OR F

HOME ADDRESS_____

NUMBER AND STREET   CITY   ZONE   STATE

BIRTH DATE_____ NAME OF PARENT OR GUARDIAN_____

MONTH   DAY   YEAR

ENTERED { NAME OF SCHOOL _____   WAS GRADUATED
                                                        WILL BE GRADUATED }
         { LOCATION OF SCHOOL _____ ENTRANCE DATE_____ WITHDREW } _____
                                                                              MO. YR.

APPLICANT RANKS_____ IN A TOTAL GRADUATING CLASS OF ____. PASSING MARK: ____. COLLEGE RECOMMENDING MARK:____

1. IF THE APPLICANT IS CURRENTLY IN ATTENDANCE, PLEASE CHECK (✓) IN APPROPRIATE SPACES THE SUBJECTS TO BE COMPLETED IN THE SENIOR YEAR.
2. DESCRIBE YOUR MARKING SYSTEM, IF UNUSUAL: _____
3. LIST OTHER SECONDARY SCHOOLS ATTENDED: _____

CLASS RECORD

CIRCLE MARKS OR CHECKS FOR HALF-YEAR SUBJECTS.

SUBJECT	GRADE ➤ YEAR ➤	9 19	10 19	11 19	12 19	N.Y.S. REGENTS EXAM.	EXTRA 19	UNITS*
ENG.								
LANG.								
MATH.								
SCIENCE								
SOC. ST.								
OTHER SUBJ.								

NOTES: SPECIFY LABORATORY PERIODS, VARIATIONS IN TIME ALLOWANCE FOR SUBJECTS OR OTHER INFORMATION NEEDED TO INTERPRET THIS RECORD. SUCH OTHER INFORMATION AS ADDITIONAL REGENTS (INCLUDING FAILURES) MARKS, AND/OR A RECORD OF A FIFTH YEAR MAY BE ENTERED IN THE EXTRA COLUMN. IF A SCHOOL DOES NOT USE MARKS, PLACE HERE AN ESTIMATE OF SUCCESS ACHIEVED.

*A UNIT REPRESENTS THE STUDY OF A SUBJECT A FULL SCHOOL YEAR, FIVE PERIODS A WEEK, OR THE EQUIVALENT.

TEST RECORD

NAME OF TEST	DATE	RAW SCORE	I.Q.** %-ILE	BASIS	NAME OF TEST	DATE	RAW SCORE	I.Q.** %-ILE	BASIS

**GIVE BASIS ON WHICH PERCENTILES WERE COMPUTED. INCLUDE ANY AVAILABLE INTERPRETATION ON AN ENCLOSURE.

DATE_____ SIGNATURE_____ TITLE_____

ADAPTED FROM N.A.S.S.P. SECONDARY SCHOOL RECORD (MASTER) BY THE NEW YORK STATE REGENTS' COLLEGE-HIGH SCHOOL ARTICULATION COMMITTEE.

TO THE PRINCIPAL: THIS TRANSCRIPT IS NOT TO BE ENTRUSTED TO THE STUDENT BUT MUST BE MAILED DIRECTLY TO THE DIRECTOR OF ADMISSIONS, SYRACUSE UNIVERSITY. ITS RECEIPT WILL BE ACKNOWLEDGED.

SECONDARY SCHOOL PERSONALITY RECORD (CONFIDENTIAL)

PERSONAL CHARACTERISTICS OF_____

LAST NAME   FIRST NAME   MIDDLE NAME

SCHOOL_____ TOWN OR CITY_____ STATE_____

THE FOLLOWING CHARACTERIZATIONS ARE DESCRIPTIONS OF BEHAVIOR; THEY ARE NOT RATINGS. IT IS RECOMMENDED THAT WHERE POSSIBLE THE JUDGMENTS OF A NUMBER OF THE PUPIL'S PRESENT TEACHERS BE USED.

1. SERIOUSNESS OF PURPOSE	PURPOSELESS	VACILLATING	POTENTIAL	SELF-DIRECTED	PURPOSEFUL
2. INDUSTRY	SELDOM WORKS EVEN UNDER PRESSURE	NEEDS CONSTANT PRESSURE	NEEDS OCCASIONAL PRODDING	PREPARES ASSIGNED WORK	SEEKS ADDITIONAL WORK
3. INITIATIVE	SELDOM INITIATES	CONFORMS	VARIES WITH CONDITIONS	SELF-RELIANT	ACTIVELY CREATIVE
4. INFLUENCE	PASSIVE	RETIRING BUT CO-OPERATIVE	VARYING	CONTRIBUTING	STRONGLY CONTROLLING
5. CONCERN FOR OTHERS	ANTISOCIAL	INDIFFERENT	SELF-CENTERED	SOMEWHAT SOCIALLY CONCERNED	DEEPLY AND GENERALLY CONCERNED
6. RESPONSIBILITY	UNRELIABLE	SOMEWHAT DEPENDABLE	USUALLY DEPENDABLE	CONSCIENTIOUS	ASSUMES MUCH RESPONSIBILITY
7. EMOTIONAL STABILITY	HYPEREMOTIONAL / APATHETIC	EXCITABLE / UNRESPONSIVE	USUALLY WELL-BALANCED	WELL-BALANCED	EXCEPTIONALLY STABLE

SIGNIFICANT SCHOOL ACTIVITIES:

SPECIAL INTERESTS OR ABILITIES:

SIGNIFICANT LIMITATIONS (PHYSICAL, SOCIAL, MENTAL):

ADDITIONAL INFORMATION WHICH MAY BE HELPFUL, SUCH AS PROBABLE FINANCIAL NEED OR WORK EXPERIENCES, OR GENERAL COMMENT:

SCHOOL'S RECOMMENDATION (SPECIFIC STATEMENT CONCERNING THE APPLICANT'S FITNESS FOR THE COURSE FOR WHICH HE IS APPLYING)

ACCREDITATION STATUS OF SCHOOL: THIS SCHOOL IS FULLY ACCREDITED BY   THE STATE EDUCATION DEPARTMENT ☐
THE REGIONAL ASSOCIATION ☐

DATE_____ SIGNATURE_____ TITLE_____

ADAPTED FROM N.A.S.S.P. SECONDARY SCHOOL RECORD (MASTER) BY THE NEW YORK STATE REGENTS' COLLEGE-HIGH SCHOOL ARTICULATION COMMITTEE.

IMPORTANT: THIS FORM IS TO BE MAILED TO THE DIRECTOR OF ADMISSIONS, SYRACUSE UNIVERSITY.

Figure 4

COLLEGE ADMISSIONS CENTER

610 CHURCH STREET   EVANSTON, ILLINOIS

INSTRUCTION SHEET

In order to continue to give good service to students and colleges, we request your cooperation in carefully following the registration procedures outlined below:

REGISTRATION PROCEDURES:

I. **For ALL STUDENTS who wish to register with the College Admissions Center:**

  1. Complete pages 1, 2 and 3 of the registration form. Please type.

  2. Complete side *A* of *both* of the information cards. Please type.

  3. Make out a check or money order for $10 (ten dollars) to the College Admissions Center to cover the registration fee. Please do *not* send cash. This fee is not refundable.

II. **For STUDENTS WHO HAVE NEVER ATTENDED COLLEGE BEFORE:**

  1. Take or send the completed registration form, the two information cards, and the check to your high school guidance counselor.

  2. Ask your counselor to complete *page 4* of the registration form.

  3. Ask your counselor to enclose a copy of your high school transcript and forward it, along with the registration form, the two information cards, and the check, to the Center in the envelope provided. Please stamp the envelope.

  4. Discard the COLLEGE TRANSFER FORM, page 3-a and 3-b.

III. **For TRANSFER STUDENTS ONLY:**

  1. Complete the COLLEGE TRANSFER FORM, page 3-a.

  2. Complete *both* sides (A & B) of *both* of the information cards.

  3. Take or send the COLLEGE TRANSFER FORM to your college dean, advisor, counselor, or registrar, and ask him to complete page 3-b which is addressed to him.

  Then request that he forward to the College Admissions Center the COLLEGE TRANS-FER FORM, an official copy of your college transcript, and the material you have previously assembled — the two information cards, the completed registration form (pages 1, 2, and 3), and the $10 registration fee. Please stamp the enclosed envelope, and give it to

him to use in mailing the material to the Center.

  4. Request your high school to send an official copy of your transcript to the Center.

  5. If you have attended more than one college, you must have official transcripts of the work you have done at each college sent to the Center. However, page 3-b of the COLLEGE TRANSFER FORM must be completed by the appropriate person in the college most recently attended. (See III, step 3).

The Center will send you a card when your registration has been received. If your registration is not complete, you will be informed of the missing materials. It is your responsibility to see that your registration is filed and complete.

After your registration is complete and placed in the active files of the Center, you may begin to hear from colleges. If you have any questions about the colleges that express an interest in you, please discuss these questions with your college counselor. The Center cannot answer questions about the colleges or their programs. If a college counselor is not available, a teacher or a reference librarian in your local library may be able to help you.

You are under no obligation to respond to all of the colleges that write to you, and the colleges that write to you are not obliged to accept you for admission. After discussing the colleges that write to you with a counselor, you should formally apply for admission to a few of the colleges in which you are most interested. In most cases, you will have to supply each college with a complete set of credentials (transcripts, test scores, letters of recommendation). If necessary, the Center will send photostatic copies of your records to colleges at your request. You will be charged $1 per set of credentials (one transcript and one letter of recommendation).

As soon as you accept admission to a college, please inform the Center and your school counselor of the name of the college. The $10 registration fee entitles you to have your registration kept active with the Center for one calendar year (which will include review by the colleges for both fall and mid-year admission), or until you have accepted college admission, whichever occurs first.

The College Admissions Center does not guarantee college admission, but it does assure you that your credentials will receive careful consideration by a large number of colleges.

* Reprinted by permission of College Admissions Center of the Association of College Admissions Counselors, Evanston, Illinois.

COLLEGE ADMISSIONS CENTER
610 Church Street   Evanston, Illinois

COLLEGE TRANSFER REGISTRATION FORM

If you have attended or are now attending college, please fill out this form. (If you have never undertaken any college work, please discard this sheet.)

PLEASE TYPE

Name _____ Address _____
                Last   First   Middle

Name of College(s) Attended	Address	No. Credits Earned Semester Quarter	Dates of Attendance
_____	_____	____ ____	_____
_____	_____	____ ____	_____
_____	_____	____ ____	_____

Total ____ ____

Indicate degree program you have followed to date, i.e., Liberal Arts (history major), Pre-Engineering (electrical), etc. _____

In transferring, what degree program do you propose to follow? _____

_____

What is the total number of quality or grade points earned in all courses taken in all colleges (use a 4.0 scale: A-4, B-3, C-2, D-1, E or F-0 _____

Did you work while you were in college? _____. Hours per week _____

Type(s) of positions held while in school _____

Briefly state your reasons for wanting to transfer_____

_____

What is your academic status? Good standing _____ Probation _____ Other _____

Were you ever dismissed from any college for academic or social reasons? _____

If answer is yes: Date of dismissal _____. Will you be permitted to return? _____

If so, what are the terms of readmission? _____

Discuss briefly the reasons for your academic or social difficulties, if any.

_____

_____

What is the name, title, and address of the person in the college *most recently attended* who is most familiar with your academic record? _____

_____

Take this sheet to the person named above for completion of the other side of this registration form. Ask that an official transcript of your college record be attached and both returned to the College Admissions Center, along with 1) the registration form, 2) the two information cards which you have completed on both sides, and 3) your check or money order for $10 made out to the College Admissions Center. Stamp the enclosed envelope and give it to the person named above to use in mailing in all this material to the College Admissions Center.

(3-a)

TO THE COLLEGE DEAN, ADVISOR, COUNSELOR OR REGISTRAR: This registration form will be reviewed by many college admissions counselors at the College Admissions Center. In order to help these college representatives determine whether or not this student meets the admission requirements of their colleges and can be accepted as a transfer student, we ask that you answer the following questions accurately and completely. It will be most helpful if you can indicate rank in class against those students who are continuing their college education.

This student is a 1st, 2nd, 3rd, 4th year student (please circle). What is the size of his class? _____

What is his rank in class? _____. What is his grade point average? _____

How is this average computed? _____

_____

Use the space below for your evaluation of him as a student. Please discuss his academic abilities, motivation, performance, strengths and weaknesses, and any pertinent factors which contributed to his desire to transfer.

Please return this sheet and *a copy of the student's college transcript* to the College Admissions Center, 610 Church Street, Evanston, Illinois.

Date _____ Signature _____

(3-b)

(A)

Name _____
             Last   First   Middle

Home Address _____
              Street   City   State

High School _____
              Name   City   State

Year of Graduation _____ Age _____ Sex _____ Race _____

Religion _____ Church Affiliation _____

Citizenship _____ ☐ Married ☐ Single

Financial Aid ☐ yes ☐ no ☐ would help

Academic Interest: (circle first choice) Humanities, Social Sciences, Physical Sciences, Biological Sciences, Business, Education, Engineering, Fine Arts, Agriculture, Other

_____

Vocational Plans: (circle first choice) Nursing, Medicine, Architecture, Law, Forestry, Home Economics, Applied Arts, Drama, Teaching, Social Work, Business,

Other _____

Would you like to hear from selected colleges not accredited by a regional accrediting agency? ☐ yes ☐ no

DO NOT WRITE IN THIS SPACE

Withdrawn _____	Book _____
Complete _____	Form _____
Rank _____	Fee _____
Class _____	Cards _____
SAT V _____	Trans H) _____
M _____	C) _____
School Code	Ratings 1) _____
_____	2) _____
_____	Pict _____

77	Trans		Church	83
78	Yr of Grad		Fin Aid	84
79	Geo Sec		Acc	85
80	Age		Acad Int	86
81	Sex		Voc Int	87
82	Race		Cycle	

(B)

If you have attended or are now attending college, please fill out this side.

List colleges starting with most recent one attended.

	Name	Address	Dates of Attendance
1			
2			
3			

Total number of credits earned in all colleges _____

Total number of quality or grade points earned on four point scale (A-4, B-3, C-2, D-1, E or F-0) _____

Academic status: _____ in good standing; _____ probation; Other _____

Reasons for wanting to transfer: _____

basis of the autobiography alone. However, it provides a part of the impression the college gets of you.

It is not easy to write about yourself. Before you write, think about what you wish to say and how you want to express it. It will be to your advantage to prepare a draft of the autobiography. Develop each idea. Ask a teacher, a parent, or friend to make suggestions for improvement before you prepare the final copy. Instructions will state whether you may type the final copy.

Typical Application Forms and Secondary School Transcript

Official application forms are not uniform in the amount and nature of information requested, their size, or organization. Sometimes the student and his high school are asked to complete separate sections. Examples of application forms will acquaint you with practices used by offices of admissions. You will want to read carefully catalogs from the institutions to which you plan to apply.

The University of Colorado provides a clear statement of when and how to apply in its 1965 bulletin.

How to Apply
1. The application for admission form for freshmen may be obtained from the Office of Admissions at the University of Colorado. A Colorado resident may also secure this form from the office of the vice principal or guidance counselor.
2. Freshmen applicants should complete Part I of the application and submit it to his high school office for record and test data.
3. The high school will send the completed application directly to the University.
4. The freshmen applicant, including the Colorado resident, should take the Scholastic Aptitude Test early in his senior year, preferably the December or January series, and have the scores sent to the University of Colorado.
5. A non-resident applicant must submit a $10 fee to cover the expense involved in processing the application as part of his credentials. This fee, in the form of a check or money order (not cash), must accompany the application. It will not be applied to the student's tuition if he is accepted nor will it be refunded if the applicant is refused admission.

When to Apply
1. An applicant currently enrolled in high school may apply as soon as his seventh semester grades are completed; he knows his courses in progress for the last semester; and he has a tentative rank in class. When these requirements have been met, the applicant may be given provisional admission until the work in progress is completed and reported to the Office of Admissions. It is the student's responsibility to see that a supplementary transcript of his last semester's work is sent to the Office of Admissions when such work is completed. Failure to submit this supplementary transcript may result in refusal of admission.
2. The application for admission may be submitted any time during the period between the beginning of the eighth semester and one month prior to beginning of the term for which admission is sought. Non-resident applications will be received until the established out-of-state quota has been filled.
3. A freshman student may make application for the Fall or Spring semester or either of the summer terms.

At the University of Pennsylvania, a form for application for admission may be obtained from the Office of Admissions, Logan Hall, University of Pennsylvania, Philadelphia, Pennsylvania 19104:

Candidates are urged to file their applications before January 1. Although the necessary procedures in applying for admission to the University can be completed satisfactorily by mail, it is desirable for candidates to visit the Admissions Office if they can conveniently do so. Alumni groups in various parts of the country regularly interview candidates on behalf of the Office of Admissions, and if there is such a group in the applicant's area, an alumnus will contact him.

The General Catalog for M.I.T. suggests the following application procedure to interested students:

A preliminary application, on a form which may be obtained from the Director of Admissions, may be filed as early as desired in advance of the anticipated date of entrance. This assures that the applicant will receive Final Application forms at the proper time, as well as any announcements which may be issued. The final application form is sent in the fall preceding the desired date of entrance to candidates who have filed Preliminary Application forms.

Students applying for entrance to Michigan State University may obtain forms from Michigan high schools or directly from the office of admissions. Students are instructed to complete one portion of the application; the remaining part is to be completed by the principal or counselor. The high school sends the completed application to Michigan State.

Two forms are needed for applying to Bowling Green University. One is titled "High School Certificate"; the other, "Application for Admission." The High School Certificate is to be completed by the high school principal and mailed directly to the director of admissions. The Application for Admission has three parts: personal information to be filled in by the student, a part to be completed by a student applying for a room in university dormitories, and a health examination form. Copies of these forms may be obtained by writing to the Director of Admissions, Bowling Green University, Bowling Green, Ohio. Completed forms, with a $25 nonrefundable fee, are sent to the same address.

Candidates for admission should address all communications to the Office of Admissions. Applications should be filed as far as possible in advance of the desired date of entrance. Admission is granted when the Admissions Committee has satisfactory evidence that the applicant shows promise of successfully completing a program of college study.

ALL APPLICANTS

All applicants for admission are required to:

File a formal application and photograph.

Pay a matriculation or registration fee.

Submit an official copy of the secondary school record.

Submit a certified copy of all previous college or university records. The applicant must request the registrar of the institution previously attended to mail directly to the Admissions Office a transcript of his record.

A Final Check. If you are accepted by more than one college, you may find it difficult to make the final choice unless you have ranked the institutions in order of personal preference before receiving notices of admission. When you have reached a decision and accepted one college, you should inform each of the colleges to which you have applied of your decision. To be certain that the college of your choice has all the information it needs, check with your high school counselor or principal to see that your last year of work is forwarded to the office of admissions, since acceptance by a college is not final until it has received all of your high school credits. The final step is up to the college. You will receive housing registration and other instructions through the mail.

In summary, the "how" and "when" of applying to a college are:

1. Write to the office of admissions indicating your interest in attending, and request application forms and other information needed.
2. Complete and return applications for admission, housing, financial aid, etc. Check for completeness, accuracy, clarity, and neatness. Enclose fees as instructed. (See figure 3.)
3. Request your high school to send an official transcript of your credits, test results, school's recommendation, and other information requested by the admissions office.
4. Arrange to take needed tests, request letters of recommendation, and other information as needed.
5. On acceptance, make a decision and notify the office of admissions and your high school guidance counselor.
6. Notify all colleges to which you applied of your decision.
7. Request your school to send final year's work to the college admissions office.
8. Arrange for room and board.
9. Make final personal arrangements for attending college.

Your Alternatives if Rejected

What can you do if you are not accepted? Don't panic. There is still hope, but it is time to change your tactics. Colleges with vacancies may be interested in students with your abilities. It is better for you to find an institution that more nearly matches your record and achievements. You will be happier and have a better chance of succeeding in such a college.

Under ordinary circumstances, a student will not know that he has been unsuccessful in gaining college admission until well into the second semester of his senior year. If you have not been accepted by the colleges to which you have applied by May it will be time for action. Consult your counselor or high school principal for suggestions regarding other colleges where you may apply. Should they have no suggestions, there are a few agencies that help students find colleges with vacancies, such as college admissions centers and other "clearing houses." These nonprofit organizations provide this service for a fee of $10 to $25. It is estimated they receive requests for placement assistance from about thirty thousand students annually. If you use the service provided by these centers, you will be asked to complete forms similar to college application forms and to provide transcripts of your high school records. Figure 5 is an example of forms to be completed. These records are made available to representatives of colleges that have vacancies. A very high percentage of students using the services of these clearing houses are accepted by one or more colleges.

While college admissions centers and clearing houses cannot guarantee results, they are your best bet for college admission if you have not been accepted by May of your senior year in high school. If you need their help, write to one of the following agencies:

College Admissions Assistance Center
535 East 80th Street
New York, New York 10021

College Clearing House Association
2169 Nelson Place
Westbury, New York 11590

The College Admissions Center
610 Church Street
Evanston, Illinois 60201

Catholic College Admissions and Information Center
500 Salisbury Street
Worcester, Massachusetts 01609

Chapter Five

Understanding Entrance Examinations

You have taken many tests in school. For students a generation ago, standardized objective tests provided reason for worry and apprehension but you are experienced in test-taking and there is no reason for concern. As a matter of fact, there is very good reason for not being concerned, for if you become overly concerned, you may not do as well on the entrance tests. Some suggestions will be discussed about what you can do to ease your mind about entrance examinations, but most of all, you should understand their purpose and how they serve you.

College entrance examinations are developed to test the kinds of abilities you have. They are a means to an objective evaluation of your development and potential development by criteria not dependent on the type or size of high school you attended or other differences in background.

Scholastic ability is made up of several different abilities. The widely used Scholastic Aptitude Test measures your ability to learn the type of things taught in college. Chief among the abilities needed by college students, due to the abstract nature of college studies, is the ability to grasp and effectively use language, arrive at the correct solution to problems with speed, comprehend arithmetical relations, and solve mathematical problems. Some abilities are needed by all college students while others are needed for successful achievement in particular fields. Much of college learning stems from the extensive use of books, words, symbols, and other abstractions. Your grades in social, studies, mathematics, and English may reflect your aptitude and abilities in these areas.

As already stated, although you may not be a candidate for an Ivy League school, you can be admitted to an accredited college if you have average mental equipment and a strong interest in a college education and are willing to make considerable effort. Some institutions do not require entrance examination. Several of these are state universities. Institutions not requiring entrance examinations admit students on a "certificate plan of admission." In this case, applications are, in reality, approved by the local school officials who certify the fitness of the applicants. The subject matter taken in high schools operating under this plan will likely be much the same as the usual college preparatory curriculum found in other high schools.

Some institutions that use entrance examinations have a cut-off score, which is used differently by each institution. Many state colleges and universities use it to place students in special classes or under a selected adviser who will direct them into special study groups to improve their chances for success. Other colleges will use the cut-off score to deny applicants admission unless other favorable evidence can be provided. When a cut-off score is used to place students in a group for special study courses, they are usually placed "on trial." They may be given a semester or a year in which to prove they are of college material. Students presenting less than a "C" average in high school courses may also be placed on trial. Students on trial are given the same rights and privileges as other students, but probably take some noncredit courses and courses designed to improve their reading skill and comprehension and other skills.

The commonly used entrance examinations are generally of two types: achievement and scholastic aptitude tests. Both seek to measure a student's ability. Achievement tests are designed to measure the amount a person has learned in a given area of subject matter. Tests of mental ability are designed to measure an individual's general ability to do school work.

Achievement Tests

Achievement tests are used for several specific purposes by colleges and universities. They show how much you already know about a given subject. Some tests, for example, the Cooperative American History Test, yield an estimate of how much knowledge you have acquired in a particular subject area — American history, in this case — when compared with other students having a similar amount of training in the same area. Achievement tests have proved to be equal or superior to scholastic aptitude tests for prediction of college success.

A trained counselor can determine how well you are achieving in relation to your capabilities by comparing your scholastic aptitude and intelligence scores with your achievement scores. If you are achieving above that indicated by your intelligence and aptitude scores, your effort is producing results. Some students with energy and drive achieve higher grades than do others with higher IQ and scholastic aptitude scores.

Colleges and universities assist you through the use of achievement tests as a part of entrance examinations. They are sometimes used to place students in more advanced work. Other times, they may be used to place students in "zero credit" or remedial courses. In either case, you will be placed in courses specifically designed for you and your classmates. For example, a high score on an English achievement test will place a student in advanced work at many institutions. Often, a high score, above 85 percent of the class, will place a student in a course designed for advanced students that replaces two freshmen English courses. By contrast, in the mathematics area, a score lower than 50 percent of the college freshman class may be used to place a student in a remedial mathematics course. In both cases, the student benefits by not being placed in courses too difficult for his present level of understanding or not difficult enough to challenge him. Achievement tests prove useful to the college and to you by:

1. Placing you in courses with persons of near-equal ability.
2. Offering you a better understanding of your ability and anchievement levels.
3. Enabling your advisor at college to understand your areas of strength and weakness.
4. Providing a record of your ability and achievement so that the college is in a position to advise you.
5. Exempting you from selected beginning courses.

Scholastic Aptitude and Intelligence Tests

Scholastic aptitude tests and intelligence tests attempt to show how much native ability you have to acquire knowledge. Commonly referred to as IQ tests, they differ from achievement tests in that intelligence test scores are a measure of your potential to learn, whereas achievement test scores are a measure of how much you have already learned about a subject.

IQ, which stands for intelligence quotient, is expressed numerically and is based on your age. To obtain an IQ score, counselors divide mental age, which is based on the raw score, by chronological age and then multiply by 100. For example, a typical fourteen-year-old freshman in high school might earn a mental age score of 16.8. To calculate his IQ score the counselor would use the following procedure:

$$\frac{16.8}{14} \times 100 = 120 \text{ IQ}$$

In this example, the fourteen-year-old has mental ability equal to the average person who is between sixteen and seventeen years of age. His IQ of 120 is a numerical statement of that fact. An IQ score of 90 to 110 is considered average. About 45 percent of the nation's youth earn scores in this range.

Scholastic aptitude tests measure your innate ability to do academic work. They may be viewed as intelligence tests designed for a special purpose. The American Council on Education's Psychological Examination (ACE) and the College Entrance Examination Board Scholastic Aptitude Test (SAT) are commonly used scholastic aptitude tests. They were specifically designed to measure academic aptitudes and were developed for use at the high school graduation and college entrance levels.

"College boards" are entrance examinations that deserve special explanation. College boards are examinations developed by the College Entrance Examination Board. More than five hundred and fifty colleges had membership in this association in the 1964–65 academic year. The number of members is growing and indications are that this group of examinations will become increasingly important to college-bound students. If the college of your choice is a cooperating member of the association, you will be asked to take the Preliminary Scholastic Aptitude Test or the Scholastic Aptitude Test. You may be asked to take some of the College Entrance Examination Board's achievement tests. These will not be too different from the examples given on the preceding pages. They may, however, be on different subjects.

If the college you hope to attend is a College Entrance Examination Board member, which of the tests do you have to take?

The college board test used by most colleges and universities is the Scholastic Aptitude Test. The Scholastic Aptitude Test seeks to measure your aptitude for college work. Insofar as it is possible, the test measures your aptitude for academic development rather than your knowledge of high school courses. It has two sections: verbal and mathematical. The time allotted for this examination is three hours. It is given in the mornings, and most counselors do not recommend that you take other examinations on the same day that you take the Scholastic Aptitude Test.

The Preliminary Scholastic Aptitude Test (PSAT), a short version of the Scholastic Aptitude Test (SAT), is used to guide students in the transition from high school to college. A service available from the College Entrance Examination Board, the PSAT is given by the high schools themselves on one of two testing dates in the fall of the year. It may be taken by juniors and seniors. It gives school counselors and principals "valid, reliable and inexpensive data" for helping students to estimate their ability to do work at various kinds of colleges.

Although the PSAT was formerly used as a screening test for various scholarship sponsors and may still be listed in some books as required, the College Entrance Examination Board is helping these sponsors to find other screening devices because high schools do not necessarily give the PSAT.

The College Entrance Examination Board states that the PSAT is not considered a replacement for the SAT and is not used for admission to any college it knows of. But the test is recommended for two groups — for students who have had relatively little experience with timed multiple-choice tests and who feel anxious about these tests, and for juniors who expect to take the SAT in the spring or not until the senior year and who want an early estimate of how they will do, especially if they wish to apply for college admission under the early decision plan.

The PSAT test is two hours, with another half-hour or less needed for distributing materials and giving instructions. Ask your high school counselor if the test will be offered. You will be charged 75 cents or more, and 75 cents per student will be sent to the Educational Testing Service along with your answer sheet for scoring. Your scores will be recieved by your high school about mid-December.

A PSAT *Bulletin for Students* will be furnished to you by your high school prior to the testing. This will give you additional information about the purpose and nature of the test and will provide sample questions. The PSAT measures the same verbal and mathematical abilities as does the SAT, and your score will be a good predictor of your SAT scores, whether you take the SAT in the spring of your junior year or during your senior year.

The Scholastic Aptitude Test, unlike the PSAT, is required for admission to the five hundred and fifty member colleges, and is recommended by many more. The SAT is designed to give you a way of comparing yourself with other prospective college students. The verbal test measures your ability to see word and idea relationships and to comprehend what you read. The mathematical test measures your understanding of the use of mathematical symbols in problem-solving. SAT scores are used along with your high school record, official recommendations, and interview reports to predict how well you will do in a particular college and/or in a particular curriculum. Though no one would claim that SAT scores will always predict correctly for every individual, they are one of the best methods of judging you in relation to the college you select.

The SAT and more than twenty subject-matter Achievement Tests, available to American college-bound students almost anywhere they live in the world, must meet certain standards year after year. The tests must predict satisfactorily for students of varying background and ability, from all kinds of high schools, and seeking entrance to all kinds of colleges. The scores must have the same meaning regardless of which year you take the tests and even though the tests you take have never before been given.

For these reasons it is impossible to "cram" for the college boards. Your best preparation is to study as well as possible on all your school work throughout your school career, for the tests place a premium on long-term, steady educational growth.

Prior to taking the SAT you will receive a booklet prepared by the College Entrance Examination Board called *A Description of the College Board Scholastic Aptitude Test*. The booklet will contain practice questions of the types used on the SAT along with explanations of the correct answers.

The colleges you are interested in will tell you in their catalogs when they wish to have your SAT scores or at what date you should take the SAT. December or January of the senior year is the usual time, although the early admission and early decision plans will mean that the SAT should be taken in the spring of your junior year. When you receive your SAT scores from your high school you will also receive a leaflet telling you how the scores you made compare with the scores of students from all over the country. By looking at your scores your high school counselor can judge what colleges will look favorably on your application and in which colleges you might find academic expectations lesser or greater than your apparent ability. Remember that it is just as discouraging to go to a college that will not challenge you as it is to attend a college that emphasizes academic ability and background you do not possess.

The College Entrance Examination Board Achievement tests are given in December, January, March, May, and July. They are one-hour tests given in the afternoon of test dates. A student may take no more than three tests in one day. The Achievement Tests are:

English Composition

American History and Social Studies

Biology

Chemistry

Mathematics, Level I

Physics

Latin

German

French

Spanish

Two Achievement Tests are given only in January — Hebrew and Russian. Given in January and May only are European History and World Cultures, and Mathematics, Level II.

Supplementary Achievement Tests may be given by interested schools early in March. Supplementary examinations requiring one and one-half hours include Greek and Italian. Shorter tests, requiring only one-half hour, include French Listening Comprehension, German Listening Comprehension, Italian Listening Comprehension, Russian Listening Comprehension, and Spanish Listening Comprehension.

Another examination, the Writing Sample, may be taken in December or January and may be taken with one or two achievement tests on a single date. It consists of an essay to be written on an assigned topic in a one-hour period.

College Entrance Examination Board tests are not free. According to the 1965–66 *Bulletin of Information,* published by the College Entrance Examination Board, from which the above information came, the following fees are charged:

Scholastic Aptitude Test: $4.50

Achievement Tests (any one, two, or three): $6.75

Writing Sample: $2.00 (no separate fee if taken in combination with one or two Achievement Tests in December)

The College Entrance Examination Board serves two useful services: it offers test scores to universities across the nation from a single test; and it serves you by allowing you to take the various examinations at an institution near your home for evaluation by a cooperating college anywhere in the nation. With this information, institutions can make better decisions about applications with minimum effort and expense on the part of prospective students. Colleges and universities are just as interested in admitting the right students as students are in being admitted to the right institution.

Should you plan to take the college boards, consult the *Bulletin of Information.* It lists all the tests, provides an application for taking the tests, explains how to select the right test, and gives a testing calendar and schedule. It also offers some sound advice for preparing and taking the college boards. Write to:

College Entrance Examination Board

Box 1025

Berkeley, California 94701

or

College Entrance Examination Board

Box 592

Princeton, New Jersey 08540

The following question and answer sheet was prepared by a counselor in a large suburban high school to help students understand more about college boards.[1]

Questions and Answers About College Board Tests

Q. How do I know if I have to take the college boards?

A. Check the catalogs of the colleges in which you are interested. Under the section on admission will be stated which of the tests, if any, should be taken. If a catalog mentions that Achievement Tests are required but does not state which ones for your particular major, write to the college and inquire.

Q. When are the application cards due?

A. Due dates are charted on pages 20–21 of the *Bulletin of Information.* Students applying for the December tests must have their applications in by November 5 or pay a penalty. They will not be accepted after November 19, however, for the December test date, even if a penalty is paid.

Q. When should I take the tests?

A. Check the college catalogs. Usually the December date is preferred. If they do not indicate a date, it is advised that they be taken as early as possible.

Q. How do I indicate which tests I want to take on the application card? They do not list the Achievement Tests separately.

A. Simply put a check in the box following the letters ACH. If you are to take the Scholastic Aptitude Test, check the box following SAT. If you are to do the Writing Sample, check WS. If you are taking Achievement Tests, you may take as many as three on the test dates they are given. You pay $6 whether you plan to take one, two, or three. On the day of the tests, you will be given a booklet containing all of the Achievement Tests. You may take the one, two, or three that you wish.

Q. Item 15 on the back of the application card asks for "code numbers." What is this for?

A. Here is where you list names of colleges to which you want to have your scores mailed. You may list three without charge. Additional listings cost $1 each.

Q. Suppose I don't know which colleges yet?

A. List the one or ones about which you feel most certain. When your scores are reported to the school, they will be placed on your permanent record which will be photographed and sent to all colleges with your applications.

Q. Do I give the application card to the counselor?

A. No! Each booklet contains an envelope to assist

[1] Reprinted by special permission of Mrs. Shirley Perry of High Point High School, Beltsville, Maryland.

you in mailing the card directly to the College Entrance Examination Board.

Q. Do I keep any part of the application card?

A. No! You will not be admitted to the testing center if you do. Mail the entire contents of the envelope. The association will return one side which you use as a ticket of admission to the testing center.

Q. Are scholarships awarded on the basis of any of these test scores?

A. Many sponsoring agencies do require these test scores. Check the details of the scholarship information to see exactly *which* tests if any.

Q. What do I do if I have more questions?

A. See your senior counselor.

The trend is for more colleges and universities to make use of college boards. As competition for college admission increases, the need for predicting probable success in college becomes critical. Institutions that do not require college boards are pleased to see and use the scores in evaluating a student's record. Emphasis is likely to be placed on the Scholastic Aptitude Test. A majority of the learning that takes place in college is through the use of symbols, words, or numbers. These are part of what the Scholastic Aptitude Test examines. If the college of your choice requires college boards, you will want to prepare for them. Specific examples of items on the Scholastic Aptitude Test may be seen in:

> *How to be Accepted by the College of Your Choice,*
> by Benjamin Fine
> Channel Press, Inc.
> Great Neck, New York

> *Complete Planning for College,* by Sidney Sulkin
> McGraw-Hill, Inc.
> New York, New York 10036

> *College Entrance Tests,* by Samuel I. Altwerger and
> Wilbert J. Levy
> Youth Educational Systems
> 2612 Grand Central Building
> New York, New York 10017

Other Tests and Inventories

You may be asked to take a battery of examinations that will include many types of tests, such as aptitude tests, personality tests, interest inventories, and other scales. There are aptitude tests designed to indicate your potential in specific areas, rather than over-all academic abilities. Aptitude tests may be added to a testing program for students entering specialized colleges within a university, or be required of all students entering an institution.

Although in limited use, personality tests provide an objective measure of a student's social adjustment and qualities such as extroversion or introversion, emotional stability, and similar behavioral tendencies. When selection is made to assure a composite of personalities on campus, students may be requested to take personality tests.

Interest inventories attempt to identify areas for for which you are likely to have motivation, and enthusiasm for study and activity, and the areas that you are likely to enjoy most. Your interest in an area does not necessarily mean that you have an aptitude for it, however. But you will find that you draw on your interest in an area to support your ability to learn in it. Because successful achievement usually requires both interest and aptitude, and since interest can be developed, it is wise to become interested in areas of your potential ability, as shown by aptitude test scores.

A Typical Testing Program

A typical Eastern university that is not a College Entrance Board Examination member requires entering freshmen to take six entrance examinations. They will serve as an excellent example, for the entrance examinations are characteristic of those administered in many colleges and universities across the nation. Note in particular the use made of scores.

1. *Cooperative English Test: mechanics of expression*
   (Educational Testing Service)
   The Cooperative English Test is a test of your ability in the mechanics of English expression. This test will measure your knowledge of grammatical usage, punctuation, capitalization, and spelling. You will be asked to determine what is acceptable English usage and to demonstrate use of skills essential to composition.

   If you score at or above the 85th percentile of the entering freshman class, you will be exempt from the first course in English but will be required to take an advanced English course.

2. *Cooperative English Test: reading comprehension*
   (Educational Testing Service)
   This test will provide measures of vocabulary, speed of reading, and level of comprehension. Performance on the three parts of the test is combined to yield a total score as well.

   The first part consists of sixty synonyms used to test your vocabulary. The second part contains reading paragraphs covering a varied assortment of subjects. The reading items are arranged in such a way that separate scores may be obtained for speed of reading and level of comprehension.

3. *Cooperative Test in American Government*
   (Educational Testing Service)
   This test covers a wide range of concepts usually taught in American government courses at the

secondary school level. It will require you to combine factual knowledge with the use of critical judgement.

Students whose scores place them at or above the 90th percentile of entering freshmen are exempt from taking the first course in government and politics.

4. *Cooperative American History Test*
   (Educational Testing Service)
   This test samples the wide range of material covered in secondary school courses in American history as well as material covered in college survey courses. It measures your knowledge of basic facts and trends in the economic, social and political developments of the United States. If your score is at or above the 90th percentile of the entering freshmen class, you will be exempt from taking history.

5. *Cooperative Elementary Algebra Test*
   (Educational Testing Service)
   This test measures your knowledge of material usually taught in high school algebra courses. It tests your ability to manipulate algebraic symbols and the more general quantitative skills.

Scores for predicting final course grades are based on the performance of entering freshmen. Students are classified into three groups. Students who score at or above the 85th percentile are placed in group I. Students who score between the 50th and 85th percentile are placed in group II and those who score below the 50th percentile are placed in group III. Each student's classification is forwarded to the appropriate college for use by advisors during the registration period in placing students in appropriate courses.

6. *American Council of Education's Psychological Examination for Freshmen*
   This test is designed to measure your general academic, book learning ability. The test has two parts: Linguistic (L score) and Quantitative (Q score). The L score measures your ability to deal with words and word symbols. The Q score measures your ability to deal with quantitative concepts and relationships.

The above example is a clear and concise description of the abilities tested for admission and placement of students in college courses. These are abilities that you need to develop to do college work.

Every college seeks good students and outstanding students will find few if any doors closed.[1] The average student may not be admitted to the top ten or twenty universities in the nation, but his range of choice is still great in the remaining two thousand institutions. Each year some spaces at very good colleges go unfilled because qualified students were reluctant, felt their chances were not good enough, or did not think of applying there.[2]

To gain admission to a selective college, the typical student must understand the factors of the selection process, and utilize this knowledge to his advantage in preparing a forceful application. In the words of the National Vocational Guidance Association's slogan for the booklet, *Choose a College,* "He who chooses a college wisely seldom fails to be admitted to a college of his choice."

Selective Colleges and Average Students

The plight of the average student has tended to go unnoticed or ignored on some campuses. A good number of colleges make no effort to attract the average student. As one high school senior put it: "I don't want to attend the colleges that will admit me, and the ones I want to attend won't admit me." Some colleges are sensitive on this point and openly seek only students ranking in the top 10 to 20 percent of their class. There are about 150 "tough" schools. These include the Ivy League colleges and universities, the institutes of technology, and other prestige institutions. These colleges are proud of their "tough" policies. They point out that to attract high-caliber students, they must have high standards. They say that about 50 percent of a beginning freshman class graduates, and they want to be sure they have the best students in the beginning.

Not every high school student will be admitted to college. Not every outstanding student is going to be admitted to his or her first-choice college. Yet, there is a place for all high school graduates of average ability, and there is a chance that typical students with average high school records and better than average scholastic aptitude scores will be admitted to a selective college, and perhaps a prestige one. How so, you ask. By choosing the right college, by living in the right part of the country, by applying at the right time, by preparing a very good application and as good a final record as possible, and by earning higher than expected SAT or ACT (American College Test) scores. Yes, and by being a little lucky too. It is true that you will be "bucking the odds" and "going against the inevitable,"

---

[1] Richard W. Smith and Howard P. Snethen, *Four Big Years* (Indianapolis: The Bobbs-Merrill Company, Inc., 1960).

[2] Gilbert C. Wren, *The Counselor in a Changing World* (Washington, D.C.: American Personnel and Guidance Association, 1963).

Chapter Six

Applying to Selective Colleges

but it is possible for an average student to be admitted to a selective college.

Colleges and universities look for different qualities in students. Colleges that select their students do so on the basis of scholarship, as shown by high school grades and rank in graduating class; intellectual capacity, interest, and abilities, as revealed by examination; geographical distribution, to provide a cosmopolitan student body; participation in extracurricular activities; and character and personality, as shown by letters of recommendation by school authorities and by interview reports.

Generally, outstanding students who apply are admitted first to selective schools, moderately good students are admitted first to semiselective colleges if they apply, and average students are admitted to institutions with open-door admissions policies as long as there is room. But there are exceptions and you could be one of them. It is possible for a student of modest demonstrated ability to be admitted because selective colleges prefer to have students from all parts of the country, because they desire to have a certain composition of students, and because they admit transfer students who have demonstrated their ability to do acceptable academic work at another college. Students who are first rejected at a selective institution and who enroll in another college or university may later transfer to the selective institution to which he or she was denied admission. Likewise, students who are not admitted to a state university may enroll in a junior college, community college, or college of continuing studies and at a later date transfer to the university.

It is generally thought that private colleges and universities are more selective in their admission of students than are public institutions. Undoubtedly, this is true for a number of the older institutions that enjoy a high level of respect; however, it is not true of the majority of private colleges and universities. This is another of the myths that becloud colleges and their admissions standards. Further, the American Council of Learned Societies found that among a sample of forty-one private liberal arts colleges there was no consistent showing as to the qualities of the student bodies. In one case, of two private colleges in adjoining states, one had a median SAT score at the sixteenth percentile and the other had its median at the sixtieth percentile.[3]

Although admissions requirements are presented by institutions in terms of grades, averages, and class ranks, it is important for you to know that many colleges of all types and levels of prestige are more flexible in their admissions than their printed policies suggest. In other words, there is a difference between what the institutions claim their requirements are and the characteristics of individuals who are admitted. Quite often colleges are willing to accept an unconventional or incomplete record if it is offset by

[3] Dael L. Wolfle, director, *America's Resource of Specialized Talent,* Commission on Human Resources and Advanced Training (New York: Harper & Row, 1954).

compensating strength or promise. If you have some outstanding ability, or very strong interest in an institution, it may carry weight that would compensate for a class rank that is less impressive. A simple factor such as class rank or a test score will seldom in itself guarantee admission or lead to rejection. A decision to admit a student to a selective institution is a result of consideration of all the evidence of a person's likely success and his individual qualities. You should not discontinue your interest in a selective or even a prestige institution if you do not meet its strict printed requirements until you correspond with the admissions office.

Using Geography as an Advantage. Your place of residence and its relation to the college you hope to attend may be a factor in, for example, your being accepted by a selective institution in another state while rejected by a semiselective institution near your home. Many colleges, particularly selective colleges, attempt to attract students from various regions of the country as well as foreign countries in an effort to have well-rounded student bodies with national and international qualities on their campuses. Also, including students from various parts of the country, the influence of the institution is widened. One Ivy League university had students from every state of the union and eighty-one foreign countries during a recent year. Because of this practice, your chances of being admitted to a selective institution in another region may be increased. Colleges that consider geographic distribution contend that out-of-state students add a desirable cultural dimension to the personality of the campus, and so welcome applications from distant areas and frequently accept students of modest ability from another state or region ahead of a student of equal ability whose residence is in a nearby community.

Students from the West or Southwest can add to the personality of a campus whose students are primarily from the Northeast. Students who live in the mid-Atlantic and Atlantic seaboard states, most of whom have had strong high school programs, are favored in Western, Southwestern, and Southern colleges and universities. The reverse is true in the Atlantic seaboard institutions, but the opportunity is limited because of the small enrollment in many institutions, the competition, and the traditional enrollment patterns.

If you can accept the idea of living a long distance from home, and the difference in cost is not a limiting factor, you have a better chance of being admitted to a selective college or university in another region than you do to one of similar stature near your home.

Admission by Test Scores. Selective colleges recognize that they may miss potentially outstanding students and leaders if they consider only high school records. The door is left ajar by permitting students to enter by examination. To be admitted by examination, students' scores must be relatively high.

U.C.L.A. is an example of a selective institution that permits students to enter by presenting outstanding test scores:

High school graduates who are ineligible on their high school records and who have had no college work subsequent to graduation from high school may qualify for admission by examination.

The University does not offer entrance examinations but accepts the results of examinations given by the Educational Testing Service for the College Entrance Examination Board.

To qualify by examination, the applicant must present scores in the Scholastic Aptitude Test and three Achievement Tests. The three Achievement Tests are to include English Composition and one from each of the following two groups:

1. Social Studies and Foreign Language
2. Mathematics and Sciences

The test must be taken after completion of the first half of the eleventh grade. The first repetition of a test will be accepted, but the verbal and mathematics scores on the Scholastic Aptitude Test must be at least 1,000; the scores on the three Achievement Tests must total at least 1,650, and the scores on any one Achievement Test must not be less than 500.

Admission by Transfer.   It may be that the college you are interested in will not accept you as a beginning freshman. Admission by transfer is one of the more common ways that students with average high school records can gain eventual admission to the colleges they prefer to attend. Students who demonstrate their ability to do acceptable college work in a nonselective institution can frequently transfer their earned credits to the institution of their choice after one or two years of college work. Admission is usually granted on the basis of grades earned in college, although high school records are considered. A student with a good record in an accredited college normally can transfer to another college without difficulty. It is possible for a student with a modest high school record who has earned "A's" and "B's" in a less selective institution to be admitted to a selective, or even prestige, college. However, you should recognize that the greater the selectivity of an institution, the fewer the students who drop out. Therefore, fewer vacancies exist for transfer students.

Nearly all colleges accept some students by transfer. The University of California, for example, gets a majority of its new students as transfers from state colleges and junior colleges within the state. Colleges with open-door admissions policies and some colleges that do not have space for average freshmen students will admit upperclassmen by transfer. All junior colleges and community college students who continue their education at a four-year institution gain admission by this procedure. Some transfer to state universities, and others apply for admission to selective institutions. Many students find they can begin their college education in one college and, by transferring, earn a degree from the college they originally preferred, for financial and personal reasons.

The admission of students by transfer is not an in-

volved process. In general, admissions procedures and fees are the same as those for students being admitted from high school. Admission is based on available room in the college and the student's achievement in the institution from which he is transferring. Usually, only a student in good standing at the institution he last attended will be admitted. However, some institutions, including selective institutions, through their evening division or college of continuing studies, will admit students who are on probation or on a provisional status. If a student has demonstrated that he can succeed in college he has a good chance of being admitted. Only students with failing grades experience difficulty in transferring.

If you feel the need to adjust to college life at a slower pace, or if you have a financial problem, you can attend a junior college, community college, municipal college, or a college of continuing studies near your home. It may be to your advantage to transfer to a more demanding college after gaining some experience. Many students earn basic requirements for degree programs and save money by staying at home during the first year or two of their studies.

The following are some suggestions to guide students who plan to transfer from one institution to another.

1. Select courses in the first institution that are acceptable to the institution from which you plan to graduate.
2. Review the terms of admission of the college where you plan to continue your education.
3. Admission by transfer is selective. Your grades in college work are the basic criteria for your selection. It is important that you demonstrate your academic ability in the college you first attend.
4. Arrange to have sent to the college to which you are transferring a copy of all required records, including a transcript of college courses you hope to have accepted.
5. Request a statement indicating that you are a student in good standing at the institution from which you are transferring. If you are on probation, a statement so indicating will also be needed.
6. Comply with admissions requirements by providing high school records, examination scores, and other information requested by the admissions office for transfer students.

Randolph–Macon, a selective women's college, admits well-qualified transfer students. Application for admission with advanced standing (credit for college courses) will be considered only from a student with good general scholarship and no academic failures. A transfer student must also meet the requirements specified for students entering as freshmen. The Scholastic Aptitude Test is required, but need not be retaken if satisfactory scores were made on the test in the senior year of high school. An application from a transfer student should be accompanied by a transcript of her high school record and a preliminary transcript of her college record, with a letter of recommendation from the dean of that college.

A small number of students are admitted to Harvard each year from other accredited colleges. The 1964 general catalog states:

> A student entering Harvard by transfer is required to spend at least two years in residence to qualify for a Harvard degree, so candidates who have spent more than two years at another college cannot be considered. Transfer students are eligible for scholarship assistance during the first year in residence.
>
> Transfer candidates are required to take the Scholastic Aptitude Test of the College Board. April 1 is the last date for filing a transfer application and candidates are notified of the decision of the Committee at the end of June.

Evening college or colleges of continuing studies will offer many typical students an opportunity to continue their education by transfer. Typical of the policies governing transfer students to these institutions is Northwestern University's policy.

> A student who transfers from another college or university, including another school of Northwestern University, must be in good standing in that institution in order to register in the Evening Divisions. A student excluded from another school may be permitted to register if he has been out of school at least a year and if his Application for Admission on a Probationary Status is approved by the registration committee. A student on probation in another school may be permitted to register if his Application for Admission on a Probationary Status is approved by the registration committee.

The policy governing the admission of transfer students to Oklahoma State University is typical of state universities.

A. Residents of Oklahoma. An Oklahoma resident, transferring from another institution, must meet the minimum requirements listed below:
  (1) must have been honorably dismissed from the college or university which he last attended.
  (2) must have a "C" overall average.
  An Oklahoma resident transferring from another institution with less than a "C" average overall on work attempted may be admitted on probation if he earned at least 1.5 for his immediate past academic year AND his grade overall average is equal to or above that stipulated in the schedule below:

Total Hours Attempted in all Colleges	Minimum Grade Point Average
LESS than 36	1.5
36 through 54	1.6
55 through 73	1.7
73 through 90	1.8
91 through 108	1.9
OVER 108	2.0

B. Non-Residents of Oklahoma. (All out-of-state applicants must file with their application for admission a $10 application fee which is not refundable.) A non-resident of Oklahoma, transferring to Oklahoma State University, must meet the minimum requirements listed below:
  (1) must have been honorably dismissed from the college or university from which he is transferring.
  (2) must have made satisfactory progress (an average of "C" or better) in the institution from which he is transferring.
C. Resident Credits from Institutions of equal standing with Oklahoma State. Credits transferred from accredited senior colleges will be given full value in similar courses wherever possible. The amount of credit for courses studied in other institutions may not exceed the amount given at Oklahoma State in the same length of time of instruction. Students may not transfer credits to satisfy more than one-half the major courses required for a department unless he has the approval of the head of that department.
D. Transfer of Resident Credits from a Junior College. Credits will be accepted by transfer from a junior college to meet lower division requirements only. This means that students will not receive credit by transfer from a junior college for more than 65 hours. A minimum of 60 semester hours must be earned in a senior college.

Admission to Programs of General Studies. Programs of general studies offer mature students who have not distinguished themselves entry into institutions with a reputation for excellence. The requirements for study in programs of general studies are sometimes less rigid than regular admissions.

Admission to Columbia's School of General Studies is as follows for high school graduates who followed college preparatory programs:

> High school preparation must include the following courses (entrance units): English, four years; elementary algebra, one year; intermediate algebra, one-half year; plane geometry, one year; physics, chemistry, or biology, one year. If you meet these requirements you may be admitted as a degree candidate.
>
> If your preparation lacks one or more of the entrance units, but is otherwise satisfactory, you may be admitted with entrance conditions. You will be required to include in your college program prescribed courses in those subjects in which you lack entrance units. The prescribed courses must be completed within three terms of your admission to degree candidacy, or within the first 30 points of college work, whichever is sooner; they will be counted toward the degree.
>
> If your preparation is inadequate in quality you may be admitted as a provisional degree candidate and must achieve a "B" average in a representative group

of courses for a prescribed period of time (usually one, two or three terms, depending on whether you enter and whether you study full time or not). You will then be admitted as a regular degree candidate.

In addition to these opportunities, the school provides through its Validation Program for the admission of applicants with incomplete high school educations, applicants with General Education or Equivalency Diplomas, and graduates of commercial or vocational high schools who have not completed the normal college preparatory program. The Validation Program consists of specific courses to be completed by students to prepare them for college work, to make up entrance deficiencies, and to advance students toward their degrees.

Making the Most of Your Interview

An interview is one part of the application to some selective colleges and universities. However, less than one-half of the nation's college students will have been on campus before arriving for their first year of study. Even fewer students have interviews with admissions officers. Interviews are required by more small liberal arts colleges than any other type of institution. Colleges that admit students of average ability, have an open-door policy, or admit students on a first-come, first-served basis do not require an interview. However, most all colleges welcome the opportunity to meet prospective students and talk with them about their aspirations for college and a career.

Interviews are usually conducted after you have filed your application so that admissions officers can review your application before the interview. The purpose of an interview is for the college to learn more about you than they can from records, application forms, and letters of recommendation. It gives them an opportunity to raise any questions and clarify any points not made clear on the application form. During the course of the conversation, admissions officers will attempt to evaluate your intellectual and personal qualities. Your high school record, entrance examinations, and vocational and professional interests may be discussed, as well as your extracurricular activities, reading interests, and so on. You should be prepared to discuss your reason for going to college and why you chose this particular one.

The interview is a business meeting. The common-sense rules of good manners and courtesy that apply when being interviewed for a job apply to being interviewed for admission to college. Your parents will be invited into the conference room if and when desired by the interviewer. If they are invited to join you, they should refrain from giving answers to questions unless specific questions are directed to them. It is you, not your parents, that the college is admitting. It may be helpful to prearrange with your parents what their role is at the interview. Be prepared to raise any questions that the

catalog does not answer, but do not ask unimportant questions. Before the end of the interview, ask about your chances of being admitted. The admissions officer will understand and appreciate your concern. If he can tell you, he will. If the necessary information is not available and the admissions officer cannot give you the answer, he will tell you.

Highly selective institutions that have a limited enrollment attempt to interview all new students. Colleges with enrollments so large they cannot interview each student arrange to interview when possible, but do not require an interview with each student they admit. Other institutions arrange for alumni who live in the student's area to interview the candidate. The typical student may enhance his chances by making a good impression at interviews. It is an opportunity to present the factors strongly in your favor. So that you may know the kinds of things asked and looked for during an interview, an example of an interview form used by a large independent Eastern university follows.

To arrange the interview, write a brief, well-composed letter to the director of admissions requesting a date and hour for the interview. On the day of the interview, arrive at the designated place on time. Interviews are conducted on schedule, and your being prompt is important to you and the admissions officer. Should you be early you will have the opportunity to become familiar with the campus and other offices. Allow time for parking, a problem common to most campuses. Your dress should be in good taste and appropriate for the occasion.

Swarthmore, a selective college, serves as an example of the instruction given students about interviews.

An admissions interview with a representative of the College is a requirement in making application to Swarthmore. Applicants are expected to take the initiative in arranging for this interview. Those who can reach Swarthmore with no more than a half-day's trip are urged to make an appointment to visit the College for this purpose. Other applicants may request a meeting with an alumni representative in their own area. Interviews should be completed before March 1 of the senior year. Candidates will not be able to have campus interviews from March 1 to mid-April but a tour of the campus may be arranged during this period. Appointments at the College may be made by calling or writing the Office of Admissions.

Vassar College uses a similar system. Prospective students are interviewed by members of the admissions office staff or of the Committee on Admissions. Appointments are made well in advance so that all students have an opportunity to be interviewed. Students who cannot come to the university campus for an interview can usually arrange for an interview elsewhere.

Figure 5
INTERVIEW REPORT
of
Cornell University Alumni Secondary School Committee

Name of Applicant ....College.....................................
                            Last   First   Initial

Address .... School ....
              City   State

1. What type of significant contributions of a nonacademic nature, (if any) would you expect this candidate to make to the   community? (Dramatics, music, publications, sports, etc.)

2. What types of general questions did the candidate ask? (Please list them in order of apparent importance to the candidate.)

3. What do you feel are the candidate's motives for wanting to attend Cornell?

4. What was the candidate's main source of interest in Cornell. (Check (√) appropriate answer (s).)

.... Parents   .... School teachers or counselors

.... Other relatives   .... Candidate's friends

.... Neighbors or   .... Others (Please list)
        family friends
                                                  ....

over

5. a: Please indicate your impressions of the candidate's characteristics by checking (√) the appropriate place on the rating scale below.

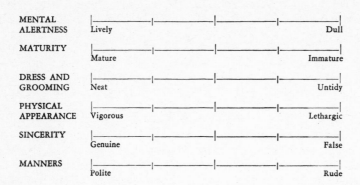

b: How would you rate the candidate's probable success as a Cornell student? Please check (√).

c: Assuming the candidate could do the academic work, how would you rate his success as a graduate of Cornell and a citizen? Please check (√).

6. Summary comments: Please make any comments regarding the candidate or his background which you feel would be helpful to the selection committee.

- -

Interviewer .... Class .... Course ....

Committee .... Date ....

PLEASE SEND COMPLETED REPORT AS EARLY AS POSSIBLE TO R. P. JACKSON, OFFICE OF ADMISSIONS
DEADLINE DATE: JANUARY 15

Other Possibilities

Other possibilities open to students depend on the practices followed by individual institutions. These may not be stated in the admissions policies, and so there is little general guidance that may be given. It is true that the student who has earned a good SAT or ACT score holds promise for academic development and success. Selective colleges give favorable consideration to a limited number of these students. A combination of good scores and being an out-of-state resident may increase a student's chances of being admitted.

Selective institutions with a strong sense of tradition give sons and daughters of alumni preference over other students. This does not mean that the weight is overriding, but given two students of equal ability, these colleges will select the child of an alumnus.

Your Extracurricular Activities

Strong extracurricular activity records can be a positive factor in support of your being admitted to your first choice college, especially if you have an outstanding ability or if the institution is a small or medium-sized private liberal arts college. However, you should recognize that extracurricular activities are not a substitute for grades; they can only improve your chance for admission.

Your participation in extracurricular activities reveals your interests and qualities of your personality. The essential point that colleges considering extracurricular activities look for is an indication that you will bring to the campus characteristics that will contribute to the college environment and community and that will help you make a quick and satisfactory adjustment to college life. Your activities should be intellectually and socially broadening, but participation in too many activities may indicate a superficial interest. If students are otherwise equal, participation and leadership in such activities may be of considerable value. Football, basketball, and other sports are classic examples, but experience as editor of the yearbook or as a member of the band may give your application preferential consideration at some institutions.

Value of Your Personal Qualities

Selective institutions take special notice of students having outstanding personal qualities and abilities. A college's decision may not always be determined wholly by students' ability to do school work They are also interested in personal experience and background not directly related to intelligence and your high school record. These personal qualities derived from your experiences become positive factors contributing to your admittance to and successful achievement in college. Personal qualities, sometimes referred to as "intangibles" or nonacademic factors because they are not measurable, are significant because they are carefully assessed by selective colleges in the belief that unusual and outstanding personal qualities will influence your success in college and later in life.

Managerial abilities and qualities that may have helped you excel in dramatics, mechanics, music, or journalistic writing do not show up on academic records and tests. You may be able to offer evidence of initiative, desire, leadership, and creativity in these and other fields that will offset an academic record that is less impressive. Admissions officers consider what you have to offer compared to the backgrounds of other potential students. These factors may be evaluated and given more or less importance, depending on the individual circumstances of your case and the kinds of students the particular college plans to attract.

Your outstanding personal qualities may be brought to the attention of admissions officers through interviews, recommendations from counselors, teachers, and your principal. Sometimes colleges will admit students with average records simply because their principals and counselors have given them strong support. Upon recommendation of counselors and principals, college admissions officers will often accept students whose rank in class, academic average, and test scores are lower than the average for other students that they would otherwise accept. Although pressure is growing, particularly in prestige institutions, many will frequently give special consideration to students when unusual circumstances are indicated and such a request is made by high school officials. Recommendations indicating outstanding motivation, character, leadership, or ability in music, art, or a sport are helpful. Should you have an interview, do not hesitate to talk about both your academic and nonacademic experiences, achievements, and aspirations. Most colleges like to think that each student has, in addition to being an acceptable student, unique qualities that will enable him to participate in the life of the campus.

Admissions officers in selective colleges know there is more to an individual than what is reflected from formal course work and the limitations of tests. The qualities they look for by assessing your experiences and personal qualities include motivation, stability, and drive. One of the most important and distinguishing characteristics looked for, usually through interviews and recommendations, is a genuine desire to learn. This is the mark of a student. So are your perseverance, tenacity, and intellectual curiosity. Your sense of values, responsibility, and humor are also important. Questions will be asked to assess your sincerity, dedication to purpose, and enthusiasm. Your maturity, motivation, and initiative, as well as your record and application, will be evaluated. These and other qualities comprise your philosophy of life, which, in the total analysis, is what is being considered.

It is encouraging that a number of outstanding colleges have waived the usual emphasis on grades for granting scholarships for some of the nation's most needy students. Participating institutions include Wayne State, Michigan, Michigan State, and Wisconsin. Highly regarded U.C.L.A. and Cornell have similar programs. The colleges of the City University of New York have announced a plan to admit five hundred new students from "pockets of poverty" who may not have the grades ordinarily required for admission. These scholarships are awarded to students who show strong motivation, leadership, and creativity. The forward-looking action of these institutions recognizes that test scores, grades, and class rank do not adequately measure the native ability of students deprived of the cultural environment of their peers.

Suggestions to Typical Students

It has been shown that the average student has a good chance of being admitted to a good college. If you are an average student and if you are still in high school, there is a great deal you can do to improve your chances for admission to a selective institution.

Do not feel that you must attend a famous or prestige college. For the student of average ability, it is most important to choose a college where he can mesh his abilities with his objectives and career aspirations. Reputations of most prestige colleges are earned at the graduate level of study and through research efforts of faculty members. It may be better for the typical student to earn a good undergraduate record from a state college or some other institution that is recognized in the student's chosen field of study, and plan for graduate study in a selective university. This is the route taken by most graduate students who study in selective institutions.

Planning and a realistic appraisal of yourself are the best ways to improve your chances of being admitted to college and staying there. This is true for all students, but is particularly true for students of average scholastic ability and those with specific problems. Your strengths and weaknesses have been identified through course work and by the school's testing program and your interest and abilities in extracurricular activities. Plan to strengthen your weaknesses and build upon your strengths.

Some ways you can best improve your chances of being admitted are:

1. Start planning for college as early in your high school program as possible. Discuss with your teachers and counselors areas needing improvement. Enlist their aid in working toward progressive development in these areas.
2. Present the best school record possible to the institution to which you seek admission. One of the most important things you can do to gain admission to a selective institution is to show improvement during your last two years of high school.
3. Make application to more than one institution but before you make application to any institution, carefully review college catalogs, admissions requirements, etc. Apply to those colleges with programs which most closely match your personal qualifications and career plans. Be sure that requested information and materials are supplied, including transcripts of your high school records, letters of recommendation, or references and autobiographical letter if required. Go for interviews where required.
4. Continue to prepare for college by broadening and deepening your understanding through reading outstanding books and other literature.

Chapter Seven

Applying to Junior Colleges

Junior and community colleges are emerging as a special type of institution where the typical American student can begin his studies. Because about half of the high school graduates now enter college and because predictions indicate that by 1970 almost 70 percent of the jobs will require some college education, these two-year colleges offer the brightest opportunities for 80 percent of the present high school students. They appear to be a most logical place for the millions of average students whose "C"-or-better grades are not quite good enough for selective and Eastern universities or for those whose occupational ambitions do not require a four-year college education. Junior and community colleges today offer the average student a chance for at least two years of low-cost college education with credits applicable to a full four-year college degree if the student wants to go on. Because they are locally available and relatively inexpensive, they are a ready-made solution to the financial problem of the typical, middle-income, suburban family faced with the question of how to finance a college education for two or three teen-agers. Yearly costs average less than $500, or one-third the cost at a public four-year college, and about one-fifth the cost at a private four-year college. In some cases, junior college tuition is free. A major factor in the low cost, of course, is that students live at home and commute to school.

Why Apply to a Junior College?

If you attend a junior or community college, you will be doing what a million other students do. One in four college freshmen go to a two-year college in the United States, according to the American Association of Junior Colleges. In states like California and Florida, where there are state-supported junior college systems, some counties reported that 80 to 85 percent of their college freshmen enrolled in local junior colleges. By 1970, states like New York, Michigan, Mississippi, and others that are financing junior college systems expect at least 50 percent of their freshmen to begin college in the two-year local public institutions.

In fact, the junior or two-year college is expected to make educational opportunity available to thousands of students for whom room will not be available in public four-year colleges and universities as the college-going population continues to grow. Although some private junior colleges have very selective admissions policies and high tuition rates, almost all public junior colleges have relatively unselective admissions policies and accept high school graduates and adults with equivalency diplomas or satisfactory General Educational Development Test scores.

The open-door junior or community college usually does have some prerequisites for courses of study. Some may demand, for instance, that a student entering the engineering program or the beginning chemistry course have the required mathematics background, or that for entrance into the first credit course in required English, the student have the requisite reading and writing skills. The junior college differs from the four-year college in this important respect, however: if the student does not have the background or prerequisites for a course or a curriculum, the junior college usually will offer the necessary remedial courses so that the student can qualify for the courses of his choice.

Community and junior colleges stress guidance and counseling, and orientation to college work, by helping students discover their objectives and interests, helping them fix on tentative career goals if they have not already done so, aiding them in finding part-time work if they must pay part of their way through junior college, and by helping them to find employment after leaving college or assisting them in making a smooth transfer to a four-year college. Although some four-year colleges stress student counseling, one of the big complaints from students at these institutions is that they do not receive enough guidance, especially in adapting their course requirements to their occupational goals.

The second area that the junior colleges stress is the quality of freshman and sophomore instruction. Numerous articles have appeared that criticize large classes and the impersonal treatment students are receiving at the big colleges and universities. Some authorities think student unrest grows out of the desire of students to be recognized by their instructors and to be taught by mature teachers instead of inexperienced instructors or graduate assistants. Junior colleges select faculty members for their ability and interest in teaching rather than for their ability in research or the training of graduate students.

The junior college courses of study are designed for three kinds of students: those who want to complete one or two years of college work and transfer to a four-year college; those who wish to earn a two-year degree in a transfer or terminal curriculum and go directly to work; and those who wish to enter a vocational institute for advanced training. And then there are many students who simply want to try college to see what it is like, or who wish one or two specialized courses to assist them in their vocations. The public junior college is also organized to assist these students.

There is great variety in cost at the nation's two-year colleges, ranging from about $3,000 annually to less than $50. Even institutions with free tuition will usually charge small fees for application, laboratory breakage, or materials. California, for example, has tuition-free public junior colleges, while Maryland expects each full-time student to contribute about one-third of the tuition cost, now about $100 a semester.

Variety also characterizes the kind of control and size of student body. There are about one hundred and seventy-five church-related, one hundred independent, and almost five hundred publicly controlled junior colleges in the United States. Eighty-five percent, or about 750,000, of all junior college students were enrolled in accredited public junior or community colleges having enrollments of four hundred or more students. Deep Springs College in California, a public college of nineteen students as of October 1962, was probably the smallest recognized junior college in the United States at that time, while, by contrast, Long Beach City College, also in California, had 24,047 students! However, 19,454 of them were part-time students.

A variety of courses is available. The curriculum most common to all junior colleges is liberal arts, used for transfer and for pre-professional training. Business administration is the next most common, followed by engineering. The variety of technical, trade, and industrial courses depends on the size and the needs of the community's industries. Junior colleges may teach embalming, radio and television techniques, computer programing, cosmetology and hair-dressing, law enforcement, agriculture, architecture, health science technologies, or watch repair. They may train airline hostesses, forest and wildlife officers, military personnel, food and hotel managers, and electronics technicians. If you are interested in a particular geographic location, a specific technology or course of academic study, a men's or women's, rather than a coeducational, college, consult *American Junior Colleges,* a matching volume to *American Colleges and Universities.* The variety of size, cost, student body, and curricula in America's junior colleges is best discovered from two authoritative directories probably available in your local public or high school library. These guides are:

The Junior College Directory (annual edition)
American Association of Junior Colleges
1315 16th Street, N.W.
Washington, D.C. 20036

American Junior Colleges (sixth edition, 1963)
American Council on Education
1785 Massachusetts Avenue, N.W.
Washington, D.C. 20036

Since *American Junior Colleges* is published only every four years, a small supplement, *Directory,* is published annually. The *Directory* is a compact source of up-to-date information on new junior colleges, which are being organized at the rate of thirty a year. It gives the exact mailing address and name of the administrative head, accreditation, the size and type of student body — whether coeducational or for one sex only — and the affiliation or control of all the junior colleges.

American Junior Colleges gives the following information about individual colleges in all fifty states:

Description
Recognition (by what agencies accredited)
History
Calendar (semester, quarter, trimester; important
  dates)
Requirements for admission and graduation
Fees

Student aid available
Staff; degrees held by faculty
Curricula offered
Buildings and grounds
Administrative officers
Enrollment by sex
Out-of-state and foreign students: number
Graduates: categories by degrees and/or curricula
Library facilities and materials held
Publications: student and institutional
Financial resources

The appendices of *American Junior Colleges* list the curricula for transfer and terminal students, unusual courses of study available, and the affiliation of the colleges — public, church-related, or private. Here one learns of the colleges that are in the process of becoming four-year colleges.

Junior College Accreditation

Are junior colleges inferior educationally? Do they largely repeat the work of the high school or "give" good marks to inadequate students? The answers to such questions must always be based on exact information about a specific college. Generally speaking, the answer for American public and private junior colleges is an emphatic "no."

The same regional organizations that accredit other colleges and universities also accredit junior colleges, and they are accredited in the same manner as other institutions of higher education. Although a new junior college may be several years in qualifying for regional accreditation, it usually has already been "accredited" by the state university and/or four-year colleges, so that transfer students are accepted without difficulty at senior institutions, providing, of course, that they can meet entrance requirements and that there is available space.

In many junior colleges, the teaching staff of elementary courses may actually be somewhat educationally superior to that at the state university, where, typically, many courses required of freshmen are taught by graduate students. A good way to assess the qualifications of the junior college faculty is to study the catalog faculty listing to determine where the instructors earned their graduate degrees and the number of instructors holding doctoral degrees.

Transferability of Junior College Credits

How well do junior college graduates and students transferring without a two-year degree do when they attend four-year colleges? More information is becoming available from throughout the United States, but the best estimate is that based on various studies of California, the state with the most publicly supported junior colleges. While 65 percent of those entering the junior colleges enroll in transfer programs, only 20 percent actually do transfer to a state college or the state university. Because only the top 11 percent of California's high school graduates may enter the University of California and only the upper 33 percent may enter the state's four-year colleges, its junior college transfers must meet rather high admissions standards at the senior institutions. The California figures show, as do those of other states supporting a junior college system, that the transferring students usually do as well or better than they did at junior college, especially after the first semester following transfer.[1]

A recent study of public junior colleges in ten states shows fewer than half of the transfer students graduating in four years from the time they entered junior college. Of the transfers who dropped out of the four-year colleges, about one-third did so for scholastic reasons. The study also suggests that the junior college students with a 2.50 average or better (high "C" or low "B" average) should have little difficulty in earning a baccalaureate degree at a public college in their home state.[2]

Do these figures on transferring from junior college and completing a four-year degree seem discouraging? Not if a realistic picture is formed about what happens to each year's entering class of the nation's four-year colleges. Approximately 50 percent of these students drop out of college or are dismissed for academic or other reasons, the loss varying from about 12 percent to about 82 percent, depending on the specific college. Although there are only estimates of how many entering college students finally complete college, it is known that only 40 percent graduate on schedule, that is, at the end of four years.[3] If the junior college student has been delayed in graduating because he did remedial courses or because he had to make up courses with grades of "D" before he could transfer them to a senior college, the junior college transfer picture is not a discouraging one at all.

Typical Junior Colleges

So that you may have an idea of the variety represented by America's junior colleges, the following descriptions of two colleges have been developed from information appearing in *American Junior Colleges*.

Schreiner Institute, Kerrville, Texas, is a privately controlled military junior college for men with a four-year high school department as well. The junior college specializes in liberal arts and pre-professional science, engineering, electronics, and other curricula. Military

[1] Nevitt Sanford, ed., *The American College* (New York: John Wiley & Sons, Inc., 1962), pp. 176–177.
[2] Dorothy M. Knoell, "Focus on the Transfer Program," *Junior College Journal,* May 1965, pp. 5–9.
[3] Sanford, *op. cit.,* pp. 630–31.

training is not required of the two hundred students, most of whom are from Texas. Room, board and tuition costs about $1,550 a year, as of 1962-63, and that year Schreiner awarded thirty-nine associate of arts degrees. One hundred percent of its graduates entered four-year colleges. The school is accredited by the Southern Association.

Stephens College, Columbia, Missouri, a private liberal arts junior college for women, added the four-year degree of bachelor of fine arts in 1959, but emphasizes its two-year curriculum. English proficiency is important for admission to Stephens. Some 60 to 70 percent of its two-year graduates go on to four-year colleges. Tuition, room, and board at Stephens in 1962-63 was $2,450 a year, and the enrollment was 1,775 women of whom more than 1,660 were from out-of-state. It awarded 16 B.F.A. and 670 A.A. degrees at the end of that same year. Stephens College is accredited by the North Central Association.

Typical Junior College Students

Who transfers successfully from the junior college to the four-year college or university? The following true stories illustrate the variety of reasons for attending junior college before transferring to a four-year college.

Harold B. is typical of the average junior college transfer who, for financial reasons, attends the local junior or community college for the first two years of academic work. Because Harold B. was an average student and could not be assured of financial aid, he chose to live at home, carry a part-time job, and commute to a local two-year institution. Harold B. completed the pre-law curriculum of the public St. Petersburg (Florida) Junior College with a low "B" average and transferred without loss of credit to a private multipurpose college, the University of Tampa. He brought sixty-four semester hours of credit with him. In one year at the University of Tampa he accumulated thirty more hours of work, majoring in history and political science, and then applied to Stetson University College of Law in St. Petersburg. Harold had a better-than-"B" average while at the University of Tampa, and he was able to qualify for a law student loan program for his three years at Stetson, which he completed successfully. He is now a practicing attorney in Pinellas County, Florida.

Selina J., a physically handicapped student, attended her local public junior college in New York State for two years. While there, she participated in the chess club and the People-to-People Organization, and worked part time in the college offices as a switchboard attendant. She graduated with a two-year degree after completing the liberal arts curriculum. Because of her difficulty in climbing stairs and with icy sidewalks, it was her ambition to be accepted at a four-year college in a warmer climate and, preferably, at a college with few stairs to climb. During a summer visit with her

grandparents in the South, Selina looked over several institutions and found a college in Georgia with high standards in her major, foreign languages, and with few multistoried buildings. Selina is a successful language major and a senior at this college, having had all of her junior college credits accepted.

DeLancey S. was dismissed from the physical education program at a state college at the end of his freshman year because of his poor average in all courses except his major. He did not fail anything, but earned only "D" in everything but courses in his major, in which he achieved all "A" grades. The college considered it impossible for him to succeed in his second year with such a poor record, but stated that it would readmit him on probation if he attended an accredited junior college for one year and successfully repeated the courses in which he had "D." On the basis of a letter of recommendation to this effect from the state college, the junior college in his hometown accepted DeLancey on probation. DeLancey applied himself so vigorously to his work that he succeeded in making better than a "B" average throughout two semesters at the junior college. He did not return to the state college, however, for his family was moved to a new location by the branch of military service in which his father was a regular officer. DeLancey now applied to a public four-year institution in his new home state and was accepted as a sophomore. He lost all of the state college credits except ten hours of physical education, but he transferred all of his junior college credits of thirty-two hours, giving him forty-two hours of credit at his new college, which was not quite enough to classify him as a second-semester sophomore. By attending two summer sessions and taking a maximum number of credits during his remaining time in college, DeLancey was able to graduate at the end of the summer following the June in which he would have finished at the state college. He is now a successful high school physical education teacher and coach.

Tom R. was not accepted at the state universities in Florida because of a low rank both in his high school class and on the statewide twelfth grade examinations. Nevertheless, he was determined to study pharmacy at the University of Florida in order to enter into his father's drug business. Tom sought the help of his local junior college in planning a program that would parallel the work of a University of Florida freshman, and such a program was set up minus qualitative chemistry, which was not available at the junior college. Because Tom's test scores and records were not promising, the junior college counselor suggested diagnostic testing, which revealed the need for remedial reading. After working with Tom in the reading laboratory, the reading instructor advised a thorough eye examination, which resulted in Tom's being fitted with glasses to compensate for an eye imbalance. Tom registered for remedial reading, English, chemistry, mathematics, and physical education the first semester. He made a study schedule and spent as much time as possible in the reading laboratory. During the second semester, by which time his reading speed and comprehension had been greatly improved, Tom used the available hours for the required American Institutions courses, planning to finish the sequence during his sophomore year at the University of Florida. Having finished his required mathematics, he replaced that course with speech. His average for the year was a high "C," with no grade below "C" and with an "A" in mathematics. He was able to transfer during the summer session to the University of Florida and study qualitative chemistry. He had enough hours of credit and the proper courses to be classified as a sophomore when the fall trimester opened. Although Tom was behind in chemistry and social studies at the time of transfer, he was able to complete the professional pharmacy degree within three months of when he would have finished had he entered the university right from high school. By correcting his eyesight problem

and improving reading and study habits, Tom proved that test scores and high school marks do not always accurately predict college success or failure. Without a year at a junior college, however, Tom could not have realized his ambition to become a pharmacist.

Sample Application Forms

Application forms to junior and community colleges and procedures for completing them are much like those for four-year institutions. One of the examples presented below is a form used by a group of institutions in Colorado, including both junior and senior colleges. The second example is one of a typical suburban junior college of the type growing in prominence.

Figure 6

Not Write In This Space

NAME:

Print name of institution to which you are submitting this application.

APPLICATION FOR ADMISSION TO ANY OF THE FOLLOWING COLLEGIATE INSTITUTIONS

Adams State College, Alamosa	Loretto Heights College, Loretto	Regis College, Denver
Colorado School of Mines, Golden	Mesa College, Grand Junction	Trinidad State Junior College, Trinidad
Colorado State College, Greeley	Northeastern Junior College, Sterling	University of Colorado, Boulder
Colorado State University, Ft. Collins	Otero Junior College, La Junta	University of Denver, Denver
Ft. Lewis A & M College, Durango	Pueblo Junior College, Pueblo	Western State College, Gunnison
Lamar Junior College, Lamar	Rangely College, Rangely	

PERSONAL INFORMATION

PART I

To be typewritten or printed by student in ink

Please answer all questions completely. Page I, Page 2, and the top of Pages 3 and 5 should be filled in by the student and then presented to the high school for completion.

Full Legal Name: (Mr. ....) (Miss ....) (Mrs. ....) ....

(Last Name)   (First Name)   (Middle Name)

Mailing Address ....

(Street and Number)   (City)   (Zone)

(County)   (State)   (Telephone Number)

Birthplace .... Birthdate .... Present Age ....

(City)   (State)

Permanent Home Address ....

(Street and Number)   (City)   (State)

Length of residence there? .... Are you married? (Yes ....) (No ....) Number of children ....

If you are less than 21 years of age, where did your parents last pay state income tax? ....

.... What year? ....

If you are 21 years of age or more, where did you last pay state income tax? ....

.... What year? ....

Is your permanent home, at present, the same as your father's? (Yes ....) (No ....) If not, with whom, at present, do you make

your permanent home? ....

(Name)   (Relationship to You)

If your permanent home is in Colorado, when did this residency begin for you? ....

(Month)   (Year)

For your father? .... For your mother? ....

(Month)   (Year)   (Month)   (Year)

Of what country are you a citizen? ....

Were you in the Armed Forces? (Yes ....) (No ....) Dates of active duty .... to ....

EDUCATION AND EXPERIENCE

Give name and location of EACH high school, college and university attended. This information must be accurate and complete. The student must request each college or university attended to send official transcripts of all work attempted.

Have you attended any college or university since graduating from high school? (Yes ....) (No ....)

Have you completed any correspondence courses or work by extension since high school graduation? (Yes ....) (No ....)

If so, indicate below.

HIGH SCHOOLS ATTENDED

(NAME OF HIGH SCHOOL)	(CITY)	(STATE)	(MONTHS AND YEARS OF ATTENDANCE)	(DATE OF GRADUATION)
1.			to	
2.			to	
3.			to	

COLLEGES AND UNIVERSITIES ATTENDED

(NAME OF COLLEGE)	(CITY)	(STATE)	(MONTHS AND YEARS OF ATTENDANCE)	(DATE OF GRADUATION)
1.			to	
2.			to	
3.			to	

— FAILURE TO LIST ALL INSTITUTIONS PREVIOUSLY ATTENDED MAY RESULT IN LOSS OF CREDIT OR DISMISSAL —

Revised 1961

PART I (Page 2)

PERSONNEL OFFICE INFORMATION

Father's Name .... Mailing Address ....
(Street and Number)

....................(City).................... ....(Zone).................... ....(State)....................

Place of Birth .... Is he living? (Yes .....) (No .....) If deceased, when? ....

Schooling completed by father   Grade School   High School   College

(Circle last grade attended) 0 1 2 3 4 5 6 7 8   1 2 3 4   1 2 3 4 5 6 7 8

Occupation .... Business Address ....
(Street and Number)

....................(City).................... ....(Zone).................... ....(State)....................

Mother's Name .... Mailing Address ....
(Street and Number)

....................(City).................... ....(Zone).................... ....(State)....................

Place of Birth .... Is she living? (Yes .....) (No .....) If deceased, when? ....

Schooling completed by mother   Grade School   High School   College

(Circle last grade attended) 0 1 2 3 4 5 6 7 8   1 2 3 4   1 2 3 4 5 6 7 8

Occupation .... Business Address ....
(Street and Number)

....................(City).................... ....(Zone).................... ....(State)....................

How many brothers and sisters older than self? .... Younger than self? ....

Rate the following as excellent, good, fair, poor: General Health .... ; Eyesight .... ;

     Hearing .... ; Speech ....

Name handicaps, if any ....

Have you ever had a serious physical illness or been under treatment for an emotional illness? (Yes .....) (No .....) If yes, give details and treatment ....

Name academic, social, and athletic activities you participated in, and check appropriate columns:

ACTIVITY NAME	TOOK PART	HELD OFFICE	ACTIVITY NAME	TOOK PART	HELD OFFICE

Name academic, social, and athletic honors awarded to you: ....

If either of your parents or another member of your family is an alumnus or former student of this institution, complete the following:

(NAME)	(DATES OF ATTENDANCE)	(RELATIONSHIP TO YOU)
	to	
	to	

COLLEGE PLANS

If you graduated from high school more than six months ago, what jobs have you held since?

(EMPLOYER)	(DATES)	(TYPE OF WORK)
	to	
	to	

Consult with your high school principal, counselor, and parents when answering the following questions. If possible, refer to the college bulletin, and use the name of the course of study, major, or curriculum given in the bulletin.

Which term and year do you expect to enter college? (Fall .....) (Winter .....) (Spring .....) (Summer .....) Year 19...........

What will be your major field of study in college? .... (Undecided .....)

For what type of vocation or profession do you wish to prepare? (Example: Accountant, chemist, lawyer, physicist, engineer, teacher, etc.) .... (Undecided .....)

If undecided, in what subjects or field of study are you primarily interested? ....

If you plan to prepare for teaching, for which level do you plan to prepare? (Elementary .....) (High School .....) (College .....)

Have you taken either of these examinations? (College Boards .....) (ACT .....) When? ....

     (See College Bulletin for entrance examination requirements)

     I hereby certify that to the best of my knowledge the foregoing information is true and complete without evasion or misrepresentation. I understand that if it is found to be otherwise, it is sufficient cause for rejection or dismissal.

Date of application .... Applicant's Signature ....

Print name of institution to which you are applying.

PART II (Page 3)

SECONDARY-SCHOOL RECORD

To be completed by student down to red line and then presented to high school for completion.

Legal Name: (Mr. ......) (Miss ......) (Mrs. ......)

....
(Last Name)   (First Name)   (Middle Name)

Home Address ....
(Street and Number)   (City)   (Zone)   (State)

Birth Date .... Name of parent or guardian ....

(Please insert carbon for duplicate record.)

Entered {

(Name of School)   Entrance Date .... (Month) (Year)   School accredited by NCA ☐

(School Telephone Number)   Was graduated .... (Month) (Year)   Others (please specify)

(Street)   (City)   Will be graduated .... (Month) (Year)   Type of School: Public ☐

(County)   (State)   Withdrew .... (Month) (Year)   Independent ☐   Parochial ☐

Class periods are .... minutes, ... times a week, ... weeks a year. Passing mark is .... College recommending mark is ....

1. List your complete marking system, highest to lowest: ....

2. List other secondary schools student attended: ....

IMPORTANT

PRINCIPAL OR COUNSELOR PLEASE NOTE:
The following items need to be included on this form before admission status of this student can be determined:

1. Show grades for 7 semesters.

2. Star (*) courses in progress.

3. Show rank in class at end of 7th semester.

4. Circle all advanced level courses the student has taken while in high school.

INFORMATION

A. A unit represents the study of a subject a full school year four or five times per week.

B. One unit equals two credits or ten semester hours unless otherwise defined.

C. Use extra column for extra school year.

APPLICANT RANKS EXACTLY............ IN A GRADUATING CLASS OF............ STUDENTS.

SUBJECTS	Grade Year	9th 19......	10th 19......	11th 19......	12th 19......	Post Grad. 19......	Units	Leave Blank
ENGLISH	English							
FOREIGN LANG.								
MATH.	Algebra							
	Geometry							
	Trigonometry							
SCIENCE With Lab. / No Lab.	Biology							
	Chemistry							
	Physics							
SOCIAL STUDIES	World History							
	U. S. History							
	American Gov't.							
OTHER SUBJECTS								

(In the 12th column: *If submitted before high school graduation star (*) courses in progress in this column*)

Total number of units school requires for graduation ....

School computed above rank in class by using official record beginning with .... grade and ending with .... semester in .... grade.

Grade Point Average is computed on the basis of the following system:
     A—4 points per complete unit; B—3 points; C—2 points; D—1 point; F—0 points.

Were the courses listed above as "other subjects" included when computing the grade point average and rank? (Yes......) (No......)

Date.......................... Signature.. Title..........................

Revised 1961   (Permission to print obtained from National Association of Secondary-School Principals)

PART II (Page 4)

PERSONALITY RECORD (Confidential)

(A duplicate record is required; please insert carbon)

TEST INFORMATION AND RATING

OF PERSONAL CHARACTERISTICS OF ....

(Last Name)   (First Name)   (Middle Name)

I.	**HIGH SCHOOL TEST RECORD**						

Entrance	CEEB (SAT) SCORES	V =	M =		Date Taken		
	Others:						
	ACT SCORES (College Bound National Norms)	Eng._____ Math._____ Social Studies_____ Nat. Sci._____					
		Composite_____ Date Taken_____					

TYPE OF TEST	NAME AND FORM OF TEST	DATE GIVEN	RAW SCORE	LOCAL NORM	NATIONAL NORM	PERCENTILE
Mental Ability						
Achievement						
Additional Tests						

2. The following sections may be completed by the principal or counselor, or teachers may be consulted if desired.

Please rank the student according to the numerical scale:
 	
    4 = Above Average   2 = Below Average
    3 = Average   1 = Very Low
 	
1. _____Desire to secure advanced education
2. _____Emotional stability
3. _____Honesty and integrity
4. _____Motivation to achieve academic success
5. _____Self-reliance
6. _____Ability to do college-level work
7. _____Respect for authority
	Comments or additional information:

3. Principal's or counselor's estimate of applicant's probable success at the college or university to which this application is being submitted: (Above Average_____) (Average_____) (Below Average_____) (Little Success_____)

Comments on above rating:

4. Do you consider the student's selection of vocation or area of study appropriate for him?

5. What information can you furnish that may be helpful in advising this student in setting up his academic program, such as his course area weaknesses, financial need, physical limitation, if any?

6. List other colleges or universities to which this student plans to apply.

Date ....   Signature ....   Title ....

School ....   City ....   State ....

Print name of institution to which you are applying.

PART II (Page 5)

SECONDARY-SCHOOL RECORD

To be completed by student down to red line and then presented to high school for completion.

Legal Name: (Mr. ____) (Miss ____) (Mrs. ____)

....
(Last Name)   (First Name)   (Middle Name)

Home Address ....

....
(Street and Number)   (City)   (Zone)   (State)

Birth Date .... Name of parent or guardian ....

(Please insert carbon for duplicate record.)

Entered {

....
(Name of School)

....
(School Telephone Number)

....
(Street)   (City)

....
(County)   (State)

Entrance Date ....
                            (Month)   (Year)

Was graduated ....
                            (Month)   (Year)

Will be graduated ....
                            (Month)   (Year)

Withdrew ....
                            (Month)   (Year)

School accredited by NCA ☐

Others (please specify)

Type of School: Public ☐

Independent ☐   Parochial ☐

Class periods are .... minutes, ... times a week, ... weeks a year. Passing mark is .... College recommending mark is ....

1. List your complete marking system, highest to lowest: ....

2. List other secondary schools student attended: ....

IMPORTANT

PRINCIPAL OR COUNSELOR PLEASE NOTE: The following items need to be included on this form before admission status of this student can be determined:

1. Show grades for 7 semesters.
2. Star (*) courses in progress.
3. Show rank in class at end of 7th semester.
4. Circle all advanced level courses the student has taken while in high school.

INFORMATION

A. A unit represents the study of a subject a full school year four or five times per week.

B. One unit equals two credits or ten semester hours unless otherwise defined.

C. Use extra column for extra school year.

APPLICANT RANKS EXACTLY_____ IN A GRADUATING CLASS OF_____ STUDENTS.

SUBJECTS	Grade Year	9th 19....	10th 19....	11th 19....	12th 19....	Post Grad. 19....	Units	Leave Blank
ENGLISH	English							
FOREIGN LANG.								
MATH.	Algebra							
	Geometry							
	Trigonometry							
SCIENCE With Lab. / No Lab.	Biology							
	Chemistry							
	Physics							
SOCIAL STUDIES	World History							
	U. S. History							
	American Gov't.							
OTHER SUBJECTS								

(Note in 12th grade column: "If submitted before high school graduation star (*) courses in progress in this column")

Total number of units school requires for graduation ....

School computed above rank in class by using official record beginning with .... grade and ending with .... semester in .... grade.

Grade Point Average is computed on the basis of the following system:
A—4 points per complete unit; B—3 points; C—2 points; D—1 point; F—0 points.

Were the courses listed above as "other subjects" included when computing the grade point average and rank? (Yes ....) (No ....)

Date .... Signature .... Title ....

Revised 1961

(Permission to print obtained from National Association of Secondary-School Principals)

PART II (Page 6)
PERSONALITY RECORD (Confidential)
(A duplicate record is required; please insert carbon)

TEST INFORMATION AND RATING
OF PERSONAL CHARACTERISTICS OF ....

	(Last Name)	(First Name)	(Middle Name)

I.	HIGH SCHOOL TEST RECORD						

Entrance	CEEB (SAT) SCORES	V =		M =		Date Taken	
	Others:						
	ACT SCORES (College Bound National Norms)	Eng._____ Math._____ Social Studies_____ Nat. Sci._____ Composite_____ Date Taken_____					

TYPE OF TEST	NAME AND FORM OF TEST	DATE GIVEN	RAW SCORE	LOCAL NORM	NATIONAL NORM	PERCENTILE
Mental Ability						
Achievement						
Additional Tests						

2. The following sections may be completed by the principal or counselor, or teachers may be consulted if desired.

Please rank the student according to the numerical scale:	Comments or additional information:
4 = Above Average 2 = Below Average 3 = Average 1 = Very Low 1. _____Desire to secure advanced education 2. _____Emotional stability 3. _____Honesty and integrity 4. _____Motivation to achieve academic success 5. _____Self-reliance 6. _____Ability to do college-level work 7. _____Respect for authority	

3. Principal's or counselor's estimate of applicant's probable success at the college or university to which this application is being submitted: (Above Average......) (Average......) (Below Average......) (Little Success......)

Comments on above rating:

4. Do you consider the student's selection of vocation or area of study appropriate for him?

5. What information can you furnish that may be helpful in advising this student in setting up his academic program, such as his course area weaknesses, financial need, physical limitation, if any?

6. List other colleges or universities to which this student plans to apply.

Date................................. Signature................................. Title.................................

School................................. City................................. State.................................

NOTE—This blank should be detached and filled out by the principal of the school and mailed directly to the Director of Admissions, Montgomery Junior College, Takoma Park, Md. 20012

MONTGOMERY JUNIOR COLLEGE
Takoma Park, Md. 20012

APPLICANT'S HIGH SCHOOL RECORD
(Secondary-School Record Revised)

Name, in full _____   Curriculum requested _____
       Last Name   First Name   Middle Name

Home address _____
          Number and Street   City   State

Name of Parent or Guardian _____ Birth Date _____ Sex _____

School accredited by _____

Entered _____   Was graduated)
        Name of School   Will be graduated } _____
                                    Withdrew   Month   Year
_____
Month   Year   Location of School

Class periods are _____ minutes, _____ times a week, _____ weeks a year. Passing mark is _____ College recommending mark _____

1. List your complete marking system, highest to lowest: _____ Honor marks _____

2. List other secondary schools attended: _____

Are all failing marks for each year listed? ☐ yes ☐ no CLASS RECORD		1st Sem 9		1st Sem 10		1st Sem 11		1st Sem 12		Extra		Standard Exams	Units or Cred.
Subject	Grade → Year → 19													
English														
Lang.														
Math.														
Check Special Lab Periods Yes No														
Science														
Soc. Studies														
Other Subjects														

Check (√) all subjects where no marks are given.
Star (*) all subjects in progress.

Notes

A unit represents the study of a subject a full school year four or five times per week.

One **unit** equals two credits unless otherwise defined.

Use **extra** column for extra school year.

Use **exams** column for special exams as Regents, *etc.*

TEST RECORD

	Name and Form of Test	Year Given	Score	%-ile Gr. Level	Basis*
Mental Ability					
Reading					
Achievement					
Others					

ADDITIONAL INFORMATION

*Give available interpretation of tests on an enclosure.

TOTAL number of units school requires for graduation _____.

Applicant ranks ☐ exactly ☐ approximately _____ in a graduating class of _____ students

School completed above rank in class by using official record beginning with____grade and ending with____semester in____grade:

☐ Marks weighted as recommended by NASSP and AACRAO
☐ Includes all subjects given school credit
☐ Major or full-time subjects only
☐ College preparatory students only

Date _____ Signature _____ Title _____

Permission to reproduce granted by the National Association of Secondary-School Principals of the NEA, 1201 Sixteenth Street, N.W., Washington 6, D. C.

PLEASE COMPLETE DATA ON REVERSE SIDE

Personality Record (Confidential)
(REVISED)

Room...

Grade..

PERSONAL CHARACTERISTICS OF ....

<table>
<tr><td>Last Name</td><td>First Name</td><td>Middle Name</td></tr>
</table>

School.. Town or City .... State..........................

The following characterizations are descriptions of behavior; they are not ratings. It is recommended that where possible the judgments of a number of the pupil's present teachers be indicated by use of the following method or by checks:

Example: MOTIVATION

1		M (5)		2
	∨	∨∨∨∨		∨∨
Purposeless	Vacillating	Usually Purposeful	Effectively motivated	Highly motivated

M (5) indicates the most common or modal behavior of the pupil as shown by the agreement of five of the eight teachers reporting. The location of the numerals to the left and right indicates that one teacher considers the pupil *vacillating* and that two teachers consider him *highly motivated*. If preferred, the subject fields or other areas of relationship with the pupil may be used to replace the numerals.

1. MOTIVATION	Purposeless	Vacillating	Usually Purposeful	Effectively motivated	Highly motivated
2. INDUSTRY	Seldom works even under pressure	Needs constant pressure	Needs occasional prodding	Prepares assigned work regularly	Seeks additional work
3. INITIATIVE	Seldom initiates	Conforms	Does routine assignments	Consistently self-reliant	Actively creative
4. INFLUENCE AND LEADERSHIP	Negative	Co-operative but retiring	Sometimes in minor affairs	Contributing in important affairs	Judgment respected— makes things go
5. CONCERN FOR OTHERS	Indifferent	Self-centered	Somewhat socially concerned	Generally concerned	Deeply and actively concerned
6. RESPONSIBILITY	Unreliable	Somewhat dependable	Usually dependable	Conscientious	Assumes much responsibility
7. INTEGRITY	Not dependable	Questionable at times	Generally honest	Reliable, dependable	Consistently trustworthy
8. EMOTIONAL STABILITY	Hyperemotional / Apathetic	Excitable / Unresponsive	Usually well-balanced	Well-balanced	Exceptionally stable

Significant school activities and special interests or abilities. Listed membership and offices held in school activities.

Significant limitations (physical, social, mental):

Additional information which may be helpful, such as probable financial needs or work experience:

Prinicpal's comments (Specific statement concerning the applicant's fitness for acceptance by this college or employer):

Principal's estimate of applicant's future success, based on the purpose of this application.

☐ Little success ☐ May encounter some difficulty ☐ Average ☐ Above average ☐ Superior

Principal's recommendation ☐ Recommended ☐ Not recommended for this college or position ☐ Prefer not to make recommendation.

Date .... Signature .... Title ....

This Personality Record (confidential) is available as a **separate** form; *i.e.,* the Secondary-School Record is omitted, leaving one side blank.

MONTGOMERY JUNIOR COLLEGE

Takoma Park, Maryland 20012

APPLICATION FOR ADMISSION
(Special students should use simplified form)

ATTACH A RECENT
PHOTO

To the Applicant: Please fill in pages 1 and 2 of this form legibly in ink and in your own handwriting and mail (or bring it) with the $10.00 matriculation fee to the Director of Admissions, Montgomery Junior College, Takoma Park, Md. 20012. Fill in your name at the top of page 3 and give that sheet to the proper secondary school official. It is the responsibility of the applicant to have his complete records furnished to the college. NO ACTION IS TAKEN UNTIL THEY ARE RECEIVED.

Date _____, 19 ____

1. *Personal Data:*

    Name in full (please print) Mr. Miss Mrs. _____
                                           (first)   (middle)   (last)

    Home address _____ Home Phone _____
              (number, street)   (town or city and zone)   (county)   (state)

    How long have you lived at the present address? _____
                                        (years and months)

    If under six months, give previous address _____ How long? _____

    Where will you live while attending the College? _____

    Place of Birth _____ Date of Birth _____
             (city or town)   (state)   (month, day, year)

    Citizenship _____

    Are you married _____ Single? _____ Divorced? _____ Live with parents? _____

    If you have children, give their ages: Boys _____ Girls _____

    If you have a legal guardian, give name and address _____

2. *Family Data:*   Father   Mother

    Name in full _____   _____

    Address _____   _____

    Telephone _____   _____

    Occupation _____   _____

    Highest education _____   _____

    Status of parents: Married _____ Divorced _____ Separated _____ Father remarried _____ Mother remarried _____

3. *Scholastic Record:*

    List all schools and colleges attended since the completion of eighth grade including summer school. (Failure to give full and accurate information will be considered adequate grounds for denying admission, or dismissal after admission.)

Name of School	Address	Attendance From (date) to (date)	Date of Graduation

    Have you taken the ACT? _____ If so, give date _____

    Have you previously made application to M.J.C.? _____ Date _____

    Have you previously attended M.J.C. _____ Date _____

    Have you made application to any other college(s)? ☐ Yes ☐ No   If yes, list institution and dates of application(s):

    _____

    Have you ever been dismissed from or placed on probation at any school or college: for poor scholarship? ____, for disciplinary reasons or any other cause? ____. If either answer is yes, attach a letter of full explanation.

4. *Service Record:*

    If you are or have been in the Armed Forces, describe your present status:

    Entered active service _____ 19 ____ Branch of service _____ Rank _____

    Discharged _____ 19 ____ Reason for discharge _____

    Service schools attended _____

    Will you be receiving V. A. benefits under P. L. 16? _____, P. L. 894? _____, or P. L. 550? _____

5. *College Plans:*

Montgomery Junior College conceives its program to be a unified entity; the curriculum and learning experiences are planned progressively and sequentially; courses are selected and planned so that the student gains most and is best prepared for transfer to another institution or for employment only after completing the entire curriculum. Students are not accepted otherwise than with this understanding except by special ruling of the Admissions Committee.

What is your educational objective?

If employment, state type of position you hope to hold _____

If junior year of a four-year college or university, give name _____

If other, describe briefly _____

Check if you wish to attend: Full-time _____ Part-time _____ Day _____ Evening _____.

Underscore curriculum in which you desire to register:

Art-Advertising	Electronic Technology	Liberal Arts (Sci.-Math. Seq.)	Pre-Medicine
Art-Cultural	Engineering	Medical Secretarial	Pre-Nursing
Business Administration	Engineering Aide	Medical Technology	Pre-Pharmacy
Dental Assisting	General Business	Music-Cultural/Professional	Physical Education
Education (Elementary)	General Education (Hum.-Soc. Sci. Seq.)	Music-Education	Radiation Science
Education (Secondary)	General Education (Sci.-Math. Seq.)	Police Science	Radiation Technology
Education for Industry	Home Economics	Pre-Dentistry	Secretarial
Electronic Data Proc.	Liberal Arts (Arts Seq.)	Pre-Law	Other (specify)

6. *Employment:*

Do you expect to earn part of your expenses while in college _____ If so, how? _____

How many hours a week do you expect to work while in college? _____

If you have been out of high school longer than one semester, and you have not registered in a college or university, state what

you have been doing in the meantime _____

Employment record:

Employer	Position held	Dates	Full or part time

7. *Extracurricular Activities:*

Underscore your high school activities, adding any not mentioned:

LITERARY—School paper, school annual, and literary societies, _____

DRAMATIC, DEBATING; MUSIC and ART; Band; _____

ATHLETICS—Baseball, basketball, football, track, hockey, tennis, golf, swimming _____

CLASS OFFICES: _____

MISCELLANEOUS—Boy Scouts, Campfire Girls, Sodality, YMCA work, YWCA work, social service, church work, _____

OTHER: _____

8. *Honors:*

What special recognition, if any, have you received for excellence in school work, such as honors, scholarships? _____

9. *Admission Date:*

When do you wish to enter the College? _____

I prefer to attend (check preference) Takoma Park _____ Rockville _____ Campus.

10. *Certification:*

I certify that the information on this application is correct and complete. If admitted, I agree to abide by the rules and regulations of Montgomery Junior College.

_____ _____
(If applicant is under 21 years, signature of parent or guardian)   (Signature of applicant)

Date you filed this application _____
                                 (month)   (day)   (year)

Write a brief informal autobiography below in own handwriting. (Do not repeat a listing of schools attended)

_____

_____

_____

_____

_____

_____

_____

_____

5M—R—1-66

The amount of money required to go to college has doubled since 1940, and is likely to double again by 1970. As the number of teen-agers going to college increases, college costs will go up to pay for dormitories to house them, dining rooms to feed them, classrooms and laboratories to educate them, professors to teach them, and student unions and football stadiums to entertain them. In a single statement: going to college is expensive, and it is going to become more so.

Analyzing College Costs

Rapid increases in enrollment coupled with the rising cost of educating each student resulted in tuition and fees rising 75 percent in the 1950's. In the past five years, the more expensive colleges have raised student charges by about 40 percent, and all colleges have raised them by an average of 30 percent. A majority of the nation's colleges have passed on increased costs to students in the form of tuition and fees of one kind or another in that same period of time. It is estimated that college costs of 1970 will double those of the mid-1950's. With little doubt, this spiraling effect will continue throughout the 1960 decade.

Rising college costs reflect increases in living costs — food, room and board, clothes, travel, and commercial entertainment — rather than increases in educational costs, such as tuition, fees, books, instructional supplies, and equipment. A study has shown that educational costs for students attending public colleges amounted to only one-sixth of the cost of attending college. Five-sixths of the expenses were classified as living costs.[1] Students who attended private colleges spent one-third for educational costs and two-thirds for living costs. Tuitions, fees, and room and board generally comprised 40 to 60 percent in public colleges, and 60 to 80 percent in private colleges of the total amount a student will spend each year.[2]

The cost of attending college varies. Private colleges cost more to attend than do public colleges. Specialized four-year technical institutes are more expensive than other kinds of institutions, generally speaking. It will cost more to attend a university offering graduate programs than to attend most colleges that offer bachelor's degrees only. Distance from home will affect the cost of going to college. College expenses vary with the part of the country. Attending college full time as compared to part time will make a substantial difference in the cost of going to college each year. Whether you live in a dormitory, a private home, or a fraternity house usually makes a difference in college expenses. The personality of a campus and the social and economic background of students' families will make a difference in

---

[1] Ernest V. Hollis and Associates, *Cost of Attending College,* Bulletin 1,957, No. 9, U.S. Office of Education (Washington, D.C.: U.S. Government Printing Office, 1958).

[2] Richard C. McKee, "College and University Aid For Students," *College Aid For Students,* U.S. Office of Education (Washington, D.C.: U.S. Government Printing Office, 1965).

Chapter Eight

Determining College Costs

what college will cost. Boys usually spend more than girls at college. Attending as a single or as a married student makes a big difference in cost. Having a car may seem very important and it cannot be denied that many students have them; but this, too, adds to the expense of going to college.

Married students are becoming more common on campuses each year. The Census Bureau estimates that one out of four full-time students are married. The financial situation for married students presents a picture very different from that of unmarried students living in dormitories. Married students have financial obligations to their budding families, and, to establish a desirable family living, they spend more money for insurance, medical needs, and for food and apartments. If one partner of a married couple attends college the other is likely to be employed, with the earnings spent on college expenses. Under these conditions, college costs married students whatever they make.

College students' spending ranges from an austere economy figure of $200 to a luxury budget of $5,500 for a school year. This wide range is influenced by the type of school attended.[3] A research team at the University of Michigan studied how much college costs on the average and how people managed to pay for college. They found that college expenses for the average unmarried full-time student totaled $1,550 a year. Of this sum, $950 came from the student's parents, $360 was earned by the student, $130 was supplied by scholarships, and $110 came from a variety of other sources. This study found that about one-half of the families experienced difficulty in meeting college expenses. Two out of ten families said they not only found financing college difficult but also felt that the amount they could provide was inadequate. The families included in the study managed their finances in several ways. Some saved money for college expenses and some borrowed money; mothers went to work and, in a few cases, fathers took on a second job.[4]

The U.S. Office of Education reports that the average cost of attending college for a single person in 1966–67 was $1,640 for students who attended public colleges and $2,570 for those attending private ones.

You may note from the following table that by attending your state college you may save hundreds of dollars in educational expenses over the cost of attending an out-of-state private one. The reported costs are averages; to attend a specific college may cost more or less than these amounts.[5]

Although private colleges and universities charge the student more than state-supported institutions charge, the actual cost of college is about the same in both

[3] Hollis, *op. cit.*

[4] John B. Lansing, Thomas Lorimer, and Chikashi Moriguchi, *How People Pay for College* (Ann Arbor: University of Michigan Press, September 1960), p. 160.

[5] Adapted from Louis A. D'Amico, *Higher Education: Basic Student Charges, 1963–64,* U.S. Office of Education, Circular 755 (Washington, D.C.: U.S. Government Printing Office, 1964). Charges of individual institutions are listed.

COST OF TUITION

Type of Institution	Public: State Residents	Public: Non-State Residents	Private
University	$268	$633	$1,200
Liberal Arts	185	503	807
Teachers College	227	454	650
Technological	250	518	1,151
Junior College	128	349	526

COST OF BOARD AND ROOM

Type of Institution	Public Men	Public Women	Private Men	Private Women
University	$692	$705	$848	$852
Liberal Arts	564	566	686	697
Teachers College	577	567	700	720
Technological	648	697	819	853
Junior College	550	547	522	589

kinds of institutions. The difference in cost is simply a matter of who picks up the tab. The state has a sizable investment in each of its college graduates. If you go to a tax-supported school, you will pay only about 60 percent of your total college costs. Construction of buildings, research, instruction, and other large expenditures run more than the amount charged students at public institutions. While some private colleges and universities have strong endowment programs, institutions must get the greater proportion of money from student charges. This does not necessarily mean that the quality of instruction in tax-supported schools is inferior. Some public institutions are highly reputable, and some private ones are not accredited.

THE AVERAGE COST

Expenses	High-cost private college	Low-Cost private college	High-cost public college	Low-cost public college (primarily commuters)
Total	$3,200	$1,850	$1,800	$1,050
Tuition & fees	1,500	550	300	100
Room	400	200	300	0
Meals on campus	500	400	500	200
Book & supplies	150	150	150	150
Transportation	250	150	150	200
Personal & miscellaneous	400	400	400	400

Source: "Get Ready for College and Go" Office of Education, U.S. Department of Health, Education, and Welfare, 1965.

Educational Expenses

What you and your family think of as "big" costs are the educational costs of attending college. These are tuition, fees, books, and educational supplies. They will include room and board if you live away from home.

You don't have to guess or estimate some of these costs, for information on the cost of tuition, fees, and room and board is listed in college catalogs. In addition, you will spend $75 to $100 on books and supplies. If college is still a few years away, these costs may be higher. The U.S. Office of Education reports that, for the 1964–65 school year, the median charge for tuition and fees was $200 for state residents at public colleges and $812 for private colleges. Many colleges plan to increase these fees, with the anticipated increase averaging about 10 percent a year.

As an example of educational costs, the following information, taken from college catalogs, lists the costs to state-resident students for tuition, room, board, and fees for the 1964–65 school year, which may be paid on a semester basis.

Institution	Tuition	Room and Board	Fees
Amherst College	$1,500	$ 850	$ 120
Franklin College (Indiana)	$1,220	$ 830	$60–100
Louisiana State University	$ 50	$616–918	$ 120
University of Arizona	$ 207	$695–832	Included
University of Wisconsin	$ 300	$ 800	Included
University of Wyoming	$ 290	$603–652	$ 5.50

All institutions have additional fees for laboratories, special courses, graduation, etc.

Tuition and fees for out-of-state students will cost as much as twice the cost to a state resident. Slightly less than 50,000 students paid from $300 to $1,000 out-of-state fees to go to a college in 1960–61. The average was about $500 a year. As the competition for more space increases, you can expect to pay even more to attend college in another state. For some of the schools mentioned above, out-of-state students had to pay the following amounts for out-of-state tuition and fees for the 1965–66 school year.

University of Arizona	$ 600
Louisiana State University	$ 570
University of Wyoming	$ 590
University of Wisconsin	$1,000

Each semester you can expect to spend $20 to $40 at the college bookstore for books and supplies. You can save by buying used books, and most texts and references are in the college library. You should remember, however, that you are in college to prepare for the future. Saving on books may be a very poor way of saving money. A wise student will take his college counselor's advice and buy the books that are needed, for they will become your stock in trade when you graduate. Your college years are just about the best time to start a personal library.

Noneducational Expenses

Don't overlook the noneducational expenses of attending college. A lack of money for needed items and activities can be a source of dissatisfaction. The noneducational costs include both some of the items and activities dear to the hearts of students, and some things that are important to success and happiness in college. You will want to dress like the other students and do what they do. If you are attending a college where most students wear expensive clothes, drive cars, and enjoy frequent or expensive recreation, then the noneducational costs may not be so little.

The educational cost of attending college remains constant from student to student on a given college campus, but not so with noneducational costs. They can get out of hand and grow into very large costs. A student's expenditure for a year of college depends on the home and community environment where he formed his spending habits, and the campus environment, with its traditions, sanctions, and the type of person it attracts to its student body. Spending habits, both in school and at home, are partly caused by social pressures. While in college, there is a strong desire to do as others do; in fact, an idea of what others do is a factor used by students in selecting a college.

Principal noneducational costs of attending college are:

Clothing and personal items
Recreation and leisure activities
Laundry and cleaning
Travel
Dues to pre-professional and social organizations
Medical needs
Grooming
Snacks
Contributions and other expenses

How much should you budget for these items? There is no set guide, since no two people spend money in the same way. Take clothing, for example. If you are attending a junior college or a state university near home, clothing may not cost you very much. But if you live in New Orleans and are to attend Jamestown College in Jamestown, North Dakota, you will need new clothes. This will cost a good bit. In this example, travel to and from college would be a substantial cost, also. Of course, most of you will not be traveling this far, and the changes in climate may not be so great.

Recreation is another item that can vary a great deal from campus to campus, depending on the composition of the student body. Some student bodies get caught up in sports and other activities, especially if the campus is close to beaches, ski slopes, and other recreational areas. Some students spend more for formal dances than they do for tuition. There is evidence, on many campuses, that $50 a month for the maintenance of a car is the rule rather than the exception. Weekends at the beach, hi-fi sets, and cameras are not considered extravagant to college students who attend on a luxury budget.

Of course, it is not a necessity to spend so much money on recreation and clothing. It is mentioned to acquaint you with the facts of campus life and to point out that the college campus is not the place to try to keep up with the Joneses unless your family can afford it.

Saving Through Selection

Keeping college costs down can begin with wise selection of colleges. The amount you spend while going to college depends on the financial decisions you and your family make. Family income and your career goals should both be considered in selecting a college. For example, state teachers colleges are a "bargain" because fees are low to encourage persons to become teachers. However, they are not a bargain, not even for low-income families, if the student does not plan to enter teaching as a career.

There is truth in the statement that there is a college to fit every pocketbook. Generally speaking, the more selective schools are the more expensive schools. But be encouraged: the more competitive colleges and universities have strong financial aid programs. They award about twice as much money for scholarships as do public colleges.

While tuition is the same for both men and women, room and board costs sometimes vary. Institutions located in New England are more expensive than ones located in other sections of the country. Those located in the West are second most expensive. It costs less to attend college in the South than in other sections, partially because the cost of food and labor is less in the South than in other areas.

College expenses can be reduced through selection and planning. Students who must forego a four-year college because of financial or other reasons find evening college the next best thing. Students who live near colleges and universities, or centers that have evening college or schools, can work full time and study at night. A recent survey estimates that college expenses can be reduced 40 to 50 percent by the student who lives at home and enters state- or city-supported colleges. Many of you have the opportunity to attend colleges close to home. Some of these may be junior colleges that have arrangements with state universities for the acceptance of credits. Cutting down the cost of attending college for the first two years may well make the difference between attending or not attending college.

You can save $400 to $500 each year by commuting to a college located near home and by taking meals at home, rather than living in a dormitory and eating lunch in a college cafeteria. It will cost you about $300 more to live in a sorority or fraternity house than to live and eat in the dormitory. A testimony to the fact that persons on limited budgets can earn a college degree is that it is being done by an increasing number of students each year.

Estimating Your College Expenses

When estimating your noneducational expenses, ask yourself these questions: What do you like to do? What do you feel you must do? What can you do without? Some students feel they must have a record player at college. You may feel that you must have a new pair of bowling shoes and go bowling one night a week, have a date each week, or buy the latest fashions. If you know some students who are going to the college that you plan to attend, find out what they do for entertainment, what the fads on the campus are, what is "expected," how much they spend, and what they spend it on. If you are to be happy in college, you must live somewhat like your classmates. But costs still depend on what is important to you and your spending habits. There are students on low budgets in every college who feel as accepted and comfortable as students who spend more on noneducational items.

For full-time students, college expenses vary from less than $1,000 at Stillman College in Tuscaloosa, Alabama, and Allen College in Columbia, South Caroline, to over $3,000 at Bryn Mawr in Pennsylvania, M.I.T. in Massachusetts, and Pomona College in California. Here are some minimum expenses for tuition, fees, and room and board for several institutions derived from the latest U.S. Office of Education statistics.[6] You should add approximately $700 at each institution for books, supplies, travel, laundry, clothing, medical needs, dues, and recreation. If you have tentatively selected two or three colleges, you will want to write for specific information so that you can prepare a budget to estimate your financial needs.

American University	$2,230
Amherst College	2,188
Auburn University	1,106
Boston University	2,435
Bryn Mawr College	2,300
College of the Holy Cross	1,830
Colorado State University	1,560
DePauw University	2,270
Goucher College	1,923
Iowa State University	1,470
Johns Hopkins University	2,450
Massachusetts Institute of Technology	2,800
Michigan State University	1,918
Oklahoma Baptist University	1,200
Stillman College	815
Texas Christian University	1,269
University of Kentucky	1,250
University of Maine	1,700
University of Notre Dame	2,260
West Virginia University	1,480
Yale University	2,550

As a guide for you to develop an estimate of the amount of money necessary for a year of college, the following budget was prepared. You may list in the blank spaces your own estimate of the college you

[6] Louis A. D'Amico, *Basic Student Charges, 1963–64: Tuition and Fees, Room and Board,* U.S. Office of Education, Circular 755 (Washington, D.C.: U.S. Government Printing Office, 1964).
Note: These have likely increased.

are considering. Estimates of the cost of attending are available from most institutions.

Education Costs	Private College	State College	Your College
Tuition and fees	$1,000	$300	———
Room and board	700	600	———
Books and supplies	100	100	———
Living Costs			
Travel	165	140	———
Clothing	225	190	———
Recreation, dues, entertainment	50	125	———
Personal and miscellaneous (haircuts, cosmetics, laundry, contributions, dates, etc.)	150	115	———
TOTAL	$2,390	$1,570	

College should not be looked at for what it costs or for its benefits toward increased earning power alone. Neither is an adequate measure of the value of a college education. A college education does cost a substantial sum of money, but it is worth it. It is an investment in you and your future. It will be worth the sacrifice you have to make to attain this worthy goal. While some colleges may have priced themselves out of the market as far as you are concerned, you can select an accredited college and work out financial arrangements so that you can attend. You can go to college if you weigh the merits of the opportunities available in light of your reasons for attending. Students with financial problems do it all the time, and you can do it, too.

Chapter Nine

Paying for College

Following the pattern of rising costs in education, money for aiding qualified students has increased sharply in recent years.

Financial aid to freshmen and first-year professional students in 1963–64 totaled $331 million, and millions more have been added since then from new sources. The total aid administered by all institutions during the 1963–64 academic year included $145 million in student employment, $131 million in scholarships, $32 million in service grants, and $24 million in loans. Employment and scholarships accounted for 84 percent of the total.[1]

Private institutions provide aid to more of their students than do public institutions. Private institutions enrolled only 36 percent of all students, but awarded 55 percent of the total aid in 1963–64. Public and private institutions differ not only in the amount of aid to students, but also in the type of aid given. Public colleges use more than 60 percent of their funds to provide jobs for students, while private colleges award more than 50 percent of their aid in the form of scholarships.

It has been estimated that total financial aid available to college students, including graduate students, is about $1 billion. There is general acceptance of the idea that no qualified student should be deprived of a college education because of financial reasons. Financing your studies is secondary to your desire and determination to gain college acceptance. Once you have been admitted by an institution, the financial aid officer at the college will assist within his capabilities. If you are an average student, you can go to college, and what's more, you can probably get financial aid.

Financial aid comes in many forms. The three primary sources of funds are the colleges and universities themselves; federal, state, and local governments; and private foundations and community organizations.

There are scholarships, loans, part-time work, cooperative work-study programs, and time-payment plans to help students and their families pay for college expenses. An increasing number of students, particularly married students who have family obligations, attend evening colleges and carry full-time jobs.

If you can be admitted to college, you have a better than equal chance of getting financial assistance of some kind if you need it. Financing a college education is a matter of planning and arranging your personal and financial program. You should know the value of the various kinds of financial aid and understand the obligations they carry. The earlier you begin planning to meet college expenses, the greater will be your chance of arranging for the necessary financial backing for college.

[1] Richard C. McKee, "College and University Aid for Students," *College Aid for Students,* U.S. Office of Education, (Washington, D.C.: U.S. Government Printing Office, 1965).

Figure 7
College and University Aid in Amounts and Percents, 1963–64
(Amounts are in millions of dollars)

	Public and Private				Public		Private	
Category	Total Percent of all aid				Amount	Percent	Amount	Percent
	Total	Public	Private					
All Aid	$331.4	100	45	55	$149.0	100	$182.4	100
Employment	144.6	44	28	16	92.3	61	52.3	28
Scholarships	130.9	40	10	30	32.3	22	98.6	54
Service grants	32.1	9	4	5	14.5	10	17.6	10
Loans	23.8	7	3	4	9.9	7	13.9	8

(Source: U.S. Office of Education)

Analyzing Financial Need

Money for college is related to family income; therefore, the need for financial assistance is related to family income. "Financial need is the difference between the amount of money the student and his family can pay for an education and the cost of the education." [2] From the institution's point of view, student aid is a single problem. The financial aid officer attempts to provide students with means of meeting their expenses by developing an overview of all the resources they and their families have to meet the total financial cost of college attendance. Each family situation is different, and financial aid is determined individually.

The system most frequently used to determine financial need was developed by the College Scholarship Service. CSS analyzes financial need in terms of the amount of financial aid needed, rather than character or academic promise. The CSS system provides financial information and a standard way of evaluating it to arrive at a preliminary "need" figure. Similar forms are used by colleges that are not members of the College Scholarship Service. The college financial aid officer, however, is responsible for studying each case and allotting aid to the student.

Family Obligation. The amount of financial support a family should expect to provide depends on its financial strength. Factors used in estimating a family's strength include the number of dependent children and the number of children attending college. In some cases, more than one child in a family plans to attend college, and, in other cases, only one will be attending at a time. Other factors to be considered are other relatives who may be able to assist, the cost of education for other children, and extraordinary expenses, such as medical bills. Special consideration is frequently given to students with unusual parental situations, such as widowed mothers and parents who are nearing retirement age.

One of the primary reasons that families are expected to contribute to the education of their children is that the greater proportion of college expenditure is spent for normal maintenance, including food, clothing, and medical care. Since these costs would be borne by the family if the student did not attend college, families should not expect the financial aid office to bear the full cost.

Income. The "modest but adequate" level of living as defined by Helen LaMale and Margaret S. Stotz in the *Monthly Labor Review* is neither minimum nor luxury maintenance. Income above this level represents money that is available for expenses other than maintenance, which includes higher education. The College Scholarship Service utilizes the concept of effective income for determining need. All income above these levels is considered effective income available for use at the discretion of the family. The following table will let you determine your possibilities for receiving financial aid.

Number of Dependent Children	Income Before Federal Tax	Typical Federal Tax (2 parents)	Income After Federal Tax
1	$6,250	$750	$5,500
2	7,350	850	6,500
3	8,175	875	7,300
4	8,750	850	7,900
5	9,225	825	8,400
6	9,550	750	8,800
7	9,775	675	9,100
8	9,825	575	9,250

Assuming there are no financial complications requiring special allowances, the following is the amount of annual support expected from family income:

| Family Income | Number of Dependent Children in Family | | | | |
	1	2	3	4	5
$4,000	$380	$270	$210	$170	$150
6,000	760	570	450	390	330
8,000	1,220	950	780	680	590
10,000	1,770	1,420	1,200	1,050	950
12,000	2,360	1,960	1,680	1,500	1,370

Assets. The analysis of need for financial assistance takes into consideration the major assets of the family. Many parents tend to disregard these assets, but they do represent one of the family's financial strengths.

---

[2] College Scholarship Service, *Manual for Financial Aid Officers* (Princeton, N.J.: College Entrance Examination Board, 1965).

Examples of assets include the equity the family has in their home, loan value of life insurance, savings, stocks, bonds, and investments. Some of these are valued at less than face value for protection of the family. Certain amounts are subtracted for family purposes. Stocks, bank savings, bonds, and similar investments are totaled and considered at face value. Equity in the family's home, life insurance policies, and similar items are considered at one-half their value. In addition, a basic allowance of $4,000 is deducted for every family, and an emergency allowance of $500 is deducted for each living parent and each child.

The Student. You, the student, are the benefactor of financial aid programs. Colleges expect you to help pay for your education by working during the year on part-time jobs, during the summer, and from savings that you may have. In analyzing your financial need, your savings will be distributed over the four years of college. The amount of money that you can logically be expected to earn will also be budgeted over the four-year period. The amount you can earn is discussed in this chapter under "Part-Time Jobs and Work-Study Programs."

Obtaining Financial Aid. If you need financial assistance after you have been admitted to college, contact the financial aid office. Some applications to college include an application for financial assistance. If the college you plan to attend is a member of the College Scholarship Service, you may obtain from your high school counselor an application for the College Scholarship Service. You will be charged a $2 fee for each college to which you want the application sent. (See figure 8.)

Colleges not using the College Scholarshp Service tend to use a single application form for all types of financial aid. The University of Washington uses such a form. It is presented as figure 9 so that you may know the kinds of questions asked by colleges when you apply for scholarship, loans, and workships.

Scholarships: Where Can You Get One?

Scholarships are the oldest, best known, and most sought-after form of student aid. However, all students will not be fortunate enough to get one. Considering the number of teen-agers talking about scholarships, and the few who do obtain them, there is some reason to suspect that too much emphasis is placed on scholarships. Only about 10 percent of today's college students receive aid from scholarship funds and 25 percent do at some time during their studies.

Understanding Scholarships. Scholarships are awards in recognition of achievement. Like loans, they are for various amounts, last for different length of time, and are from monies derived from many sources. They are

given for various reasons, and the rules for obtaining them differ widely. Though scholarships are constantly changing, there are a few principles that are true for most. While some are granted without regard to true scholarship, most scholarship sponsors would like persons who receive their scholarships to be good risks, both academically and personally. If the donor of the scholarship is a business firm, it would quite naturally, like to find a person interested in the type of business or activity of the donor, because one of the reasons that businesses, agencies, and organizations sponsor scholarships is to secure publicity for encouraging young people to enter their particular kind of work.

What are your chances of getting a scholarship? They may be better than you think. You may believe that scholarships are only for those students who earn the highest grades in high school. This is not necessarily true. Good grades are a big help, but some scholarship rules call for other qualities, such as abilities in writing essays, farming, sports, and dancing, for example.

Scholarships are valuable. In 1963–64, more than two thousand institutions awarded 388,000 scholarships worth $163 million.[3] Seventy-five percent of all scholarships go to students enrolled in private colleges. According to the U.S. Office of Education, colleges and universities in New York granted scholarships totaling $7,894,397 as early as 1957. Examples of the amount of money set aside for scholarships in other states are: Pennsylvania, $6,618,944; Illinois, $3,677,259; and California, $3,186,408. Of course, this amount has probably increased during the past few years.

It is not enough to know how much money is spent in a state. What you want to know is: What is it worth to you? Is a scholarship worth applying for? To what extent will a scholarship help defray college expenses? Will other financial aid be necessary? Answers to some of these questions will become clear if you will consider scholarships on a national basis.

Actually, scholarships vary widely in amount, ranging from less than $50 to about $2,000. Many colleges and universities grant one or more classifications of scholarships that average $1,000. A recent survey shows that scholarships have grown larger during the past few years. The average scholarship grant increased from $341 in 1959 to $420 in 1964.[4] This is in part due to an equal rise in college costs. Most colleges award scholarships, but they vary both in amount and for what they may be used. All states have scholarship programs of one kind or another. Some colleges grant several scholarships that equal less than 10 percent of the cost of attending college. Other colleges grant a few scholarships that will pay for the entire cost of college.

How, then, do you know a good scholarship when you see one? The size of a grant is not the only indicator of a scholarship's value. The National Merit Scholarship Program, for example, gives honorary

[3] McKee, *op. cit.*
[4] McKee, *op. cit.*, p. 2.

Figure 8

Colleges participating in the College Scholarship Service

The institutions listed below require students who are seeking financial aid for college expenses in the 1966-67 academic year to submit a completed Parents' Confidential Statement or Parents' Confidential Statement—Short Form. Next to the college names, in most cases, are the dates by which these institutions require candidates to file the Statement or Short Form with the College Scholarship Service. A student who applies to more than one college should indicate all his college choices on the Statement or Short Form and should file it by the earliest of the dates specified by the colleges to which he is applying. Copies of Statements or Short Forms filed after these desired receipt dates will be forwarded to the colleges, but under these circumstances a student cannot be certain of being considered for financial assistance. To the left of each college name is a four-digit college code to be entered in Item 13 of the Statement and on the Short Form. Be certain to enter the correct css college code number or the Statement or Short Form will be mailed to the wrong institution.

Note: Other colleges, state scholarship programs, and certain sponsored scholarship programs may also require these forms of some or all of their candidates. Candidates should not, however, request that copies be forwarded until they have been specifically requested to do so by the college or scholarship program. Names and code numbers of these colleges and scholarship programs are not included in this list. After receiving a request to submit a Statement, you should enter only the name of the college, sponsored scholarship program, or state scholarship program; the College Scholarship Service will enter the proper code for you.

Code Number	College	Desired Receipt Date
6001	Abilene Christian College	Feb. 21
5001	Abraham Baldwin Agricultural College	Mar. 25
2011	Adelphi Suffolk College of Adelphi University	No definite date
2003	Adelphi University	Feb. 1*
5002	Agnes Scott College	Feb. 15*
3001	Albertus Magnus College	Dec. 7*
1007	Albion College	Mar. 7
2004	Albright College	Apr. 20*
5005	Alderson-Broaddus College	No definite date
2005	Alfred University	Feb. 20*
2006	Allegheny College (Pa.)	Jan. 21
2007	Alliance College	Apr. 1*
1010	Alma College (Mich.)	Mar. 1*
1011	Alpena Community College (Mich.)	Mar. 25
3003	Amherst College	Jan. 15*
5008	Anderson College (S.C.)	Aug. 1
1030	Andrews University	No definite date
3005	Anna Maria College for Women	Mar. 1
3006	Annhurst College	Nov. 24*
1017	Antioch College	Jan. 25*
5010	Appalachian State Teachers College	Mar. 15
1018	Aquinas College (Mich.)	Mar. 1
4008	Armstrong College (Calif.)	Mar. 1
4009	Art Center College of Design (founded as the Art Center School)	Mar. 8
1021	Ashland College	Feb. 25
3009	Assumption College (Mass.)	Mar. 1*
6014	Augsburg College	Mar. 7
1025	Augustana College (Ill.)	Feb. 20
1027	Aurora College	July 1
6016	Austin College	Aug. 15
6109	Avila College	No definite date
3075	Babson Institute	Apr. 1*
1050	Baldwin-Wallace College	Mar. 23
1051	Ball State University	Feb. 7
1052	Barat College of the Sacred Heart	Jan. 20*
2037	Bard College	Mar. 7*
2038	Barnard College	Jan. 7*
5053	Barry College (Fla.)	Feb. 15
	Bates College	
3076	Men	Feb. 20*
3077	Women	Feb. 20*
6032	Baylor University	Mar. 10*
0743	Baylor University College of Dentistry	June 24
2039	Beaver College	Mar. 1*
5055	Belmont Abbey College	Mar. 1
1059	Beloit College	Feb. 20*
2042	Bennett College (N.Y.)	Feb. 1*
5058	Bennett College (N.C.)	Mar. 24
3080	Bennington College	Feb. 21*
6034	Bethany College (Kan.)	Mar. 15
5060	Bethany College (W.Va.)	Mar. 1*
6037	Bethel College (Kan.)	No definite date
6038	Bethel College (Minn.)	No definite date
4017	Biola College	Apr. 15
1064	Birmingham-Southern College	Mar. 8
6040	Bishop College	July 1
1065	Blackburn College	No definite date
2044	Bloomfield College	May 1*
1067	Bluffton College	June 1
3083	Boston College	Jan. 15*
3087	Boston University	Jan. 24
3089	Bowdoin College	Mar. 1*
3091	Bradford Junior College	Feb. 1*
1070	Bradley University	Mar. 1
3092	Brandeis University	Feb. 1
6046	Briar Cliff College (Iowa)	Jan. 24
2045	Briarcliff College (N.Y.)	Jan. 1
5069	Bridgewater College (Va.)	Apr. 23
3094	Brown University (R.I.)	Jan. 1*
2049	Bryn Mawr College	Jan. 10*
2050	Bucknell University	Feb. 1
6047	Buena Vista College	Mar. 15
2070	C.W. Post College	Jan. 25*
2072	Caldwell College for Women	Dec. 1
4031	California College of Arts and Crafts	Apr. 1
4034	California Institute of Technology	Feb. 15

Code Number	College	Desired Receipt Date
4393	California Institute of the Arts	Consult college literature
4088	California Lutheran College	Mar. 8*
	California State Colleges:	
4589	California State College at Fullerton	Aug. 7
4011	California State College at Hayward	No definite date
4099	California State College at San Bernadino	Aug. 7
4038	California State Polytechnic College, San Luis Obispo	Mar. 25
4082	California State Polytechnic College, Kellogg-Voorhis	Apr. 8
4048	Chico State College	Mar. 15
4345	Humboldt State College	Feb. 15
4682	San Diego State College	May 1
4707	San Fernando Valley State College	Apr. 1
4684	San Francisco State College	Feb. 22
4687	San Jose State College	Mar. 25
4713	Stanislaus State College	May 8
4039	California Western University	No definite date*
1095	Calvin College	Mar. 15
1099	Capital University	Feb. 15
6081	Carleton College	Jan. 25*
2074	Carnegie Institute of Technology	Feb. 8
1101	Carroll College (Wis.)	Apr. 1*
1103	Carthage College (Wis.)	Mar. 15
4042	Cascade College	Apr. 15
1105	Case Institute of Technology	Mar. 1*
3765	Castleton State College	May 15
2078	Cazenovia College	Mar. 8*
2079	Cedar Crest College	Feb. 24*
6082	Centenary College of Louisiana	Feb. 15*
6087	Central College (Iowa)	Aug. 1
4044	Central Washington State College	Mar. 1
1109	Centre College of Kentucky	Feb. 15*
0907	Chaminade College of Honolulu	Mar. 15
4047	Chapman College	Mar. 24
2081	Chatham College	Feb. 22*
2082	Chestnut Hill College	Jan. 15*
5108	Citadel, The Military College of South Carolina	Mar. 1
4054	Claremont Men's College	Feb. 22*
3279	Clark University (Mass.)	Jan. 25*
6099	Clarke College (Iowa)	Jan. 15
2084	Clarkson College of Technology	Feb. 8
5111	Clemson University	Feb. 22
6101	Coe College	Apr. 1
5112	Coker College	Mar. 1
3280	Colby College (Maine)	Jan. 15*
3281	Colby Junior College (N.H.)	Jan. 15*
2086	Colgate University	Dec. 23*
4058	College of Great Falls	Mar. 20
4060	College of Idaho	Mar. 31
1129	College of Mount St. Joseph on the Ohio	Jan. 24*
2088	College of Mount St. Vincent	Dec. 8*
2089	College of New Rochelle	Nov. 1*
4063	College of Notre Dame (Calif.)	Mar. 8
5114	College of Notre Dame of Maryland	Jan. 1
3283	College of Our Lady of the Elms	Mar. 18
6104	College of Saint Benedict (Minn.)	Mar. 1
6105	College of Saint Catherine (Minn.)	Jan. 31*
2090	College of St. Elizabeth	Jan. 7*
1131	College of Saint Mary of the Springs	Jan. 4*
6107	College of Saint Scholastica	Feb. 1
6108	College of Saint Teresa (Minn.)	Feb. 1
6110	College of Saint Thomas (Minn.)	Mar. 15*
1133	College of Steubenville	Jan. 20*
3282	College of the Holy Cross	Feb. 15
4059	College of the Holy Names (Calif.)	Feb. 8
5115	College of William and Mary	July 15*
1134	College of Wooster	Mar. 7*
2087	College Misericordia	Jan. 1*
4072	Colorado College	Mar. 1*
4075	Colorado State University	Mar. 5
4076	Colorado Woman's College	Mar. 1
2093	Columbia College (N.Y.)	Jan. 1
2111	School of Engineering	Jan. 1

*Candidates for the Early Decision Plan should consult the college's literature for desired receipt date.

Colleges participating in the College Scholarship Service (Continued)

Code Number	College	Desired Receipt Date	Code Number	College	Desired Receipt Date
5117	Columbia College (S.C.)	Feb. 20	5291	Hampden-Sydney College	Feb. 21*
8030	Columbia University School of Nursing	Mar. 1	2288	Hartwick College	Mar. 1*
6113	Concordia College (Moorhead, Minn.)	June 15*	3434	Harvard College	Dec. 17
1140	Concordia Teachers College (Ill.)	Sept. 1	4341	Harvey Mudd College	Feb. 22*
3284	Connecticut College	Jan. 8*	6270	Hastings College	May 1*
5121	Converse College	Feb. 1*	2289	Haverford College	Jan. 15*
2097	Cooper Union	Apr. 1	1292	Heidelberg College	Feb. 22
6119	Cornell College (Iowa)	Mar. 1*	5293	High Point College	Mar. 20*
2098	Cornell University (N.Y.)	Jan. 1	1297	Hiram College	Mar. 15
6121	Creighton University	Mar. 8	2294	Hobart College	Mar. 1*
6123	Culver-Stockton College	Jan. 1*	2295	Hofstra University	Feb. 1*
3351	Dartmouth College	Feb. 1*	5294	Hollins College	Jan. 7*
5150	Davidson College	Apr. 1*	2297	Holy Family College (Pa.)	Dec. 17
5151	Davis and Elkins College	May 1	5296	Hood College	Feb. 1*
3352	Dean Junior College	Mar. 1	1301	Hope College	Feb. 21*
1164	Denison University	Mar. 1	1302	Howard College (Ala.)	Aug. 1
1165	DePaul University (Ill.)	Feb. 1*	1315	Illinois College	Apr. 1
1166	DePauw University (Ind.)	Feb. 1*	1318	Illinois Institute of Technology	Feb. 1
2186	Dickinson College (Pa.)	Feb. 1*	1320	Illinois Wesleyan University	May 15*
6165	Doane College	Apr. 25	2320	Immaculata College (Pa.)	Dec. 30*
1173	Dominican College (Wis.)	Apr. 23	4357	Immaculate Heart College	Feb. 22
4284	Dominican College of San Rafael	Feb. 8	1321	Indiana Central College	Mar. 1
2192	Douglass College	Feb. 1	2652	Indiana State College (Pa.)	Apr. 15*
6168	Drake University	Mar. 1	1322	Indiana State University (Ind.)	Feb. 15
2193	Drew University, College of Liberal Arts	Feb. 28*	1324	Indiana University (Ind.)	Feb. 1
2194	Drexel Institute of Technology	Feb. 14	2324	Iona College	Feb. 22*
6170	Duchesne College of the Sacred Heart	Jan. 15	6308	Iowa Wesleyan College	Apr. 15*
5156	Duke University	Jan. 25*	3464	Jackson College	Feb. 1*
5158	Dunbarton College of Holy Cross	Mar. 1*	1342	John Carroll University	Apr. 1
2196	Duquesne University	Jan. 25	5332	Johns Hopkins University	Mar. 1*
2197	D'Youville College	Feb. 1	3766	Johnson State College (Vt.)	No definite date
1195	Earlham College	Feb. 21*	2341	Juniata College	Mar. 1
2650	East Stroudsburg State College	June 1*	1365	Kalamazoo College	Mar. 1
2220	Eastern Baptist College	Apr. 1	3472	Keene State College	Mar. 15
5181	Eastern Mennonite College	June 24	1367	Kent State University	Consult college literature
1201	Eastern Michigan University	Jan. 31			
4298	Eastern Montana College	No definite date	1370	Kenyon College	Feb. 20
4301	Eastern Washington State College	Mar. 1	2350	Keuka College	June 7*
1202	Edgewood College of the Sacred Heart	Jan. 15	2351	Keystone Junior College	May 8*
2225	Elizabethtown College	Mar. 15*	1371	King College (Tenn.)	May 15
1204	Elmhurst College	Mar. 1*	2353	King's College	Jan. 15*
2226	Elmira College	Mar. 1*	1372	Knox College	June 1*
3367	Emerson College	Jan. 1	2360	Ladycliff College	Feb. 1
3368	Emmanuel College (Mass.)	Jan. 25	2361	Lafayette College	Feb. 22*
5185	Emory and Henry College	No definite date	5362	LaGrange College	No definite date*
5187	Emory University	Apr. 1*	1391	Lake Erie College	Feb. 15*
1206	Eureka College	No definite date*	1392	Lake Forest College	Mar. 15*
1208	Evansville College	Feb. 22	1393	Lakeland College	May 15
3390	Fairfield University	Feb. 1	6360	Lamar State College of Technology	Apr. 23
	Fairleigh Dickinson University:		1394	Lambuth College (Tenn.)	No definite date
2232	Edward Williams College	Apr. 20	4380	La Sierra College	Sept. 1
2262	Madison	Apr. 20	4381	La Verne College	Mar. 25*
2255	Rutherford	Apr. 20	1398	Lawrence University (Wis.)	Feb. 15
2263	Teaneck	Apr. 20	2364	Lebanon Valley College	May 1*
2257	Fashion Institute of Technology	Mar. 1	2365	Lehigh University	Jan. 15
1222	Ferris State College	Feb. 20	2366	Le Moyne College (N. Y.)	Mar. 1
1223	Findlay College	May 1*	4384	Lewis and Clark College	Feb. 15*
1224	Fisk University	June 1	6367	Lindenwood College	Feb. 20
1853	Flint College of the University of Michigan	Jan. 24*	4387	Linfield College	Mar. 1*
5218	Florida Southern College	June 1*		Long Island University:	
5219	Florida State College	Feb. 15	2369	University Center	Mar. 1
6216	Fontbonne College	Feb. 1	4390	Loretto Heights College	Mar. 1
2259	Fordham University	Feb. 1*	4397	Los Angeles Pacific College	No definite date
4344	Fort Wright College of the Holy Names	Feb. 15	1412	Loyola University (Ill.)	Feb. 15
2261	Franklin and Marshall College	Feb. 22*	4403	Loyola University of Los Angeles	Feb. 15
1228	Franklin College of Indiana	Mar. 8	6374	Loyola University of the South (La.)	Jan. 31
5222	Furman University	Feb. 20*	6375	Luther College (Iowa)	No definite date
2270	Gannon College	Mar. 15	2372	Lycoming College	Feb. 15*
3415	Garland Junior College	May 20*	5372	Lynchburg College	Mar. 15*
2273	Geneva College	Apr. 15	6390	Macalester College	No definite date
4325	George Fox College	June 1	1435	MacMurray College	Apr. 8*
1247	George Peabody College for Teachers	Mar. 1	1440	Manchester College	Feb. 23
5246	George Washington University	Jan. 25	2395	Manhattan College	Feb. 15*
1248	George Williams College	July 1	2397	Manhattanville College of the Sacred Heart	Feb. 8*
5244	Georgetown University (D.C.)	Mar. 1*			
5248	Georgia Institute of Technology	Feb. 15	1444	Marietta College	Mar. 1
5253	Georgia Southern College	Aug. 1	1448	Marquette University	Feb. 15
5251	Georgia State College	No definite date	5397	Mary Baldwin College	Jan. 25*
2274	Georgian Court College	Jan. 15*	5398	Mary Washington College of the University of Virginia	Feb. 22
2275	Gettysburg College	Feb. 1*			
3416	Goddard College	No definite date	6397	Marycrest College	Mar. 7
4330	Gonzaga University	Feb. 15*	4480	Marylhurst College	Mar. 1
2276	Good Counsel College	Nov. 1	4481	Marymount College (Calif.)	Feb. 15
3417	Gordon College	Mar. 15*	6398	Marymount College (Kan.)	Mar. 1
1251	Goshen College	Mar. 25	2406	Marymount College (N.Y.)	Feb. 10*
5257	Goucher College	Jan. 8*	2405	Marymount Manhattan College	Jan. 3*
6249	Graceland College	No definite date	6399	Maryville College of the Sacred Heart	Jan. 1
1256	Greenville College	No definite date	2407	Marywood College	Dec. 31*
6252	Grinnell College	Feb. 20*	3514	Massachusetts Institute of Technology	Jan. 6
2277	Grove City College	Mar. 5			
6253	Gustavus Adolphus College	Mar. 24*	5408	Medical College of Virginia	Apr. 25*
2278	Gwynedd-Mercy College	Jan. 15*	4483	Menlo College	Apr. 1*
2286	Hamilton College	Mar. 15*	5409	Mercer University	May 1
6265	Hamline University	Feb. 15	2410	Mercyhurst College	Feb. 1*

*Candidates for the Early Decision Plan should consult the college's literature for desired receipt date.

Colleges participating in the College Scholarship Service (Continued)

Code Number	College	Desired Receipt Date
1465	Michigan State University	Dec. 8
1464	Michigan Technological University	Jan. 25
	Middlebury College	
3526	Men	Mar. 20*
3527	Women	Mar. 20*
1469	Milligan College	Aug. 1
1470	Millikin University	June 1
4485	Mills College	Jan. 15*
2413	Mills College of Education	Feb. 21*
6411	Minneapolis School of Art	Feb. 15*
3528	Mitchell College	Aug. 1
1484	Monmouth College (Ill.)	No definite date
2416	Monmouth College (N.J.)	Apr. 1
4488	Montana State University	Feb. 1
2520	Montclair State College	No definite date
1485	Monticello College	May 21*
2417	Moore College of Art	Mar. 24
2418	Moravian College	Mar. 15*
6415	Morningside College	Mar. 25
4492	Mount Angel College	Mar. 8
3529	Mount Holyoke College	Jan. 8*
6417	Mount Mercy College (Iowa)	Mar. 1
2421	Mount Mercy College (Pa.)	Jan. 15*
5420	Mount Saint Agnes College	Jan. 8*
3531	Mount Saint Mary College (N. H.)	Feb. 15
4493	Mount Saint Mary's College (Calif.)	Feb. 15
6419	Mount Saint Scholastica College	Feb. 1
1492	Mount Union College	Consult college literature*
5422	Mount Vernon Junior College	Apr. 1*
2424	Muhlenberg College	Jan. 1*
1493	Mundelein College	No definite date
1496	Muskingum College	Mar. 1*
3655	Nasson College	Mar. 25
1551	National College of Education	No definite date
1554	Nazareth College (Mich.)	Mar. 15
1553	Nazareth College of Kentucky	May 1
2511	Nazareth College of Rochester	Feb. 1*
3659	New England Conservatory	May 15
4533	New Mexico Institute of Mining and Technology	Aug. 1
2562	New York University	Dec. 5*
2517	Newark State College	May 7
3664	Newton College of the Sacred Heart	Feb. 1
5496	North Carolina State of the University of North Carolina at Raleigh	Feb. 1
1555	North Central College (Ill.)	Apr. 1
5497	North Georgia College	May 25
5498	North Greenville Junior College	Apr. 1
1556	North Park College	Feb. 1
3667	Northeastern University (Mass.)	Feb. 1
4540	Northrop Institute of Technology	Consult college literature
4544	Northwest Nazarene College	Mar. 25
1565	Northwestern University (Ill.)	Feb. 1*
3669	Norwich University	Apr. 1*
1566	Notre Dame College (Ohio)	Mar. 1*
2559	Notre Dame College of Staten Island	Nov. 24*
1497	Oakland University (Mich.)	May 15
1587	Oberlin College	Mar. 15*
4581	Occidental College	Feb. 20*
5521	Oglethorpe College	Apr. 15
1591	Ohio Northern University	No definite date*
1592	Ohio State University	Mar. 1
1593	Ohio University	Feb. 15*
1594	Ohio Wesleyan University	Feb. 1*
6543	Oklahoma City University	No definite date
1595	Olivet College (Mich.)	No definite date
	Oregon State System of Higher Education	
4300	Eastern Oregon College	Mar. 1
4585	Oregon College of Education	Mar. 1
4586	Oregon State University	Mar. 1
4587	Oregon Technical Institute	Mar. 1
4610	Portland State College	Mar. 1
4702	Southern Oregon College	Mar. 1
4846	University of Oregon	Mar. 1
4394	Otis Art Institute of Los Angeles County	Feb. 15
6547	Ottawa University (Kan.)	No definite date
1597	Otterbein College	Apr. 8
1599	Our Lady of Cincinnati College	Jan. 15
6550	Our Lady of the Lake College	No definite date
2635	Pace College	Mar. 15
4597	Pacific Lutheran University (Wash.)	Mar. 1
4600	Pacific Union College	June 30
4601	Pacific University (Ore.)	Apr. 1*
6575	Parsons College (Iowa)	No definite date
4605	Pasadena College	No definite date
2518	Paterson State College	Apr. 1
0703	Peabody Conservatory of Music	Feb. 15*
3688	Pembroke College in Brown University	Jan. 15
2642	Pennsylvania Military College	Mar. 1
2660	Pennsylvania State University	Jan. 15
4326	Pepperdine College	Apr. 20
2664	Philadelphia College of Art	Apr. 8
2666	Philadelphia College of Textiles and Science	June 1
3689	Pine Manor Junior College	Apr. 1*
4619	Pitzer College	Feb. 22*
3690	Plymouth State College	May 1
2668	Polytechnic Institute of Brooklyn	Mar. 1*
4607	Pomona College	Feb. 15*
6580	Prairie View Agricultural and Mechanical College	June 1*
2669	Pratt Institute	Feb. 22
5540	Presbyterian College (S. C.)	Feb. 1*
2672	Princeton University	Jan. 1
1630	Principia College (Ill.)	Jan. 26*
3693	Providence College	Mar. 25*
1631	Purdue University	Feb. 14
5560	Queens College (N.C.)	Feb. 1*
1645	Quincy College (Ill.)	Feb. 22*
3722	Radcliffe College	Dec. 20
5567	Randolph-Macon Woman's College	Feb. 1*
4654	Reed College	Feb. 8*
3723	Regis College (Mass.)	Jan. 15*
5568	Reinhardt College (Ga.)	Aug. 20
2757	Rensselaer Polytechnic Institute	Jan. 25
3726	Rhode Island School of Design	Mar. 1
6609	Rice University	Feb. 1*
2758	Rider College	Mar. 8
1664	Ripon College	Feb. 21*
5571	Roanoke College	Mar. 8*
2760	Rochester Institute of Technology	Mar. 1
6610	Rochester Junior College (Minn.)	Mar. 1
1665	Rockford College	Jan. 15
6611	Rockhurst College	Mar. 15
4660	Rocky Mountain College	No definite date
5572	Rollins College	Mar. 1
1666	Roosevelt University	Mar. 8
1667	Rosary College (Ill.)	Dec. 30*
2762	Rosary Hill College (N.Y.)	Feb. 20
1668	Rose Polytechnic Institute	Mar. 1
2763	Rosemont College	Jan. 25
	Rutgers—The State University:	
2092	College of South Jersey	Feb. 8*
2192	Douglass College	Feb. 1
2512	Newark College	Feb. 8
2765	Rutgers College	Feb. 8
1685	Sacred Heart College (Ala.)	June 1
6617	Saint Ambrose College	No definite date
5214	Saint Andrews Presbyterian College	Apr. 20*
3748	Saint Anselm's College	Mar. 23
1689	Saint Bernard College	May 31
6618	Saint Benedict's College (Kan.)	Mar. 1
6619	Saint Edward's University	Mar. 1
2796	Saint Francis College (N. Y.)	Mar. 25
2797	Saint Francis College (Pa.)	Feb. 3
1696	Saint John College of Cleveland	Mar. 1
2798	Saint John Fisher College	Feb. 15*
5598	Saint John's College (Md.)	No definite date
6624	Saint John's University (Minn.)	Mar. 23
3754	Saint Joseph College (Conn.)	Jan. 15*
5599	Saint Joseph College (Md.)	Dec. 15
1697	Saint Joseph's College (Ind.)	Mar. 25
2801	Saint Joseph's College (Pa.)	No definite date
2805	Saint Lawrence University	Feb. 21*
6629	Saint Louis University	Feb. 8
1704	Saint Mary-of-the-Woods College	Feb. 1*
4675	Saint Mary's College (Calif.)	Apr. 7
1702	Saint Mary's College (Ind.)	No definite date*
6632	Saint Mary's College (Minn.)	Jan. 25*
6633	Saint Mary's Dominican College (La.)	Mar. 15
6637	Saint Mary's University (Texas)	Apr. 1
3757	Saint Michael's College (Vt.)	Mar. 1*
1706	Saint Norbert College (Wis.)	Mar. 1*
6638	Saint Olaf College	Apr. 1*
2806	Saint Peter's College (N.J.)	Jan. 23*
1707	Saint Procopius College	Mar. 15
2808	Saint Vincent College	Feb. 1*
1708	Saint Xavier College (Ill.)	Dec. 15*
5607	Salem College (N.C.)	No definite date*
3759	Salve Regina College	Nov. 23*
4683	San Francisco College for Women	Feb. 1*
4692	Santa Rosa Junior College	Feb. 15
2810	Sarah Lawrence College	Jan. 10
1713	School of the Art Institute of Chicago	Apr. 1
4693	Scripps College	Feb. 15
4694	Seattle Pacific College	Mar. 25
2812	Seton Hill College (Pa.)	Feb. 1*
5613	Shenandoah College and Conservatory of Music	June 1
1717	Shimer College	May 1
2814	Siena College (N.Y.)	No definite date
3761	Simmons College	Feb. 1*
6650	Simpson College (Iowa)	June 15*
2815	Skidmore College	Jan. 5*
3762	Smith College	Jan. 8*

*Candidates for the Early Decision Plan should consult the college's literature for desired receipt date.

Colleges participating in the College Scholarship Service (Continued)

Code Number	College	Desired Receipt Date
4701	Southern California College	July 25
6660	Southern Methodist University	Mar. 1
1730	Southwestern at Memphis	Feb. 21
6674	Southwestern University (Tex.)	Apr. 15
1733	Spring Hill College	May 15
3763	Springfield College (Mass.)	Mar. 15*
4704	Stanford University	Feb. 15
	State University of New York:	
2522	Agricultural and Technical College at Alfred	May 1
2525	Agricultural and Technical College at Delhi	No definite date
2533	College at Buffalo	Apr. 15
2538	College at Cortland	No definite date
2542	College at Oneonta	Apr. 1
2543	College at Oswego	Mar. 20
2530	College of Forestry at Syracuse University	July 1*
2535	Harpur College	Mar. 1
2536	Maritime College	June 15
2532	State University at Albany	Apr. 1
2925	State University at Buffalo	Feb. 15*
6683	Stephens College	Apr. 15*
6684	Sterling College	No definite date
5630	Stetson University	Apr. 1*
2819	Stevens Institute of Technology	Feb. 1*
3770	Stonehill College	Feb. 24*
3771	Suffolk University (Mass.)	Apr. 8*
5633	Sullins College	Feb. 1
2820	Susquehanna University	No definite date*
2821	Swarthmore College	Feb. 1
5634	Sweet Briar College	Jan. 25*
2823	Syracuse University	Feb. 15*
6815	Tabor College	July 1
1802	Taylor University	Feb. 21
2906	Temple University	Feb. 15
6003	Texas A & M University	Apr. 1
6820	Texas Christian University	Feb. 22
2910	Thiel College	Apr. 15
1808	Transylvania College	Apr. 15
2519	Trenton State College	Apr. 30
3899	Trinity College (Conn.)	Feb. 7*
5796	Trinity College (D.C.)	Jan. 8*
6831	Trinity University (Tex.)	Feb. 1*
3901	Tufts College	Feb. 1*
6832	Tulane University	Feb. 21*
6471	Newcomb College	Feb. 21*
2920	Union College (N.Y.)	Feb. 1*
0962	University of Alaska	Mar. 8
3914	University of Bridgeport	May 1
	University of California:	
4833	Berkeley	Feb. 1
4834	Davis	Feb. 1
4859	Irvine	Feb. 1
4837	Los Angeles	Feb. 1
4839	Riverside	Feb. 1
4835	Santa Barbara	Feb. 1
4860	Santa Cruz	Feb. 1
1832	University of Chicago	Jan. 8*
1833	University of Cincinnati	Feb. 20
4841	University of Colorado	Feb. 15
3915	University of Connecticut	Mar. 25
6868	University of Dallas	Mar. 1
1834	University of Dayton	Dec. 1
4842	University of Denver	Mar. 1*
1835	University of Detroit	Aug. 1*
6869	University of Dubuque	Aug. 1
5812	University of Florida	Feb. 15*
5813	University of Georgia	Feb. 1
3436	University of Hartford	Mar. 1*
6870	University of Houston	Mar. 1
	University of Illinois:	
1851	Chicago Circle	Jan. 24
1836	Urbana	Jan. 24
1838	University of Louisville	June 1
3916	University of Maine	Mar. 1
3917	University of Massachusetts	Feb. 22
5815	University of Miami	Mar. 1*
1839	University of Michigan	Jan. 23
	University of Minnesota:	
6873	Duluth	Mar. 15
6874	Minneapolis	Jan. 15
6874	Morris	Jan. 15
6874	Saint Paul	Jan. 15
6872	University of Missouri at Kansas City	Mar. 1
4489	University of Montana	July 15
3918	University of New Hampshire	Feb. 8*
4845	University of New Mexico	Apr. 1
1841	University of Notre Dame	Feb. 20
2926	University of Pennsylvania	Jan. 1*
2927	University of Pittsburgh	Feb. 15*
4847	University of Portland	Jan. 15

Code Number	College	Desired Receipt Date
4067	University of Puget Sound	Mar. 1*
4848	University of Redlands	Feb. 15*
3919	University of Rhode Island	Mar. 8*
2928	University of Rochester	Jan. 8*
4849	University of San Diego, College for Men	Mar. 25
4850	University of San Francisco	Feb. 8
4851	University of Santa Clara	Feb. 15
2929	University of Scranton	Mar. 23*
5818	University of South Carolina	Feb. 8
4852	University of Southern California	Feb. 8
6882	University of Texas	Mar. 8
4065	University of the Pacific (including Raymond and Covell Colleges)	Feb. 19*
1842	University of the South	Mar. 15*
1845	University of Toledo	Feb. 1
3920	University of Vermont	Feb. 15
5820	University of Virginia	Feb. 15*
4854	University of Washington	Feb. 1
	University of Wisconsin:	
1846	Madison and Centers	Feb. 8
1473	Milwaukee	Feb. 8
4855	University of Wyoming	Feb. 15
4856	Upland College	June 15
2930	Upsala College	Mar. 1*
2931	Ursinus College	Feb. 8*
1848	Ursuline College for Women (Ohio)	Feb. 1
2932	Utica College of Syracuse University	May 3
5855	Valdosta State College	June 24
1874	Valparaiso University	Feb. 15
1871	Vanderbilt University	Apr. 1*
2956	Vassar College	Jan. 1*
1876	Villa Madonna College	July 1*
1895	Wabash College (Ind.)	Mar. 8*
2966	Wagner College	Jan. 26*
5885	Wake Forest College	Jan. 1*
6925	Waldorf College	July 15
4595	Warner Pacific College	Apr. 8
6926	Wartburg College	Apr. 1*
6928	Washburn University of Topeka	Mar. 25
2967	Washington and Jefferson College	Mar. 1*
5887	Washington and Lee University	Feb. 1*
5888	Washington College (Md.)	Feb. 1
4705	Washington State University	No definite date
6929	Washington University (Mo.)	Feb. 1*
1898	Wayne State University	Consult college literature
2969	Waynesburg College	Mar. 21
6933	Webster College (Mo.)	Feb. 10
3957	Wellesley College	Jan. 7*
2971	Wells College	Feb. 1*
5894	Wesley College	June 15*
5895	Wesleyan College (Ga.)	Jan. 15
3959	Wesleyan University (Conn.)	Feb. 1*
5900	West Georgia College	July 1
5904	West Virginia University	Dec. 7
3960	Westbrook Junior College	Mar. 1
1899	Western College for Women	Jan. 25*
1903	Western Reserve University	Mar. 1*
4947	Western Washington State College	Feb. 15
6936	Westmar College	July 1
6937	Westminster College (Mo.)	Consult college literature*
2975	Westminster College (Pa.)	Feb. 1*
4948	Westminster College (Utah)	Mar. 25
4950	Westmont College	Apr. 1
1905	Wheaton College (Ill.)	Feb. 1
3963	Wheaton College (Mass.)	Jan. 15
5906	Wheeling College	Feb. 15
4951	Whitman College	Feb. 15*
4952	Whittier College	Mar. 1
4953	Whitworth College	Feb. 20*
2977	Wilkes College	Apr. 1
4954	Willamette University	Feb. 18*
6941	William Jewell College	June 1
6943	William Penn College	July 15*
2978	William Smith College	Feb. 1*
6944	William Woods College	No definite date
3965	Williams College	Feb. 1*
1909	Wilmington College (Ohio)	Mar. 25
2979	Wilson College	Feb. 22*
5908	Wingate College	July 1
1922	Wittenberg University	Feb. 21*
5912	Wofford College	Feb. 25*
5252	Woman's College of Georgia	Apr. 20
3969	Worcester Polytechnic Institute	Feb. 15
1965	Xavier University (Ohio)	Feb. 23
3987	Yale University	Jan. 1
6983	Yankton College	No definite date
2990	Yeshiva University	Apr. 1*

*Candidates for the Early Decision Plan should consult the college's literature for desired receipt date.

Figure 9

UNIVERSITY OF WASHINGTON
Seattle 5, Washington

FINANCIAL AID APPLICATION

for entering freshmen

Academic Year 19____ - 19____.

Please check one, two, or three: Scholarship____, National Defense Loan____, Part-time Employment____.

PROCEDURE FOR SUBMITTING THIS APPLICATION

APPLICANT

←——a. Fill out lines 1, 2, and 3 of page 1 and all of page 2.

b. Fill out the parts of page 3 which apply to your application and give the application to your parents or guardian for completion.

c. Obtain two (2) completed recommendations on the enclosed forms which are to be returned to your high school principal for attachment to this application before mailing.

d. Obtain a College Scholarship Service Parents' Statement form from your counselor or principal and take it home to your parents or guardian for completion.

PARENT OR GUARDIAN

a. Complete the Parents' Confidential Statement included in the College Scholarship Service folder and mail the Statement to Box 27896, Los Angeles 27, California.

b. If applicant is to be considered for a National Defense Loan, complete and sign the statement under Part III, page 3 of this form.

HIGH SCHOOL PRINCIPAL OR OTHER AUTHORIZED PERSON

a. Fill out and attach your signature to page 4.

b. Attach an official transcript record and two completed recommendations.

c. Mail completed application to the Director of Student Financial Aid, University of Washington, Seattle 5, Washington.

ALL INFORMATION WILL BE TREATED WITH THE STRICTEST CONFIDENCE

**THIS APPLICATION AND AN APPLICATION FOR ADMISSION
ARE TO BE SUBMITTED BEFORE MARCH 1**

(left margin, vertical text:)
1. ____ (Last) ____ (First) (PRINT your name in space above) ____ (Middle)
2. Home (mail) Address____ (Street) ____ (City) ____ (State) Telephone____ (State)
3. High School____ (Name) ____ (City) ____ (State)

Do Not Write In This Space

Major_____   Special Field_____

FINANCIAL ASSISTANCE	EVALUATION
Scholarship	Rank in class_____ in _____
Name_____	Grade point average_____ _____
Amount_____	Tests or predictions_____ _____
Accepted_____	General Worth_____ _____
Rejected_____	Activities_____
N.D. Loan	Honors_____
Amount_____	Recommendations_____
Accepted_____	Financial Need_____ _____
Rejected_____	
Part-time Employment	TOTAL _____
Position_____	
Hourly rate_____	
Hours per week_____	

Page 1

PART I—TO BE FILLED OUT IN INK BY ALL APPLICANTS

1. Name in full_____
   (Last)   (First)   (Middle)

2. Place of birth_____Date of birth_____
   (City)   (State)   (Month) (Day) (Year)

3. What major course do you expect to follow in the college?_____

   _____ _____ _____
   (First Choice)   (Second Choice)   (Undecided)

4. What is your choice of vocation?_____

5. Are you a citizen of the United States? Yes_____ No_____. If not, are you a permanent resident of the

   United States? Yes_____ No_____.

6. Father's name_____Age_____

   Address_____

   Place of birth_____Is he living?_____ If deceased, when?_____

   Occupation_____Highest school grade completed_____Graduated?_____

   College or university_____Number of years_____ Degrees_____

7. Mother's name_____Age_____

   Address_____

   Place of birth_____Is she living?_____ If deceased, when?_____

   Occupation_____Highest school grade completed_____Graduated?_____

   College or university_____Number of years_____ Degrees_____

8. Name and address of legal guardian_____

9. Academic school year of your request: 19_____ - 19_____.

10. Proposed Budget
    Estimate as accurately as possible your expenses for the period of this financial aid request. Estimate for the same period the income you expect to have to meet these expenses. The difference should represent what you need.

EXPENSES	Autumn	Winter	Spring	INCOME	Autumn	Winter	Spring
	$	$	$		$	$	$
Tuition and required fees.........				Bank balances and cash on hand.			
Books and supplies..............				Earnings during summer and school year.................			
Room rent, furnishings, utilities...				Aid from parents or guardian....			
Board......................				Aid from relatives and friends....			
Lunches and travel for commuters.				Estate, insurance, and trust funds			
Clothing.....................				Loans—other than University....			
Laundry and dry cleaning........				Scholarships (Specify)..........			
Personal and recreation..........				Government (Specify)..........			
Organizations, clubs, church......				Tax refund...................			
Debt repayment...............				Earnings of spouse............			
Other (Specify under 11).........				NEEDED TO BALANCE BUDGET..			
	$	$	$		$	$	$
Total...............				Total...............			

11. Specify "Other" expenses_____

_____

Page 2

PART II—TO BE FILLED OUT BY SCHOLARSHIP APPLICANTS

1. List up to five of your nonacademic activities. (Examples: Secretary, student council; second violin, high school orchestra; senior patrol leader, Boy Scouts; reserve team, basketball; business manager, school annual; member, French club.)

JUNIOR YEAR	SENIOR YEAR

2. Are you the son or daughter of a former member of the Students' Cooperative Association? Yes_____ No_____
   If yes, give name (if mother, use maiden name)_____
3. List special awards or honors earned in high school._____
_____
_____

4. The Scholarship Committee is interested in your ability to think and to express yourself in writing. In the space below please write a paragraph in which you set forth your own reasons for seeking a college education._____
_____
_____
_____
_____
_____

PART III—TO BE FILLED OUT BY NATIONAL DEFENSE LOAN APPLICANTS

1. Total amount of loan requested for the academic period of this application, as determined from the proposed budget in PART I: $_____.

2. Certification:

In case I am granted a loan under the National Defense Student Loan Program, I certify that I am in need of the loan in order to attend college; that I will register as a full-time student; that I am willing to execute, as required by law, an affidavit that "I do not believe in, and am not a member of and do not support any organization that believes in or teaches the overthrow of the U.S. government by force or violence or by any illegal or unconstitutional means"; that I am willing to take and subscribe to, as required by law, an oath or affirmation that "I do solemnly swear (or affirm) that I will bear true faith and allegiance to the United States of America and will support and defend the Constitution and laws of the U.S. against all enemies, foreign and domestic"; that I will use the proceeds of the loan only for college related expenses; that I hereby acknowledge that the information submitted herewith is true and correct; and I fully understand my obligations incurred by the grant of this loan and the conditions of its repayment.

_____
Signature of Applicant

3. Statement of parent or guardian (for applicants under 21 years of age):

I_____, have read the foregoing application in full and hereby state that
(Name of parent or guardian)

with my knowledge_____is applying for a student loan in the amount of $_____
(Name of applicant)

to further (his, her) education.

_____
Signature

PART IV—TO BE FILLED OUT BY PART-TIME EMPLOYMENT APPLICANTS

Typing speed_____   Shorthand speed_____
Work preference_____
Training_____
Work experience_____
_____
Proposed major in college_____

PART V—TO BE FILLED OUT BY PRINCIPAL OR OTHER AUTHORIZED PERSON
(Attach an official transcript record.)

Name and Address of High School:

Date _____
        (Current Date)

This record to be filled out by the high school official, signed by the principal or other authorized person, and mailed to the Director, Student Financial Aid, University of Washington.

This will certify that

_____
(Student's Last Name)   (First)   (Middle)

entered this school _____ and {will be ☐ / was ☐ / was not ☐} graduated _____ with {certificate ☐ / diploma ☐}
    (Mo.) (Day) (Yr.)   (Mo.) (Day) (Yr.)

He (or she) has a grade average of _____ and ranks _____ in a class of _____.
    Class rank and grade average above are based on ALL grades earned through the _____th semester.

Grading System _____

Passing Grade _____

Grades not transferable to college _____

This school is {accredited ____3-year high school ____4-year high school / ____unaccredited high school (check one)}

(A credit is applied to work taken in high school. To count as a credit, a subject must be taught five times a week in periods of not less than 45 minutes, for a school term of 18 weeks. Two credits equal one unit)

PERSONALITY AND TEST RECORD: The checks below represent single ☐ composite ☐ judgment.

*	Below Average	Average	Above Average	Superior	Comments:
1. Motivation					
2. Industry					
3. Initiative					
4. Influence and Leadership					
5. Cooperation					
6. Concern for Others					
7. Responsibility					
8. Integrity					
9. Emotional Stability					

*Items of behavior characteristics adapted by permission from the standardized Personality Record of the National Association of Secondary-School Principals.

10. *Unusual Aptitudes:* writing____ music____ art____ speaking____ athletics____ dramatics____ business____ others_____

11. *Primary Interests:* intellectual____ social____ scientific____ athletic____ journalistic____ handskills____ others_____

12. Cumulative record of test scores (exclusive of those entered on transcript):

Science Research Associates	English Usage	Math. Usage	Soc. Stud. Reading	Nat. Sc. Reading	Word Usage	Total Composite	Selection Score
National Merit Scholarship Qualifying Test			P E R C E N T I L E S				

College Entrance Examination Board Tests	Date Given	Number Scores Verbal	Math.	Name and Type of Other Tests	Date Given	Score	%ile
Preliminary SAT							
Scholastic Aptitude Test							

13. After considering this student's scholastic record, work habits, and scores on tests, I recommend him as a superior ☐ above average ☐ average ☐ below average ☐ student, or as one who will succeed only by unusual effort ☐.

_____   _____   _____
    Date   Signature   Title

UNIVERSITY OF WASHINGTON
Seattle 5, Washington

CONFIDENTIAL
REPORT ON APPLICANT FOR FINANCIAL AID

This report is to be completed and returned to the High School Principal by February 20. He will then forward it to the Director of Student Financial Aid.

TO BE COMPLETED BY APPLICANT (Type or print in ink)

1. Name of applicant_____
       (Last)   (First)   (Middle)

2. Home address_____
     (Street and Number)   (City)   (State)

3. High School_____
      (Name)   City)   (State)

4. Type of aid: Scholarship_____, National Defense Loan_____.

  Part-time employment_____. (Check one, two, or three)

TO BE COMPLETED BY REFERENCE

1. How long have you known the applicant?_____

  In what capacity?_____

2. Your confidential evaluation of the applicant:

	Below Average	Average	Above Average	Superior	Comments:
1. Motivation					
2. Industry					
3. Initiative					
4. Influence and Leadership					
5. Cooperation					
6. Concern for Others					
7. Responsibility					
8. Integrity					
9. Emotional Stability					

10. *Unusual Aptitudes:* writing____ music____ art____ speaking____ athletics____ dramatics____ business____ others_____

11. *Primary Interests:* intellectual____ social____ scientific____ athletic____ journalistic____ handskills____ others_____

(over)

3. To what degree do you recommend this applicant for financial aid?

Highly_____; Good degree of confidence_____; Fair degree of confidence_____; With some doubt_____.

4. What is your evaluation of the student's scholastic ability?

Top 5%_____; Top 10%_____; Top 20%_____; Top 40%_____; Top 50%_____; Unknown_____.

Please comment on exceptional scholastic abilities and accomplishments._____

_____

_____

_____

_____

_____

_____

_____

5. If possible, give your evaluation of the candidate's financial need:

Very great_____; Great_____; Above average_____; Average_____; Below average_____;

Very little, if any_____; Unknown_____.

Please comment on unusual financial circumstances._____

_____

_____

_____

_____

_____

_____

_____

_____

Signed_____

Title_____

Organization_____

Date_____

awards of $100 that recognize ability, not need. Generally, the student with the greatest need gets the most money. A very good scholarship for a needy student is one that will defray about one-half of the cost of attending college. You should be happy with one that will pay for about 30 percent of college costs. This is about the level of most scholarships granted by a majority of colleges and universities.

There are other things you should know about scholarships. Usually, the more scholarships granted by an institution, the smaller the size of each scholarship. A second point worth knowing is that private institutions usually grant larger scholarships than public colleges and universities. You should remember, however, that tuition, fees, and other costs are usually higher at private colleges and universities. For example, a $750 scholarship granted by a state college in the Midwest is comparable to the average scholarship of $1,175 at Hamilton College. The Hamilton student, however, will have to pay higher tuition and other costs, which will total a little less than $2,900, as compared to the state college costs of about $1,500. Also, you should know that not all scholarships are awarded and financed by colleges. However, it is becoming the rule rather than the exception for colleges to administer scholarships for organizations and other outside agencies.

There is one basic principle that is true for all financial aid programs and is clearly applicable to scholarships. Scholarships are generally granted on the basis of academic ability, but the amount of the grant is based on financial need. Academic ability is the most frequently used kind of ability considered, but there are some notable exceptions. Football and other sports, music, and other special abilities are the basis for awarding some scholarships.

The student who has not distinguished himself as a scholar but who has other worthwhile talents should begin his search for a scholarship in his local community. Frequently, scholarships are available in the community and are overlooked by students seeking assistance from national foundations and agencies. Parent-teacher associations offer scholarships to local students. Industrial companies sponsor more than two hundred scholarships valued at about $800 million a year available to sons and daughters of employees, according to the National Industrial Board. Civic groups such as the Lions, Kiwanis, Rotary, Optimists, and others may offer scholarships as a part of their community service activities. Your community may have a local chapter of the Citizens Scholarship Foundation of America, which awards scholarships to local students from funds raised in the local community.

Here is a student's actual experience in obtaining a scholarship.

Obtaining a scholarship for the freshman year at Reed College is more difficult than getting financial aid for subsequent years. However, the procedure itself is simple. When I wrote to the admissions office at Reed for the first time to request a copy of the bulletin and an application for admission, I asked for a scholarship application too. Along with the scholarship application they sent a copy of the Parents' Financial Statement form prepared by CEEB (College Entrance Examination Board). My parents completed this six-page form and I sent it back to the admissions office with my applications.

This financial statement, when processed, indicates to the Financial Aid Committee (composed of five or six faculty members, who serve for a year or two) how great the student's need is and therefore how large the scholarship must be. The amount of the scholarship at Reed is not based on the student's high school record, though the high school transcript, together with the teachers' recommendations and the whole application, determine whether or not the student will receive a scholarship at all for his freshman year, as well as whether or not he will be accepted to Reed. But at this point it is a yes or no question and the amount of the scholarship is not the issue.

I was accepted to Reed but did not receive a scholarship. I got a job in an office in San Francisco at $250 a month with the intention of saving $2,500, or enough to go to Reed for a year. The director of admissions offered some encouragement and indicated that second-year scholarships were easier to obtain than freshman scholarships. Fifteen months after graduating from high school I entered Reed as a freshman. Since my previous acceptance was still considered valid, I did not need to reapply.

To apply for a scholarship for my sophomore year I attended a meeting (announced well ahead of time) for students who needed financial aid. This was in April of my freshman year. Here I was given another copy of the Parents' Financial Statement form and sent it home for my parents to fill out and return to the admissions office. I also received a one-page application which I filled out myself. In August, I was notified that the Financial Aid Committee had settled on the amount of $1,200 for my scholarship for the coming school year. This covered full tuition, room and board, even though I had decided to live off campus that year.

The procedure was exactly the same for the two following years, but I received slightly more because of tuition raises.

How to Apply for Scholarships. If you apply for a scholarship, you should know the rules used in selecting scholarship recipients. Each committee that selects students to receive scholarships may place more or less emphasis on certain factors. Consideration is usually given to a number of factors. Some of the more important ones are:

1. High school scholastic record. It is a measure of your seriousness of purpose, your study habits, and your probability of success.

2. Results of scholastic aptitude tests. Any one of several tests may be required for a particular scholarship. These tests attempt to measure your ability to do college work.
3. A record of your participation in extracurricular activities indicates evidence of your leadership potential. It is also evidence of your ability to get along with others.
4. Character references from teachers, counselors, and others reveal much about you as a person, your personality, drive, and enthusiasm.
5. Financial need will be established by a report of your family's financial circumstances. Many colleges are now using a branch of the Educational Testing Service to gather financial information. This branch is the College Scholarship Service, Box 176, Princeton, New Jersey 08540. If you apply for a scholarship from one of the colleges using the service, the college will usually send forms to fill out and file with the service. The CSS will send the information on to that college and to other colleges to which you apply for a scholarship, provided they use the service. If you apply for financial aid from colleges that do not use the service, you must file a confidential statement with the director of financial aid of these colleges.

Other items that may be important when applying for scholarships are: geographical area, citizenship, member of ethnic group, and high school attended. Your counselor can be of assistance in advising you on these matters.

Where to Apply for Scholarships. Scholarships are available from many sources. In fact, there are about 250,000 scholarships. The best way to locate one is to look for it. It is nearly impossible to list all the sources, but here are a few with which you can begin your search.

1. Community. Try to locate a scholarship in such organizations as the PTA, VFW, fraternal orders, and local or county boards of education.
2. Church. Each of the major faiths and denominations sponsors scholarship or loan programs. Among the funds are:

   American Baptist National Scholarship
     Program
   152 Madison Avenue
   New York, New York 10016

   Board of Christian Education
   Presbyterian Church in the United States
   Box 1176
   Richmond, Virginia 23209

   National Methodist Scholarships and
   Methodist Student Loan Fund
   P.O. Box 871
   Nashville, Tennesee 37203

   CURA Scholarship Program
   Youth Department
   National Catholic Welfare Conference
   Washington, D.C. 20005

   United Presbyterian Church
   College Scholarships and Loans
   Board of Christian Education
   Witherspoon Building
   Philadelphia, Pennsylvania 19107

3. Minority groups. Agencies such as the John Hay Whitney Foundation in New York City assist students who belong to ethnic groups. For Negro students there is:

   Fund for Negro Students
   6 East 82nd Street
   New York, New York 10028

   Scholarships for American Indian students are provided by:

   The National Congress of American Indians
   1346 Connecticut Avenue, N.W.
   Washington, D.C. 20036

4. College Alumni. The alumni of the college you wish to attend may have a fund for students in your area. Inquire of local alumni leaders, or write to the college alumni association to find out who the local leaders are.
5. Special groups. There are any number of special-interest groups providing scholarship and loan funds on a local or national basis. Two examples are:

   National 4-H Service Committee
   59 East Van Buren Street   (for 4-H club
   Chicago, Illinois 60605   members)

   P.E.O. Educational Fund
   3700 Grand Avenue   (for women)
   Des Moines, Iowa 50312

6. National. There are several national scholarships for which students qualify, usually through nationally administered examinations. Among the best known are the following:
   A. The National Merit Scholarship Program. This program, originated by the Ford Foundation, is now supported by a number of business and industrial concerns. The College Scholarship Service is used in determining the amount of money awarded to winning students. If you apply through your high school for this scholarship you will be required to take a three-hour test in April of your junior year. Semi-finalists usually take the college board examinations. There is at least one winner from every state. The amount of money granted depends on the student's financial need, varying from $200 to $2,000. You select the college to which it is applied. Certificates of merit are awarded to outstanding students who were not awarded scholarships but who did well on the examination.

This list is used by colleges and other agencies in awarding scholarships. If your high school does not participate, write to:
National Merit Scholarship Corporation
1580 Sherman Avenue
Evanston, Illinois 60201

B. The General Motors National Scholarship Program. You must make individual application. Write to:
The General Motors National Scholarship Program
P.O. Box 461
Princeton, New Jersey 08540

You will be required to take the Scholastic Aptitude Test. Should you win a General Motors scholarship, money will be awarded on the basis of financial need, varying from $200 to $2,000.

In addition to the National Scholarship Program, General Motors has a college plan that awards scholarships to students through colleges in all fifty states. If you are interested in applying for a scholarship under the G. M. College Plan, write to the director of admissions at the college you have selected and inquire if it participates in the program.

C. The Betty Crocker Scholarship Program. General Mills Food Company conducts a national search for the "homemakers of tomorrow." A home economics test is given in each school that enters the contest. Winners are selected on the basis of the test results. Check with your home economics teacher.

D. The Scholarship Qualifying Program. This program is conducted by the Educational Testing Service for a number of organizations. The one that many students are interested in is:
National Honor Society Scholarships
1201 Sixteenth St., N.W.
Washington, D.C. 20006

The Preliminary Scholastic Aptitude Test is administered to interested seniors. Students who make high scores on this test are required to take a second test. Winners are chosen by the organization awarding the scholarship. The amount of the stipend depends on financial need.

E. The Westinghouse Science Talent Search. This program is conducted through the Science Clubs of America. A test is administered in each school. Each candidate must also develop a project and write a paper about it. Selections are made on the basis of the test results, the project, the school's recommendation, and an interview. The scholarship money may apply at any college you choose. See your science club advisor about this program or write to:
Science Talent Search for Westinghouse Science Scholarships and Awards
1719 N Street, N.W.
Washington, D.C. 20006

There are other national programs, including the Alfred P. Sloan Foundation, General Electric, and Procter & Gamble, but the funds are available through colleges and not directly through the foundations.

Should you be interested in learning about other scholarships that are available, here are sources on the subject:

Financial Aid for College Students
Theresa B. Wilkens
Bulletin No. 18
U.S. Office of Education
Washington, D.C. 20202

Scholarships, Fellowships and Loans
Norman Feingold
Bellman Publishing Company
P.O. Box 172
Cambridge, Massachusetts 02101

College Scholarship Guide
Clarence E. Lovejoy and Theodore S. Jones
Simon and Schuster, Inc.
630 Fifth Avenue
New York, New York 10022

Financial Assistance for College Students
Russell T. Sharpe, *et al.*
American Council on Educational Studies
Washington, D.C. 20036

You Can Win a Scholarship
Samuel C. Brownstein, Mitchell Weiner, and Stanley Kaplan
Barron's Educational Series, Inc.
343 Great Neck Road
Great Neck, New York 11021

The College Handbook
College Entrance Examination Board
P.O. Box 592
Princeton, New Jersey 08540
P.O. Box 1025
Berkeley, California 94701

Need a Lift?
Americanism Division
American Legion
Indianapolis, Indiana 46206

New American Guide to Scholarships, Fellowships and Loans
John Bradley, editor
Signet Key Books
New American Library
New York, New York 10019

Loans: What Kinds Are There? Where to Get Them?

Loan programs are making college possible for students who, a generation ago, could not attend college. Loans make it possible for them to "learn now and pay later." There are long-term loans, short-term loans, and emergency loans. There are loans for tuition and fees, and there are loans that may cover the total cost of going to college. Loans for college expenses are available from insurance companies, loan companies, foundations, the college you plan to attend, from states, and from the federal government.

Who gets loans? In general, loans to students are worked out on an individual basis. Attention is paid to enterprise, energy, determination, and, of course, ability. While it is less true than it was before the advent of the federal loan program, willingness to work may be a factor. Most students want to work part-time to keep the size of their loans down.

NDEA Loans. According to Sterling M. McMurrin, former United States Commissioner of Education, the National Defense Education Act constitutes one of the most significant developments in governmental support of education and reflects the judgment of our lawmakers and the public that education is the bone, sinew, and blood of our country. The program provides $163.3 million in 1965, $179.3 million in 1966, $190 million in 1967, and $195 million in 1968.

It was established to increase the opportunities for qualified needy students to continue their education beyond high school. Loans are administered by approximately 1,400 colleges participating in the program. Business and technical institutions are included. Each college participating in the loan program selects students to receive loans, arranges the loans, and is responsible for their collection.

To be eligible for a National Defense Student Loan, you must be enrolled or accepted by a cooperating college, be a capable student, and be in need of financial assistance. If there is competition for federal loans, preference is given to students on the basis of academic ability, intention to teach in elementary or secondary schools, and preparation in science, mathematics, engineering, and modern foreign languages. However, you may qualify for a federal loan regardless of your major in college if you have and maintain satisfactory grades and need financial aid.

The terms are generous. A student may borrow for college expenses up to $1,000 each year during his entire college period, but may not borrow more than $5,000 in all. Repayment does not begin until you cease to be a full-time student for one year. The loans are interest-free until the beginning of the repayment period, and are then at a low rate of 3 percent a year. You must sign the note for your loan. You have ten years in which to repay the loan. If you become permanently disabled or die, the loan is canceled.

If a borrower becomes a full-time teacher in an elementary or secondary school or in an institution of higher education, as much as half of the loan may be forgiven at the rate of 10 percent for each year of teaching service. Borrowers who elect to teach in certain eligible schools located in areas of primarily low-income families may qualify for cancellation of their entire obligation at the rate of 15 percent per year.

Conditions for applying for a National Defense Student loan, as reported by the Office of Education, are:

1. You must be enrolled or accepted for enrollment as a student in an institution participating in the National Defense Student Loan Program and carry at least one-half the normal full-time academic work load as determined by the institution.
2. You must be in need of assistance and be able to maintain good academic standing.
3. You must be a citizen of the United States or intend to reside permanently in the United States.
4. Preference is given to students with superior academic background.
5. Partial loan cancellation may be earned on the basis of full-time teaching service in private nonprofit elementary and secondary schools and in institutions of higher education.
6. You must make application for the loan directly to the college.

To apply for an NDEA loan, you should find out whether the college or university of your choice has established a loan fund with federal assistance. If it has, you should make your application to the institution. Inquire, and they will tell you when and how to apply.

Guaranteed Loan Program. Guaranteed loans are available to any college student who wants to borrow, with the focus directed primarily toward students from middle- or upper-income families. The student has an obligation to repay his loan with three percent (middle-income) or six percent (upper-income) interest.

The education of young people from middle- or upper-income groups frequently places a financial burden on their families, particularly if there are a number of children who want to go to college. In many cases, the student cannot qualify for student employment or a student loan. Even when commercial credit sources are available, repayment generally runs concurrently with the years the student attends college. To help these young people and their families a student may borrow from a bank or other financial institution. A graduate student may borrow as much as $1,500 a year; an undergraduate, as much as $1,000.

A student from a family with an adjusted income of less than $15,000 a year pays no interest while he is in an eligible college, university, or technical school. Repayment of principal and interest begins when the student has ceased his course of study. At that time the federal government pays approximately one-half the interest and the student the remainder. A student from a family with an adjusted income higher than $15,000 a year pays the entire interest on the loan, but he may borrow under the Guaranteed Loan Program at six percent simple interest.

Loans are not limited to only degree-seeking students. The National Vocational Student Loan Insurance Act of 1965 authorized a program of guaranteed loans for vocational students in amounts up to $1,000 a year. The program is expected to be put in operation in the near future. Keep in touch with your vocational school, or with your state education agency.

Commercial banks, mutual savings banks, savings and loan associations, credit unions, and similar financial institutions subject to State or Federal supervision may be lenders under this program in participation with student loan guarantee agencies. In some instances colleges may

be lenders and make loans directly to their students. Four states — Florida, North Dakota, Texas, and Wisconsin — have established State agencies which make loans directly to students.

If a student cannot obtain a loan from one source, he may apply to another. A list of eligible lenders will be supplied by his college or the loan guarantee agency in his home state.

State loan programs started in the northeast, principally in Massachusetts, Maine, and New York, and they are now available throughout the nation. Each state loan program has its own rules and regulations governing it. If you need a loan and are a resident of any of the following states, write to:

NAME AND ADDRESS OF AGENCIES

ALABAMA
Department of Education
State Office Building
Montgomery, Alabama   36104

CALIFORNIA
California State Scholarship and Loan
  Commission
520 Capitol Mall
Sacramento, California   95814

CONNECTICUT
Connecticut Foundation for Financial Assistance to Higher Education
State Capitol Office Building,
  Room 207-A
Hartford, Connecticut   06115

DELAWARE
Higher Education Loan Program
University of Delaware
Newark, Delaware   19711

FLORIDA
Florida Student Scholarship and Loan
  Commission
State Office Building
Tallahasse, Florida   32304

GEORGIA
Georgia Higher Education Assistance
  Corporation
244 Washington Street, S. W.
Atlanta, Georgia   30334

HAWAII
Department of Budget and Finance
State Office Building
P. O. Box 150
Honolulu, Hawaii   96810

ILLINOIS
Illinois State Scholarship Commission
730 Waukegan Road
P.O. Box 607
Deerfield, Illinois   60015

INDIANA
Indiana State Scholarship Commission
Room 514, State Office Building
100 N. Senate Avenue
Indianapolis, Indiana   46204

IOWA
Iowa Higher Education Facilities
  Commission
1300 Des Moines Bldg.
Des Moines, Iowa   50309

KENTUCKY
Kentucky Higher Education Assistance
  Authority
First National Lincoln Bank of Louisville
216 South Fifth Street
Louisville, Kentucky   40202

LOUISIANA
Louisiana Higher Education Assistance
  Commission
P. O. Box 4095
Capitol Station
Baton Rouge, Louisiana   70820

MAINE
Maine Higher Education Assistance
  Foundation
15 Western Avenue
Augusta, Maine   04330

MARYLAND
Maryland Higher Education Loan
  Corporation
2100 Guilford Avenue
Baltimore, Maryland   21218

MASSACHUSETTS
Massachusetts Higher Educational Assistance Corporation
604 Statler Building
Boston, Massachusetts   02116

MICHIGAN
Michigan Higher Education Assistance
  Authority
700 Prudden Building
Lansing, Michigan   48933

MISSISSIPPI
Board of Trustees of Institutions of
  Higher Learning
1007 Woolfolk Building
Jackson, Mississippi   39205

NEW HAMPSHIRE
New Hampshire Higher Education Assistance Foundation
18 School Street
Concord, New Hampshire   03301

NEW JERSEY
New Jersey Higher Education Assistance
  Authority
225 West State Street
Trenton, New Jersey   08625

NEW MEXICO
New Mexico Board of Education Finance
Commission Building
Santa Fe, New Mexico   87501

NEW YORK
New York Higher Education Assistance
Corporation
159 Delaware Avenue
Delmar, New York   12054

NORTH CAROLINA
State Education Assistance Authority
1307 Glenwood Avenue
P. O. Box 10887
Raleigh, North Carolina   27605

OHIO
Ohio Higher Education Assistance
Commission
Wyandotte Building
21 W. Broad Street
Columbus, Ohio   43215

OKLAHOMA
Oklahoma State Regents for Higher
Education
State Capitol, Room 118
Oklahoma City, Oklahoma   73105

PENNSYLVANIA
Pennsylvania Higher Education
Assistance Agency
Towne House, 660 Boas St.
Harrisburg, Pennsylvania   17102

RHODE ISLAND
Rhode Island Higher Education
Assistance Corporation
Room 617, 49 Westminister St.
Providence, Rhode Island   02901

SOUTH DAKOTA
South Dakota Board of Regents of
Education
State House
Pierre, South Dakota   57501

TENNESSEE
Tennessee Education Loan Corporation
State Department of Education
115 Cordell Hull Building
Nashville, Tennessee   37219

TEXAS
Coordinating Board

Texas College and University System
San Houston State Office Bldg.
201 East 4th Street
Austin, Texas   78701

UTAH
Coordinating Council of Higher
Education
1201 University Club Building
136 East South Temple Street
Salt Lake City, Utah   84111

VERMONT
Vermont Student Assistant Corporation
109 So. Winooski Avenue
Burlington, Vermont   05401

VIRGINIA
Virginia State Education Assistance
Authority
1116 State-Planters Bank Building
Richmond, Virginia   23216

WISCONSIN
Higher Education Aid Commission
115 West Wilson Street
Madison, Wisconsin   53702

United Student Aid Funds, Inc., administers the program in the following States:

ALASKA
ARIZONA
ARKANSAS
COLORADO
DISTRICT OF
COLUMBIA
IDAHO
KANSAS
MINNESOTA
MISSOURI
MONTANA
NEBRASKA
NEVADA
NORTH DAKOTA
OREGON
SOUTH CAROLINA
WASHINGTON
WEST VIRGINIA
WYOMING
PUERTO RICO

College Loans.   Colleges and universities have money available for students who need financial assistance. As a matter of fact, institutions are lending more money each year since the passage of the National Defense Education Act than they were before. Not only are more students benefiting from more money, but more institutions have taken up the practice of providing loans to students. A recent survey revealed that some institutions are lending more money each year than they award for scholarships. In general, private colleges usually have more money for student loans than do public colleges.

There has been a notable shift in college loan policies since the passage of the National Defense Education Act of 1958. The trend is toward terms resembling the federal loan program. In general, college loans provide for rates of interest at about 2 percent, beginning one to two years after graduation. Policies vary.

If you need assistance, write for particulars from the institution you plan to attend.

College emergency loans provide a most valuable service to the student who, after enrollment, finds himself in financial difficulty. These loans are used to pay for essentials to tide the students over a particular crisis. Should you run into money problems, you will want to visit the director of financial aid.

Foundation and Association Loans.   Many foundations, associations, commissions, and organizations have provided money for student loans, and some have sizable amounts. These organizations provide a worthwhile service to families of college-bound students. The Methodist Student Loan Fund, for example, granted 3,123 student loans totaling $1,057,085 in 1964–65, according to Mrs. Dorothy Corn, Loan Officer, Methodist Church, Division of Higher Education, Nashville,

Tennessee. The addresses of a few of the church groups sponsoring scholarships are given on page 107.

An organization particularly interested in potential leaders is:

American Leaders Foundation
c/o Northeastern Pennsylvania National Bank and
    Trust Co.
P.O. Box 937
Scranton, Pennsylvania 18515

A general loan source for very needy students of good character and good past academic performance is:

Pickett & Hatcher Educational Fund
P.O. Box 1238
Columbus, Georgia 31902

There are many, many other sources of loans. Ask your guidance counselor for a list of organizations and businesses assisting students in your area of study and location.

Other Loans.   To encourage students to enter their professional area and to assist needy students who have already selected that area, many occupational organizations offer scholarships and loan assistance. Some of these are:

Fannie and John Hertz Engineering Scholarship
    Foundation
1314 Westwood Boulevard
Los Angeles, California 90024

National Committee for Careers in Medical
    Technology
Undergraduate College Scholarships for Pre-Medical
    Technologists
1785 Massachusetts Avenue, N.W.
Washington, D.C. 20006

National Foundation
Health Sciences Scholarships
800 Second Avenue
New York, New York 10017

National Scholarship Trust Fund
Education Council of the Graphic Arts Industry
5728 Connecticut Avenue, N.W.
Washington, D.C. 20015

The Nurses Training Act of 1964 makes provisions for loans to students planning to enter the nursing profession. The purpose of this program is to enable qualified students in need of financial aid, as determined by the school, to take a full-time program in nursing leading to a diploma, associate degree, baccalaureate, or master's degree by making low-interest loans available through loan funds in participating schools. To be eligible to participate in the program, the school must be a public or nonprofit institution and be accredited or give reasonable assurance that it can meet criteria for accreditation. Students can receive no more than

$1,000 in any one academic year. They may cancel up to 50 percent of the loan, through full-time employment as a professional nurse in any public or nonprofit agency, at the rate of 10 percent of the loan and its interest for each complete year of service. Another source of loans for nurses is:

Nurses' Educational Funds
10 Columbus Circle
New York, New York 10019

Banks in large cities have developed loan programs for parents for financing the education of their children. These loans are not "aid," but are commercially transacted like loans for any other purpose. Ability to repay the loan is considered more important than financial need. The rate of interest is higher on bank loans than on college and government loans. Information is available at the banks themselves

Part-Time Jobs and Work-Study Programs

Can I work my way through college? The answer is "yes," but it won't be easy. Unless you are willing to extend your number of years in college, you will not be able to earn enough money to pay for *all of your college expenses*. But the answer is still "yes." Yes, you can work your way through college just as your father might have done. There are those who say it can't be done, but there are many examples of successful people who did. Thousands of students today defray college expenses while they are in college. Virtually all colleges and universities have programs for students who find they must work to attend college. According to the Census Bureau, about six out of ten students in college work part time or during the summer months. The Midwestern Association of University Student Employment Directors reports that from 25 to 40 percent of the students work, despite academic pressures.

There are unique advantages to working while you attend college. While some say that if you are a good working-student you would be a better studying-student if you did not work, most studies comparing the achievement of working and nonworking students find evidence to the contrary. Some students find that hours spent in gainful employment is a helpful "breather" from school work. Their mental health is improved by the gratification of doing socially useful work. The student who works to pay for his college expenses has a strong sense of purpose about his actions. Working students are often more mature than many nonworking students, because of this sense of purpose. Experience gained on the job is a good way to gain practical learning useful to you after graduation.

How much should you work? How much time can you afford from your studies? What makes good financial sense may not make good educational sense. If you work to earn your support and most or all of your college expenses, it very likely will take you longer to

Figure 10

UNIVERSITY OF MARYLAND
COLLEGE PARK, MARYLAND
EXECUTIVE DEAN FOR STUDENT LIFE

OFFICE OF THE
DIRECTOR OF STUDENT AID

APPLICATION FOR PART-TIME EMPLOYMENT

Date..

I. Personal Data

Name...Age................Sex................
           Last   First   Middle

No. years at

Permanent Address...this address...........

....Home Phone:......................................

Where do you plan to live during the school year?

Dormitory.............................Sorority or Fraternity.............................At home.............................Other.............................

    Single [   ]   Married [   ]   No. of dependents [   ]

Names of Father or Guardian...

Occupation of Father or Guardian...Position..................................

Are you a citizen of the United States?.............................If not, are you a permanent resident?.............

Name of Mother...Occupation.......................................

First Enrollment..Class..
                      Month, Year

Course of study...College...

List other colleges attended...

II. Financial

List any scholarships or jobs you have or for which you have applied (circle those awarded)....................

....

Estimate amount you desire to earn during the school year...

If you desire, please list any circumstances which make employment necessary...............................

....

....

....

(OVER)

(FOR OFFICE USE ONLY)

Referred:..   ....

....

....

....

....

III. Work Experience

If you have ever been employed, please state type of work done, dates of employment and employer's name and address

....

....

....

Previous on-campus employment..

List types of work in which you are proficient (typing, stenographic rate, office machines)..................................

....

What type of employment do you desire?   (office, stenographic, food service, laboratory, mechanical, gardening, selling, etc.)

....

Minimum pay rate you will accept...Auto available..................................

Will you accept off-campus employment?.............................Type of driver's license?..................................

IV. Military Experience, including any occupational specialties

....

V. After Registration (come to Office of Student Aid and complete)

College Address..Phone...............................
                  Dormitory, home, or off campus residence

Schedule

Hour	Monday	Tuesday	Wednesday	Thursday	Friday	Saturday
8						
9						
10						
11						
12						
1						
2						
3						
4						
5						

FAILURE TO GIVE NEW SCHEDULE WITHIN TWO WEEKS AFTER THE BEGINNING OF EACH SEMESTER WILL RESULT IN YOUR APPLICATION BEING DISCARDED.
ONCE YOU HAVE BEEN REFERRED TO A JOB, YOUR APPLICATION WILL BE PLACED IN AN INACTIVE FILE AND REMAIN THERE UNTIL **YOU** NOTIFY THIS OFFICE AS TO WHETHER OR NOT YOU ARE EMPLOYED.

graduate, or may cause your grades to suffer. If you spend most of your time earning money to live at and pay for college, you can't be studying for class assignments and exams. If you are studying for class you can't be earning a living. One or the other will have to "give" or both will suffer. Seek the counsel of the financial aid officer on how much you should work. Don't work your way *out* of college. By placing too much emphasis on working, some students accept a work schedule too heavy to permit academic success.

Part-Time Jobs. If you have some money saved or if your family can pay a share of the cost of attending college, you can get part-time work on or near the campus. Most colleges recommend that students work no more than twenty hours, with fifteen hours a week being the average.

Colleges are not known for the outstanding salaries they pay. This is true for student labor, too. You can expect to earn $1.25 or more an hour if you work for a college or university. Off-campus work usually pays about 50 percent more. The hourly pay varies with the type of work. The kind of work varies, and for this reason you should not have difficulty in getting a part-time job. Most colleges have a student employment or financial aid office. Some institutions place all students who request work, and others need additional student helpers.

Capitalize on the educational value of part-time and summer work. If you are selective you may be able to find a job in your chosen career field. Alumni frequently give students part-time and summer work, and your college advisor may be able to help you get a job. Work in the post office is seasonal but is a well-paying job for boys. Working as a telephone operator is an example of employment available to women students, both on and off the campus. Working as an accountant, draftsman, barber, and bartender are examples of better-paying jobs. Specialized work on school farms may pay well also. The office of financial aid will give you information on jobs available and what they pay.

Many students earn $300 to $600 while studying and earn that and much more during the summer months. A job fifteen hours a week at $1.25 an hour will pay a student $600 in two semesters. It is not uncommon for a student to earn $500 to $750 during the summer months. A thousand dollars will go a very long way in paying the cost of attending college. If you could earn this much and attend one of the many accredited state colleges where the cost is equal to the national average, $1,500, you would earn two-thirds of your college expenses.

Educational Opportunity Grants. Under the authorization of a new program supported by the federal government colleges and universities make Educational Opportunity Grants available to a limited number of undergraduate students with exceptional financial need who require these grants to attend college. To be eligible, the student must also show academic or creative promise.

Eligible students who are accepted for enrollment on a full-time basis or who are currently enrolled in good standing may receive Educational Opportunity Grants for each year of their higher education, although the maximum duration of a grant is four years.

Grants will range from $200 to $800 a year, and can be no more than one-half of the total assistance given the student. As an academic incentive to students, an additional award of $200 may be given to those students who were in the upper-half of their college class during the preceding academic year.

The amount of financial assistance a student may receive depends upon his need—taking into account his financial resources, those of his parents, and the cost of attending the college of his choice.

Work-Study Programs. Students who will work their way through college will be interested in colleges having cooperative work-study programs. These institutions, about eighty of them, have a philosophy that working is a necessary part of a student's education. Work-study programs are designed to develop essential academic understanding and work experience applicable to a particular career field. Most of the fields of study can be found in a college that offers work-study programs. The level of work experience is the equivalent of a technician as compared to an engineer, or a bookkeeper as compared to an accountant. This kind of program is found in both junior and senior colleges. Credit may be given for work experience, but this is less often the case in four-year institutions. Usually, five years are required to complete a work-study plan.

The Student Work-Study Program at Southern Illinois University is outstanding. It is based on the belief that the academically capable, financially needy high school graduate should have an opportunity to develop his potential in college. Considerable effort is made to find work related to students' major fields. The program offers on-campus work, off-campus work, summer employment, and cooperative work-study programs. The purposes of the Student Work-Study Program at SIU are:

1. To provide work experience which is educationally worthwhile for any student, which contributes to the student's maturity and to the development of the student into a useful, productive citizen, and which is, whenever possible, related to the student's academic program.

2. To provide employment on a part-time basis for those students with great financial need who are academically capable of working and going to college. The on-campus program is designed so that the student with extreme need can finance his entire college education through employment with the University.[5]

[5] "The Counselor's Handbook—A Guide to the Student Work Program at Southern Illinois University" (Carbondale, Illinois: Southern Illinois University, 1960).

Applicants for student work are interviewed and the extent of need is determined. The interviewer determines need for financial assistance on the basis of the following factors:

1. A statement from the high school principal or guidance counselor.
2. Other financial assistance that the student may have received. (scholarship, loan, or G.I. Bill of Rights)
3. Personal savings as listed by the student.
4. Occupation of parents and the number of dependents of the family income.
5. A personal statement by the student.
6. Marital status of the student.[6]

A College Work-Study Program of major importance for needy students who can qualify is provided for in Part C of the Economic Opportunity Act of 1964. The purpose of the work-study program is to stimulate and promote part-time employment of students. Institutions in this program make grants for operation of work-study programs. Students are employed in work-study programs for no more than fifteen hours a week when classes are in session. Employment is furnished only to students who (a) are from low-income families, (b) are in need of employment in order to continue study at such institution, (c) are capable of maintaining good standing in the institution while employed, and (d) have been accepted for enrollment as full-time students at an institution or who are already enrolled as full-time students.

Sarah Lawrence College in Bronxville, New York, has a work-study program that prepares liberal arts students for careers in social work. Antioch College in Yellow Springs, Ohio, has a similar program for other career fields. If you have a particular interest in work-study plans, a list of colleges that provide them may be obtained from the Division of Higher Education, Office of Education, Washington, D.C. 20025.

Suggestions for Working Students. There are some cautions you should observe. Don't work so much that it interferes with your studies. You wouldn't want working in college to hinder your future professional advancement. Working need not cause you to earn lower grades, however. It doesn't for many students, according to research conducted on this subject. If working does result in lower grades, then you should not work so much, or at all.

There are good reasons not to work during the first semester of college. The adjustment to college life is dramatic for some students. Until you learn what professors want in college classes, develop study habits, and have learned to adjust to the normal routine of college life, it would be best not to work. But if you must work to attend college then by all means work, even if it means working during the first semester you are on campus.

[6] *Ibid.*

You should not work so much that you miss some of the many extracurricular activities that are available on a college campus. Intramural sports, special weekends, lectures, and exhibits are only a few of the opportunities available to you. They are a part of your education, too.

If you do take a campus job while going to college, you should do well in your job. When college advisors are asked to recommend graduates for positions, their part-time work may be a part of their college record. To do a poor job of your job assignment could signify to a potential employer that you are a poor risk.

A majority of college students who work part time do so to help meet rising college expenses and to get those extras they feel are important. If a student must work in order to go to college, he can do so. You have heard it said that necessity is the mother of invention. By bending this cliché a little one can say that, if you want to go to college, necessity will become the mother of initiative. Money earned on part-time jobs matched with money from home, a student loan, or a scholarship makes it possible for any student to have a college education. Yes, it will take initiative, drive, perseverance, and a willingness to put out an extra bit of effort. But stop and think: Aren't these the things success is made of? Won't this kind of experience be of value to you later in life? Start planning today to meet college expenses.

Other Ways to Meet College Expenses

You should make every effort to save money needed to meet college expenses. Savings make it unnecessary to rely on a scholarship, which may not materialize. Savings ease the burden of costs during the college years, reduce the amount of time that a student may have to work while in college, and keep debts for college expenses to a minimum. Life insurance is the principal means of saving, according to a study by the Ford Foundation, and is used by 60 percent of the families with college savings plans.

Paying for college has fallen in line with other buying habits of our society and time. As a nation, we are an "installment plan" people. We buy cars, clothes, and houses on time. Why not a college education? College expenses can be met just as we meet current expenses, or car and house payments. Installment payment of college expenses can be arranged through some colleges and banks, commercial credit companies, and certain agencies that specialize in college funds. It will be easy for you to check on educational programs offered by banks in your area. Should you be interested in learning of pay-as-you-study plans offered by colleges, write to the colleges you are considering for specific information. Most will have some arrangement for an installment payment plan.

There are several financial plans offered by agencies specializing in arranging funds for education. Most of these agencies lend money to parents for their sons' and daughters' education regardless of the section of the country in which they plan to attend college. Like the NDEA loan program, many plans carry insurance benefits. Should your father become disabled, or die, money for college is assured. Financial plans supply the money as you need it, and your parents pay a certain sum each month to reduce the debt. Financial plans are of most value to families who provide money for educating their children from earned income. It lessens the impact of college expense by spreading the normal payments faced in a four-year college program over a period of six or more years.

Money from these plans can be used in any accredited college for fees, tuition, room and board, books, supplies, laundry, travel, and so on. The average minimum amount of money that may be borrowed ranges up to $1,250 per semester.

Some of the agencies specializing in arranging educational finance plans are:

Education Funds, Inc.
10 Dorrance Street
Providence, Rhode Island 02923

Figure 11

ILLUSTRATION OF
INSURED TUITION PAYMENT PLAN

Prepared For:

THE PARENT OF A STUDENT ENTERING COLLEGE IN THE FALL OF 1965

Account No.

INSURED TUITION PAYMENT PLAN will pay:

THE COLLEGE TO BE NAMED LATER

$750 per semester for 8 semesters (4 years), a total of $6000

commencing September 15, 19 65 , provided that the payments below are made in full and on time. In the event the insured parent loses his earning power through death or total and permanent disability, all remaining monthly payments will be made by the insurance company, subject to the provisions of the policy.

If the plan's payment to the school or college for credit to the student's account is greater than the amount of the charges against the student's account, the school or college returns the difference to the parent or to the student, in accordance with its regulations. If the Plan's payment to the school or college is less than the charges against the student's account, the parent pays the difference directly to the school or college.

PAYMENTS TO BE MADE TO INSURED TUITION PAYMENT PLAN:

1. Initial fee (once only) .... $ 25.00

2. 60 monthly payments commencing as of

   February 1, 1964 .... $105.30

(assumed age – 40 to 60)

Each of the above monthly payments includes $ 4.80 for life and disability insurance and fifty cents for banking service. The disability benefit terminates on the date when the assured attains the age of sixty-five years; the life insurance benefit continues throughout the term of the contract.

Payments are completed with the January payment of the final year of the educational program.

Funds for Education, Inc.
319 Lincoln Street
Manchester, New Hampshire 03103

Insured Tuition Payment Plan
38 Newbury Street
Boston, Massachusetts 02116

The Tuition Plan, Inc.
One Park Avenue
New York, New York 10016

Security Tuition Plan
Security Life and Trust Company
Winston-Salem, North Carolina 27102

In addition to these sources of financial aid, there are literally thousands of sources available throughout the country. While there is probably no one listing that includes them all, the most complete one is "Credit for College," by W. W. Hill, published by College Life Insurance Company of America, Indianapolis, Indiana.

Billy Plans a Program

Billy Smith faced the problem of arranging a program for financing his college education while he was a junior in high school. Billy had decided he was going to college and reviewed the cost of attending. He found that college costs varied considerably among institutions. Since money for college was a problem for his family, he decided to go to the state university, which would cost about $1,650 a year. His guidance counselor had arranged a high school program for Billy that would meet the requirements of the university.

Billy knew that his parents had an obligation to his brothers and sisters. He recognized that he would have to plan well if he were to go to college. He discussed this problem with his parents and counselor. They explained the various ways that Billy could save money before entering college. No money had been set aside for Billy's education because his father had bought his own business only two years before. The guidance counselor told Billy's father, who owned a gasoline station, that Billy's education was an investment in his future just as a delivery truck was an investment in the family's business. She pointed out that the cost of Billy's room and board would be an expense even if he stayed at home. She also mentioned that families could pay for college costs on a pay-as-you-go basis, but that it was not always possible to pay for all the expenses. The counselor cautioned that Billy's college budget should not be so limiting that he would not benefit from the many valuable experiences while attending college or that he would have to work so much that he would make low grades in college. She said that the plan should be only a guide.

Billy's performance in high school and his results on examinations showed that he would probably be successful in college, but that his chances for receiving a scholarship were very slim. Considering the family situation, the counselor suggested that the family save as much as possible for Billy's, and the other children's education. She helped Billy's parents estimate how much they could provide for college from the family budget by reducing some of the family's nonessential items. Billy helped by working part time in his father's gasoline station. It was decided that Billy should be paid for this work rather than add to the family's savings by saving his father the expense of hiring an attendant. His earnings were tax deductible. Despite Billy's working and his family's economizing, they all knew that not enough money could be set aside for meeting all of Billy's college expenses.

A college loan was the obvious alternative. Billy's counselor explained the various loan programs available at the state university. Mr. Smith was surprised to learn how low the interest rate and how liberal the repayment plan were. He said he wished that he could get credit like that for operating his business. The counselor told them that Billy had a good chance of receiving a college loan because he could make application almost a year before he needed it.

This was the Smith family's financial situation:

1. Because of the demands of the family business, no savings were set aside for Billy's education.
2. Billy had saved $200.
3. It was estimated that Billy could earn $500 each summer by working in the gasoline station.
4. The counselor suggested that Billy not work during his first semester on campus but that he could earn approximately $150 each of seven semesters. She told them that they would need to make a specific plan showing how much the family could contribute, how much Billy could earn during the summer months, and the amount he could earn while attending college.

This was the Smith family's financial situation:

BILLY'S PROGRAM

	One Year	Four Years
Savings		
Family savings	0	0
Billy's savings	$200	$200
Pay-as-you-go from family income	300	1,200
Billy's earnings		
Summer months	500	2,000
Part-time at college*	150	1,050
	$1,150	$4,450

Amount of Loan Needed

	One Year	Four Years
Cost of college	$1,650	$6,600
Less total savings and income	1,150	4,450
Amount of loan needed	$ 500	$2,150

* One-year figure is computed for one term of work: four-year figure is total of seven semesters or terms of work.

Chapter Ten

What Parents Should Do, Can Do, and Cannot Do

FOR PARENTS ONLY

This section is written directly for parents concerned with the welfare of their college-bound teen-agers. It is the hope of the author that many of the anxieties, questions, and concerns of parents may be alleviated and answered in this section.

The fact that colleges have drastically changed during the past twenty years is a basic reason why parents feel inadequate to advise their sons and daughters. To become aware of this fact, one needs only to open a college text, visit a campus, or discuss course work and campus activities with students presently enrolled in college. Information presented in this chapter will be helpful to parents in assisting their children find answers to the questions raised in preceding chapters.

You can gain a thorough understanding of college costs and the sources of financial aid to students in preceding chapters. Supplemental facts and information regarding how parents pay for college and programs for which parents must excerise prudent planning is presented in this section. As a parent you will find the information useful in planning a financial program to fit individual family needs. The information is presented in this form in the belief that it is in this manner that parents seek solutions to pertinent problems.

As a parent you are probably acutely aware of college enrollment pressures as they apply to your son or daughter. Your concern for your teen-ager's college education is not unique. It is shared with parents of approximately five million high-school-age students who entered college in 1965. The U.S. Office of Education has estimated that almost eight million students will be enrolled in college by 1973. The percentage of new students seeking a degree is increasing by about 10 percent a year, and this trend is expected to continue throughout the present decade. This increase didn't just happen; never before has so much pressure been placed on students to earn a college degree.

Most parents have heard or read about how difficult it is to be admitted to college. Much of what has been written would lead you to believe that unless your teen-ager took a straight college preparatory program in high school, earned very good marks, and achieved a score of 550 or better on college board examinations, he would not be admitted to college. This is not necessarily true. There is a place in college for every high school graduate. There are more than two thousand colleges and universities in the nation. Many of them would like to have more students than they enroll. Certainly, the more selective schools want to attract the very best students they can find, and so they discriminate on the basis of marks, rank in class, and scores earned on certain examinations. That is why they are called "selective" institutions. The fact that an institution has a highly regarded reputation and many ivy-covered buildings, however, is not sufficient evidence to say that it is the school your teen-ager should attend. If your son or daughter has average intellectual ability and has achieved average marks in high school, he or she can be admitted to an accredited college.

There are good schools, fully accredited, with fine reputations, that will accept students who have shown no great spark of brilliance.

Parents are concerned for the happiness and success of their children. And well they should be. A college education is not something to be taken lightly. We have made "getting a college education" an achievement of importance in our society. To some, "getting in" is more important than the "why" of going, and this is unfortunate. Nevertheless, there is the misplaced emphasis because, in our society, a college education is a prestige factor in many circles; it is a passport to the professions; it is almost a union card for the right to work in many positions; and it has become the certificate of admission to many of the white-collar jobs and the more desirable occupations.

You are concerned because you want to give your children "something better than what I had." "Only the best is good enough for my boy" and "they need a college degree to get a 'good' job" are the laments of concerned parents. And parents are right: college is a good place to prepare for tomorrow. It is here, during the years from seventeen to twenty-two, that great and lasting personal decisions are made. These may include the choice of a life's work, which is so important to success, the development of lifelong friendships, and perhaps meeting the man or woman your child will marry. There is no better place in American society than college to make these decisions.

Parents' Role in Preparing Children for College

Many parents are not fully aware of the important role they play in the academic success of their college-bound children. There are many things that parents can do to help prepare their sons and daughters for college. To be sure, there are limiting factors, and some opportunities may have lapsed, but there are other things that parents can do for their children that will increase their chances of being admitted to college and succeeding after they get there.

What should be the role of the parent in planning for college? Before the answers can be given to the many questions parents have concerning the subject of planning for college, certain questions should be asked. What is of value in the high school program that prepares youth for college success? Which college is the best? How much will it cost? Will there be room for my child? What sources of financial aid are available? When and how is college application made? What can parents do to help their child get "settled" in college? These questions imply what parents can do and what they should do. What parents cannot do will also become apparent.

Before you can be of any lasting assistance in preparing your child for college, you must be relatively sure there is a place for him in college. Any boy or girl who has graduated from high school and has average ability can be admitted to an accredited college. This is a fact and will continue to be true for a good many years to come. There are some things you can't do because it is too late, but there are so many things you can do that you shouldn't lose too much time thinking of the past. If your teen-ager is college material, leave no stone unturned to prepare him for it. You can help this goal become a reality by:

1. Developing and nurturing your child's interest in attending college.
2. Understanding the needs and limitations of your teen-agers.
3. Gaining a knowledge of how colleges operate—their purposes, policies, and practices.
4. Becoming acquainted with what colleges look for in students.
5. Recognizing and making use of available opportunities.
6. Helping your college-bound youth arrive at realistic choices for life's work and a college that will prepare him for it.
7. Planning a financial program that will provide the necessary money for college attendance.

Parents have always been one of the strongest influences causing students to go to college Sometimes parental expectations are strong motivators and in other cases they are more subtle. When students in a Mid-Western survey were asked who or what exerted the most influence on them to attend college, they reported:

Family	30 percent
Teachers	10 percent
Friends	10 percent
Counselors	10 percent
Scholarship	2 percent
Don't know, or other	38 percent

One of the most important things parents can do in preparing their children for college is to develop and nurture the aspiration of going to college. Passively waiting for teen-agers to decide to go to college, instead of instilling and cultivating the desire, has been disastrous to the plans of some parents and their children. What good is it to have the financial means, interested parents, and uninterested youth? Parents can develop a positive attitude in their children toward a college education as a means of achieving a richer and fuller life, both professionally and personally. Attitudes, interests, and aspirations of teen-agers are dynamic motivating forces worthy of developing and directing toward a desirable end.

Parental attitudes and expectations are necessary, but must be handled with care. There are some decisions about going to college that must be made by the person going. The choice must be a realistic one. Rather than suggesting specific colleges, a parent's role may be best played by being certain that all the pertinent facts are considered in their correct perspective. When this is done, have faith in your teen-ager to make a sound decision and give his decision support. After all, it is your child who will spend four years on the campus.

Parents can take a cue from the findings of research conducted on the psychological problems of students. It has been found, for example, that student problems are most frequent when students come from families that provide little emotional support and where the parents' high aspirations for their children are shown by critical attitudes. Further study of student problems indicates a lack of consistent goals due, in part, to the fact that they are not free to select goals for themselves. To some degree, parental goals were imposed on students included in these research studies.

Too much parental pressure can cause psychological problems and disorders. In general, a student with personal problems does poorly in college. It has been found that when parents have insisted on both high school and prep school as a means of preparing for college, students are more likely to underachieve than overachieve in college. Some college personnel feel this reflects external and too severe a pressure on the part of parents.

Unrealistic goals, set and encouraged by parents, can be a deterrent to maximum achievement in college. Teen-agers will reject goals they are not capable of fulfilling. If preparation for that goal becomes a stumbling block, such as studying in the wrong curriculum to please a parent, a student may fail when failure was not inevitable. This has been found to be the basis for parental rejection by children. They may show it by underachieving, or by dropping or flunking out of college. Parents should be critical of their own motives for wanting their teen-agers to get a college education. There are some very good reasons for encouraging your child to go to college, but parental egotism is not one of them. Family pride should not get out of hand to the extent that it does harm to an immature, unknowing teen-ager. Encourage, but don't push; suggest, don't insist. Coerced cooperation is not very lasting, and is almost certain to bring on academic difficulties.

Planning for college should be a partnership between teen-agers and their parents. It is becoming a three-way partnership with the high school guidance counselor. Take advantage of the free assistance and information provided by the counselor. He is a professionally trained person whose help is yours for the asking. Counselors have objective information that is needed in helping you and your teen-ager plan for college. One specific way they help is by providing information on your teen-ager's potential and the specific demands of particular colleges. Use their advice and information judiciously, remembering that the final decision rests with your son or daughter. Your mature judgment is of much value because quick decisions made by uncounseled youth may lead to errors that could influence the life of your son or daughter.

The primary thing to remember about the "why" of going to college is that college is for some definite purpose. Keeping up with the Joneses, or because it is the "thing to do" is not reason enough. His or her chances for success will be greatly enhanced with a definite purpose, one that is personally meaningful. When students can apply what is learned to some future goal, they develop a desirable attitude about what is studied, which is reflected in their performance.

To emphasize this point, studies have found that a large number of gainfully employed people are improperly placed. Many, including college graduates, have little interest in their present work, although it may pay well. Success is important, but it is not always measured in dollars and cents. Happiness and success are not necessarily on the same end of the measuring stick.

College education will offer two distinct advantages for your children: the opportunity to make more money and less risk of unemployment. In addition, college education opens doors to jobs, and lifts barriers on positions that will not otherwise be available. The Bureau of the Census found that male college graduates earned about 75 percent more money than did all other males. For women, the financial value of a college degree was worth two and one-half times the salary of the average woman in the working force in 1958.

Using Census data, based on the expectancy of forty years of employment, young men entering the labor force can expect to earn $182,000 if they have had only a grade school education; $258,000 if they have completed high school; and $435,000 if they have earned a college education. Without doubt, the difference will increase during the next decade. The obvious conclusion is that college pays.

One of the more important reasons for encouraging your children to consider going to college is that future success almost demands it. According to the Bureau of Labor Statistics, the shift from farms to cities is a continuing process that has tended to increase the demand for lawyers, social workers, other professional personnel. The reduction in the number of hours worked, coupled with increasing incomes, is creating a demand for persons trained in cultural and recreational fields. The demand for teachers and college professors is well known. Shifts in our economy create jobs for research specialists, economists, statisticians, and many others. For example, a decade ago, the demand for electronic computer and data-processing workers was slight; today, they are in great demand. The thing to note is that all these positions require education beyond high school.

Unemployment is related to education. According to the Bureau of Labor Statistics, 8.5 percent of the unemployed workers had less than a high school education. This may be compared with 4.8 percent who were high school graduates and 2.4 percent who had some college education. These figures clearly indicate that education is a way of avoiding the risk of being unemployed.

Research has found that family income, education of

parents, rank of child in high school, and the sex of the child are highly correlated with attending college. Family income is considered because it provides the opportunity to attend college. Without money, students with interest may not be able to attend. The more education parents have had, the more likely the child will be to attend college. How parents see the child's ability, and their attitude toward both the child and education is important to whether college is an acceptable goal for the child. It is an acceptable goal for boys more so than for girls, based on national averages.

A look at the kind of students colleges want and what research shows regarding who is successful in college will have implications for what parents can do to help their teen-agers succeed in college. As to be expected, there is not much disagreement between these two points of view. Both sources indicate that students who have confidence in their ability to deal with new situations and to solve personal problems are preferred. Students who experience little fear in new situations achieve better in college than those who are insecure in new situations. Youths who find it easy to identify with persons with whom they are unfamiliar succeed more frequently than those who are less able to develop such relationships. Persons who can relate themselves to purposes, goals, and values of a new group with ease have a good chance for success. Students who experience difficulty in college tend to have feelings of inadequacy in relating themselves to new situations, people, and ideas.

As a parent you can plan and provide situations and opportunities for the development of your children in many ways. A look about the community, church, and school will point up many opportunities for your teen-ager to gain valuable experience through participation. The parental objective is to strengthen the weaknesses that you see in your child. The guidance counselor, high school principal, and teachers will be able to help you provide opportunities for your boy or girl to gain experiences that will develop ability and self-confidence in the areas needed for success in college.

Going away to college is a big step for most teenagers. It will break for many, if not most, the ties they have had with their clubs and close friends. Socially, it is a starting-over time. Most seventeen and eighteen year olds seek independence, but it is cast upon college students quickly and with a sharp break from their past experiences. It is an understatement to say that teen-agers planning for college are apprehensive, concerned, and anxious. The anticipation of new freedom with responsibility is often frightening to them. They need to know they have your interest, your understanding, your moral support. By sharing your time, by just being a good listener, and by providing an atmosphere of mutual understanding and acceptance, you will be providing needed encouragement to your maturing son or daughter.

There are few things you can do that will be of more lasting importance to your children than letting them know you care for them as individuals, that you respect their notions and convictions, and that you try to see and feel as they do about things that concern them. Parental love and affection is the basis for personal security. You can't expect your children to be socially secure and not be emotionally secure; you can't have one without the other. Parental concern and affection is the "key."

Satisfactory academic performance is dependent on these complex, personal relationships. They provide a setting for the development of a sense of responsibility and emotional stability that are vital to the self-discipline needed at college and for success in any field. You can make a valuable contribution toward the academic success of your child by being an understanding parent, sensitive to his needs and to your own actions.

Becoming Acquainted With College Policies

Parents should remember that good colleges come in all sizes and are found in most states. In terms of your child's personal development, happiness, and adjustment to campus life, it is important that he select a college with objectives, curricula, atmosphere, etc., that are suited for his academic and personal development. Only in this way can he make the best use of his interest and abilities to develop his aptitudes to the fullest degree. It is a poor idea to insist on a particular college if your teen-ager doesn't like it, or if it won't challenge him, or if it is too much of a challenge for him.

There is a growing body of research that points out that having taken a particular course in high school, including the so-called solids — science, English, and a foreign language — has a limited and hard-to-prove relationship to success in college In fact, there is just about as much research available to show that certain vocational courses make an equal or superior contribution to college as do some of the solid courses. Of course, English and the required courses for high school graduation are a must. Without doubt, when your teen-ager enrolls in a course, you will want to see that it is the section best for your child.

Just what courses should students take? There is no general answer to this important question, but there are some guides. When a college has been selected, or a group of three or four are being considered, review the requirements of the institution; these will be courses that should be taken in high school. A second guide is that if a high school course contributes to the abilities and understanding needed in the chosen career field, it will be good to gain the experience at the high school level.

Parents need to be well informed on certain factors about colleges before they can help students to make a logical choice. An explanation of these factors may be found in chapter III. You will want to consider with your teen-ager the following factors, any one of which may be of great or minor importance, depending on your individual situation:

- Philosophy and standards of the institution
- Career field to be followed
- Accreditation
- Cost
- Requirements for admission
- Location
- Size
- Coeducational or non-coeducational
- Work-study plan available

When discussing the selection of a college with your teen-age, it is best to emphasize two important points: career field and accreditation. While it may be true that a specific profession or job objective may change, opportunities will be open in the general professional area of the career field. As a matter of fact, unless you, your teen-ager, and guidance counselor agree, precision about a career is to be avoided. All that is desired is a field of employment to serve as a tentative objective. It is well established that people succeed more often when they have an objective to achieve. A career field serves as a "target." It is an incentive and motivator that will encourage your son or daughter toward academic success.

Here is something else to remember when assisting your teen-ager in planning for college: there is an increasing number of positions that once required only college preparation that now require graduate work above the baccalaureate degree. Recognition of this fact is too far in the future for most high school students to see, but parents' maturity, experience, and vision can be influential. The fact that some jobs require graduate work may make the selection of the first college to attend less of a problem. For example, if the field your teen-ager chooses is highly specialized, only a few undergraduate programs may be suitable. On the other hand, if a B.S. or B.A. degree from an accredited institution will suffice, he or she may be able to attend a college near home for convenience and to cut costs. Some employers, such as Campbell Soup, General Electric, and other large concerns, hire graduates from several kinds of colleges with such diversified majors as liberal arts, agriculture, business and public administration, and engineering, and provide special training by their own staff. The college selected should be fully accredited so that your son or daughter may enter graduate school in good standing and receive credit for courses taken when transferring for graduate work.

College entrance examinations are not always understood by parents of college-bound teen-agers. They are used for two purposes: to determine the readiness of a student for college work, and to place students in courses and sections in which they have a greater chance for success. The latter is, in a way, a kind of ability grouping. When tests are used for determining if students are ready for college, they aid in the decision to admit or reject students. This is a factor used by the more selective colleges and universities. As a parent, it is encouraging to learn that this is only one factor considered by admissions offices and that several other factors may compensate for a relatively low score on such examinations.

Here is how examinations are used by colleges, and why they have become necessary. Each year the number of new students is increasing on most campuses. To cope with the problem of placing students in groups of near-equal ability, universities administer examinations that may be scored electronically. Based on scores earned, advisors place students in courses and sections of courses that are compatible with their ability. If test scores indicate that a student should take remedial work, he may be placed in a beginning course or a non-credit course. If, on the other hand, your son or daughter earns a high score, he or she may be placed in an advanced course. In either case, your teen-ager benefits by being placed in courses in which he has a chance to progress at a rate equal to his ability.

How Parents Pay for College

College is expensive. As long as college costs approximately as much as a cabin cruiser, or half as much as a new house, there is little doubt that decisions about financing college expenses are going to continue to confront parents.

The cost of a college education is getting so high that parents are tempted to say "what's the use?" when they plan a detailed budget of college expenses. Before you throw in the towel consider the question, "Can we afford not to send them to college?" Failing to come to grips with this question may shape the destiny of your children to something less than that of which they are capable. A college education is an investment, the best kind of investment, in your teen-agers' future. It opens doors to opportunity, it raises salary ceilings, and it provides the foundation for a better life for your children. These are very good reasons for making sacrifices for the future of one or more of the family's members.

The solution to money problems lies in planning to meet the rising cost of sending your teen-ager to college. Parents who have planned for their children's education feel a sense of security about their childrens' future. Peace of mind is one of the benefits of planning before children enter college. Parents who plan for the education of their children usually do a better job of financing it and should feel that their contribution to their childrens' welfare has been more adequate.

The cost of a college education over and above what is may cost to support your son or daughter is not as great as it may seem. Consider the fact that, in our society, young people from seventeen to twenty-three years of age are accorded a very high status and recognized as mature citizens There are several reasons for this, and anticipation of spending time in military service is not one of the least. For most parents, this has brought on an extended time in which youth are supported by the home. There is a likelihood that your teen-ager will be dependent on your support during this period of time whether he or she will be in college or not. Many parents consider room, board, clothing, and personal expenses of their children while in college to be equal to these costs while at home. In some cases, teen-agers are able to live at home and attend college with little additional expense.

Families sending two or three children to college are becoming commonplace in many communities. Nearly all the children of college graduates and more than one-half of the nation's youth are expected to attend college by 1970. It has been estimated that from 60 to 70 percent of the children now between the ages of one and nine will enroll in college.

What will it cost a typical family to give its children a college education? Tuition and fees have increased about 10 percent a year since 1960. Some authorities estimate that college costs will rise 7.5 percent or more a year for the next ten years. Five percent a year over the next decade appears to be a conservative estimate. To point up the financial pressures on families meeting college costs, consider, for example, a family with three children. One child is in the seventh grade, one is in the fifth grade, and the youngest is in the fourth grade. The year is 1965–66. Based on $1,884 as an annual cost of attending an Eastern state university in 1964–65, with a 5-percent increase each year over the preceding year, this family's college expense are shown below. The figures have been rounded to the nearest dollar.

Year	Cost per year	Child No. 1 7th grade	Child No. 2 5th grade	Child No. 3 4th grade	Total
1964	$1,884				
1965	1,978				
1966	2,077				
1967	2,181				
1968	2,290				
1969	2,405				
1970	2,525				
1971	2,651	$2,651			$2,651
1972	2,783	2,783			2,783
1973	2,923	2,923	$2,923		5,846
1974	3,069	3,069	3,069	$3,069	9,207
1975	3,222		3,222	3,222	6,444
1976	3,383		3,383	3,383	6,766
1977	3,552			3,552	3,552
1978	3,730				
1979	3,917				
1980	4,112				
Total		$11,426	$12,597	$13,226	$37,249

Students go to college, but parents pay for it. How do parents meet the rising cost of college expenses? The answer is through long-range planning and financial aid arranged by the college attended. One of the most detailed surveys conducted on this subject found that the most direct action parents of elementary and high school students can take to finance their college education is to save money.[1] Today's parents who plan to meet college costs when their children are at these ages are making better financial provisions for college than parents were twenty years ago.

The Parents' Confidential Statement. The most widely used financial assistance program is that of the College Scholarship Service. The CSS forms and the Parents' Confidential Statement are designed for use by colleges in their evaluation of students' financial need. This form is processed by the College Scholarship Service, an organization of colleges whose members are listed on pages 96 to 99. Parents who submit these forms should understand that the forms will be evaluated by the CSS before they are submitted to colleges. Also, the CSS will preserve the confidential nature of information received by releasing copies only upon your written request.

Colleges using the CSS believe that financial aid should be awarded on the basis of ability and promise, but that the amount of aid should vary according to the relative financial need of each applicant. In keeping with this principle, the participating colleges make the final selection and determine the amount and type of award.

The Parents' Confidential Statement* comes in two forms. The regular statement is for parents whose annual income exceeds $4,000. The short form is for parents whose income is less than $4,000 a year. Figure 12 is a sample of a complete statement. Copies of the regular and short form, instructions on how to complete them, and of supplements A and B, for owners of businesses and for farm owners, operators, and tenants respectively, follow the sample completed statement on pages 129 to 136. To provide colleges with this information, the CSS charges parents $1 for the initial processing of the completed form, $3 for the copy sent to the first college listed, and $2 for each additional college.

If your son or daughter plans to attend a college participating in the College Scholarship Service, you should obtain a copy of the Parents' Confidential Statement through the cooperation of the local guidance counselor or from the financial aid officer at the chosen college or institution. The statement should be com-

[1] Lansing, *op. cit.*

* The Parents' Confidential Statement form which appears on the following pages is reproduced with permission from the 1967 edition of the form, published by the College Entrance Examination Board, New York. This form is revised biennially by the College Scholarship Service, an activity of the College Entrance Examination Board, and is supplied without cost to high schools for distribution to students who have been advised by colleges or scholarship sponsors to submit the Parents' Confidential Statement. The form may also be obtained on request by writing to College Scholarship Service, Box 176, Princeton, New Jersey 08540, or Box 1025, Berkeley, California 94701.

pleted and should accurately reflect your financial position. The completed forms should be mailed to:

> College Scholarship Service
> Box 176
> Princeton, New Jersey 08540

If you live in, or west of, Montana, Wyoming, Colorado, or New Mexico, send the completed form to:

> College Scholarship Service
> Box 1025
> Berkeley, California 94701

The College Work-Study Program. The College Work-Study Program, supported by the Office of Economic Opportunity in cooperation with the U.S. Office of Education, has as its objective the provision of jobs to enable young people to attend college. Working part time to help pay for college expenses is not new, particularly for parents of today's youth who attended college. This program was planned to stimulate students to attend who might not otherwise be able to because of lack of money. Under this program, qualified students are assigned jobs that pay $1.25 or more an hour by the director of student aid at the institution they attend. A student may work for a maximum of fifteen hours a week while attending school. More than $156 million was spent for this purpose in 1965.

Students qualify if they are capable of maintaining a good academic standing, and attend college on a full-time basis. Participating students may get an academic break: some colleges may waive the results of standardized tests for them.

The program's guidelines specify that the family must be eligible to receive assistance under a public or private welfare program, and must have a combined income of less than $3,200, other than income from assets, investments, etc. Students from large families, however, may qualify according to the following schedule:

Family members	Maximum annual income
4	$4,000
5	4,700
6	5,300
7	5,800
8	6,200
9	6,600

In addition, the financial aid officer is permitted to make allowances for special factors that "constitute an excessive drain on family resources." Also, it is recognized that an income of $3,200 in an industrial area in the Northeast is not the same as the income of a tenant farmer in a depressed area.

The most important factor in determining financial need in this program is the family. The student is eligible for the College Work-Study Program if the family cannot support him; it is not enough that the family will not support him. Married students qualify for eligibility when both sets of parents meet the above conditions.

Loan Programs. "Go now and pay later" has found its way to college campuses in a big way. During the past decade, long-term loans for students and their parents have changed from a relatively unpopular form of aid granted to students unable to qualify for scholarships to a fully accepted and eagerly sought means of funds for college. The change is in part due to the fact that loans in themselves are more acceptable to the American public, and in part to the formulation of massive federal and state loan programs.

Appendix A: Sample case studies

Description of Norman Olson case

This case illustrates the special circumstances met in computing contributions from members of the clergy. The miscellaneous business expenses incurred by clergymen, such as automobile expenses, books, and conference attendance, are common in forms submitted by clergymen and are normally

allowable nonreimbursed business expenses. A ministerial housing allowance ($1,500 in this case) is common for clergymen, and note should be made of the method of handling the allowance.

In this case the allowance ($1,500) has been reported by the parent. In cases in which no allowance is noted, no home owned, and no rent paid, the financial aid officer may wish to add an amount equal to 15 percent of the reported income to provide an imputed housing value.

In addition to the housing allowance, note should be taken of the $600 schooling expense for Sharon. Since Sharon is receiving no scholarship aid, an allowance for the amount of her reported tuition will be made.

A housekeeping allowance equal to one quarter of Mrs. Olson's estimated 1968 income is given.

Figure 13

COLLEGE SCHOLARSHIP SERVICE
Parents' Confidential Statement
Academic Year 1968-1969

Part I

(Do not send to CSS after September 1, 1968)

Submit this form after transferring information from work sheet

1A STUDENT APPLICANT | O L S O N | N O R M A N | T | (1) X M (2) ☐ F | 6 | 8 | 49 | 3 2 4 6 5 7 6 8 4

LAST NAME — FIRST NAME — MID. INIT. — SEX — MO. DAY YEAR (DATE OF BIRTH) — SOCIAL SECURITY NUMBER

1B ARE YOU A U.S. CITIZEN? YES X NO ☐   **1C WHAT IS YOUR MARITAL STATUS?** SINGLE (1) X   MARRIED (2) ☐

2A STUDENT APPLICANT'S HOME ADDRESS 122 McDonnel Street   Rhinelander, Wisconsin   5 4 5 0 1

NUMBER AND STREET — CITY — STATE — ZIP CODE

2B APPLICANT NORMALLY LIVES WITH (CHECK ALL THAT APPLY)
(1) X FATHER (2) X MOTHER (3) ☐ STEPFATHER (4) ☐ STEPMOTHER **OR** (5) ☐ MAINTAINS OWN RESIDENCE

CHECK IF ANY APPLY:
(6) ☐ FATHER IS DECEASED (7) ☐ MOTHER IS DECEASED (8) ☐ FATHER IS UNABLE TO WORK (9) ☐ PARENTS ARE SEPARATED OR DIVORCED (0) ☐ OTHER SPECIAL CIRCUMSTANCES (EXPLAIN)

3 LIST COLLEGES AND AGENCIES TO WHICH COPIES OF THIS FORM ARE TO BE SENT. (CHECK HERE IF YOU LIST MORE THAN FOUR) ☐

NAME	CITY	STATE	CSS USE ONLY	NAME	CITY	STATE	CSS USE ONLY
Rockford College			1665	University of Colorado			4841
Lake Forest College			1392	Carleton College			6081

Father or Male Guardian | **Mother or Female Guardian**

4A NAME OF FATHER Harry L. Olson   AGE 42   **4B NAME OF MOTHER** Sylvia M. Olson   AGE 40

HOME ADDRESS 122 McDonnel Street, Rhinelander, Wis.   HOME ADDRESS

OCCUPATION AND TITLE Clergyman   OCCUPATION AND TITLE General Office

EMPLOYED BY Christ the King Lutheran Church   YEARS WITH FIRM 4½   EMPLOYED BY St. Johns Toys   YEARS WITH FIRM 1

CHECK IF YOU WILL RECEIVE RETIREMENT BENEFITS FROM: (1) X SOCIAL SECURITY (2) X ANOTHER PLAN (3) ☐ NEITHER

CHECK IF YOU WILL RECEIVE RETIREMENT BENEFITS FROM: (1) X SOCIAL SECURITY (2) X ANOTHER PLAN (3) ☐ NEITHER

5A ENTER NUMBER OF CHILDREN YOU WILL CLAIM AS TAX DEPENDENTS ON YOUR FEDERAL INCOME TAX RETURN FOR 1967.......... 6

5B ENTER NUMBER OF OTHER DEPENDENTS RECEIVING FINANCIAL SUPPORT FROM FAMILY (DO NOT INCLUDE ANYONE ENTERED IN 4A, 4B AND 5A)..........

6 DO YOU OWN A BUSINESS OR ARE YOU A FARM OR RANCH OWNER, OPERATOR OR TENANT? (IF YES, COMPLETE BUSINESS OR FARM SUPPLEMENT)...... NO X   YES ☐

Parents' Annual Income and Expenses

	$ TOTAL 1966	$ TOTAL 1967	$ ESTIMATED 1968
7 SALARIES AND WAGES BEFORE TAXES A. FATHER, STEPFATHER, OR MALE GUARDIAN	$5,867	$6,167	$6,467
B. MOTHER, STEPMOTHER, OR FEMALE GUARDIAN	257	2,025	1,040
8 OTHER INCOME	1,500	1,500	1,500
9 BUSINESS EXPENSES		800	800
10 UNINSURED MEDICAL EXPENSES (INCLUDE COST OF MEDICAL INSURANCE)		461	350
11 OTHER EXTRAORDINARY EXPENSES PAID		none	none
	FOR 1966	FOR 1967	
12 FEDERAL INCOME TAX PAID	$ 478	$ 450	

Parents' Assets and Liabilities

	A. PRESENT MARKET VALUE	B. UNPAID MORTGAGE
13 HOME (IF OWNED) YR. PURCHASED 19___ PURCHASE PRICE $_____	none $	$
14 OTHER REAL ESTATE	none	
15 BANK ACCOUNTS (PERSONAL SAVINGS AND CHECKING)		$100
16 OTHER INVESTMENTS (PRESENT MARKET VALUE)		none
17 INDEBTEDNESS (DO NOT INCLUDE MORTGAGE, AUTO LOANS, INSURANCE LOANS OR CHARGE ACCOUNTS)		none
18 STUDENT'S OWN ASSETS (INCLUDE SAVINGS, ENDOWMENTS, TRUST FUNDS, STOCKS AND BONDS)		none

CSS USE ONLY | B F | A. | B. | C.

19 LIST BELOW ALL CHILDREN, STUDENT APPLICANT FIRST

CHECK HERE IF YOU LIST MORE THAN SIX ☐

FIRST NAME ONLY	AGE	NAME OF PRESENT SCHOOL OR COLLEGE (1967-68)	WILL HE ATTEND SAME SCHOOL IN 1968-69?	YEAR IN SCHOOL 1967-68	A TUITION PLUS FEES 1967-68 (DO NOT INCLUDE ROOM AND BOARD)	B TOTAL AMOUNT OF SCHOLAR-SHIP OR GIFT AID, 1967-68
APPLICANT Norman	17	Rhinelander H. S.		12		
Sharon	19	Waldorf College		Soph	$600	
Ramona	13	Rhinelander Jr. H. S.		8		
Peter	7	Anderson Elem.		2		
Paul	7	Anderson Elem.		2		
Hilda	3					

ENCLOSE CHECK OR MONEY ORDER PAYABLE TO COLLEGE SCHOLARSHIP SERVICE: $2.50 FOR FIRST COLLEGE OR AGENCY LISTED AND $2.00 FOR EACH ADDITIONAL COLLEGE OR AGENCY.

AMOUNT ENCLOSED $ 8.50

20 TOTAL RESOURCES FOR STUDENT FOR ACADEMIC YEAR 1968-1969

A. FROM PARENTS' INCOME AND ASSETS.......... $ 800
B. FROM STUDENT'S ASSETS..........
C. FROM STUDENT'S SUMMER EARNINGS.......... 600
D. FROM VETERANS BENEFITS..........
E. FROM SOCIAL SECURITY BENEFITS..........
F. FROM OTHER SOURCES..........
TOTAL.......... 1,400

(DO NOT WRITE IN THIS SPACE)

Part II

In the space below explain all circled items and any special family circumstances the college should know.

Ordained at age 40. Only limited funds available for two in college at one time. Because of church obligations, Mrs. Olson will need to give up her job some time this spring.

7. Wife will stop working.

8. Value of home provided free of charge.

9. Auto, professional books, and conference attendance not covered.

10.

	1967
Hospital Insurance	$158
Clinic	68
Doctors	208
Hospital	27
	$461

Parents' Certification and Authorization

We declare that the information reported on this form, to the best of our knowledge and belief, is true, correct, and complete. We authorize transmittal of this form to the colleges and agencies named in Item 3 and its use by the College Scholarship Service (css) as described in the *Instructions*. The css or any of the colleges and agencies named to receive copies of this form have our permission to verify the information reported. If requested, we agree to send to the css, or to any college or agency named to receive a copy of this form, an official photostatic copy of our latest federal income tax return obtained from the appropriate district office of the United States Internal Revenue Service.

Signatures of both parents (or guardian) {

_____

_____   *Date* _____

COLLEGE SCHOLARSHIP SERVICE

Confidential

FINANCIAL NEED ANALYSIS REPORT

Academic Year 1968-69

UNUSUAL CONDITIONS NOTED FOR CURRENT YEAR

A   No income tax reported last year
B   Income tax reported for last year is less than 80% of standard tax
C   Income tax reported for last year exceeds standard tax by 20% or more
D   Estimated income is zero

NAME OF APPLICANT			SEX	DATE OF BIRTH			SOCIAL SECURITY NUMBER	NO OF PARENTS	NO OF CHILDREN	CLASSIFICATION	COLLEGE CODE	UNUSUAL CONDITIONS
LAST	FIRST	M I										
Olson	Norman	T	M	6	8	49	324 65 7684	2	6	ES	1665	B

COMPUTATION OF EFFECTIVE INCOME

YEAR	NET INCOME	FEDERAL INCOME TAX	HOUSEKEEPING	MEDICAL EXPENSES	OTHER EXTR. EXPENSES	INDEBTEDNESS	SCHOOLING	OTHER DEPENDENTS	TOTAL ALLOWANCES	EFFECTIVE INCOME
1	8200	448	260	0	0	0	600	0	1308	6892
2										
3										
4										

COMPUTATION OF INCOME SUPPLEMENT FROM FAMILY ASSETS

YEAR	RESIDENCE EQUITY	OTHER REAL ESTATE	BUSINESS OR FARM	BANK ACCOUNTS	OTHER INVESTMENTS	APPLICANT'S ASSETS (over $2 000)	TOTAL ASSETS	DEBT OUTSTANDING	NET WORTH	INCOME SUPPLEMENT
1	0	0	0	100	0	0	100	0	100	6493
2										
3										
4										

COMPUTATION OF ADJUSTED EFFECTIVE INCOME

YEAR	EFFECTIVE INCOME	INCOME SUPPLEMENT	ADJUSTED EFFECTIVE INCOME
1	6892	0	6892
2			
3			
4			

COMPUTATION OF TOTAL FAMILY CONTRIBUTION

PARENTS' CONTRIBUTION	APPLICANTS SUMMER EARNINGS	APPLICANT'S ASSETS	TOTAL FAMILY CONTRIBUTION
275	300	0	575

COLLEGE BUDGET / ESTIMATED FINANCIAL NEED

COLLEGE BUDGET		ESTIMATED FINANCIAL NEED	
RESIDENT	COMMUTER	RESIDENT	COMMUTER
2775	1875	2200	1300

COLLEGE ESTIMATE

YEAR	1	2	3	4
1. College budget				
2. College adjustment				
3. TOTAL BUDGET				
4. Parents' contribution				
5. Applicant's summer earnings				
6. Applicant's assets				
7. Other resources				
8. TOTAL CONTRIBUTION				
9. FINANCIAL NEED (line 3 minus 8)				

FINANCIAL AID AWARD

SCHOLARSHIP				
LOAN				
JOB				

General Information

The Parents' Confidential Statement (PCS) is used in evaluating student financial need. Parents of students who plan to attend college during 1968-69 and who wish to receive financial aid should submit this form.

The forms are processed by the College Scholarship Service (CSS), which evaluates them in accordance with standards and procedures developed by its membership. This evaluation and a copy of the form itself are sent to each college or agency named by the parents. *The colleges and agencies make the final decisions* about candidates designated as award recipients, the type of aid to be granted (scholarship, loan, job, or any combination), and the amount awarded. Parents should understand that by submitting the forms to the CSS, they consent to this evaluation. The colleges and agencies using the CSS believe that financial aid should be awarded to students on the basis of ability and promise, but the amount of the awards should vary according to financial need.

Since the PCS generally is not considered an application for financial aid, the colleges and agencies may require other application forms. Such requirements are explained in publications of the individual colleges and agencies. These other forms should be returned directly to the colleges and agencies.

Who should complete the PCS: In most cases, the form should be filled out completely and submitted by the *parents* of the student applicant. In certain circumstances, however, it may be appropriate for someone other than the student applicant's parents to fill out the form. In these cases, the person completing the form should indicate his relationship to the student applicant and make any necessary notations specifying whose income and expenses, assets and liabilities are shown on the form.

IF YOU OWN A BUSINESS, OR IF YOU ARE A FARM OR RANCH OWNER, OPERATOR, OR TENANT, complete the Supplement Section of the Parents' Confidential Statement. The Supplement Section (A for business owners, B for farmers or ranchers) should be returned to the CSS with your original Parents' Confidential Statement. If the Supplement Section is not available in your secondary school or the college of your choice, write to the appropriate CSS office and request the Supplement from the College Scholarship Service. You can avoid delay in complete and accurate reporting to the colleges and agencies by including the Supplement Section with your original PCS.

If a student applicant is married but under the age of 25, his parents must complete the PCS. The CSS will then send the married student a supplementary form requesting additional information. Although a student may consider himself self-supporting, colleges nevertheless expect complete information from his parents. A self-supporting applicant should indicate his own financial circumstances in detail in Part II, including his income for both 1967 and 1968, his personal assets in ITEM ⑱, and the amount from his income and assets he will use toward the payment of his college expenses for 1968-69 in ITEM 20.

Submitting the PCS: The form you submit should be mailed in time to reach the CSS by the dates specified by the colleges and agencies to which you would like a copy of your PCS sent. (Consult the college catalogs or agency bulletins for deadlines.) You should enclose a fee of $2.50 for the first college or agency you list and $2 for each additional one. (See the front cover for mailing instructions.) Copies will be released only to the colleges and agencies you name on your PCS or in subsequent correspondence with the CSS. The original copy will be held on file by the CSS until October 1, 1968. If before that time you wish copies to be sent to other colleges or agencies, you should write to the appropriate CSS office and enclose $2 for each additional copy. *Do not submit another* PCS.

If your circumstances change: If the family finances change materially after the form is filed, or if the student is awarded financial aid not granted by a college, you should promptly notify the CSS, which will inform the colleges and agencies. Include in your letter the student's name (last, first, and middle), date of birth, Social Security number, and his home address. Indicate the changes in your financial position by identifying the item on your original form in which the change occurred and the dollar amount of the change. Send your letter to the CSS office with which you filed your original form.

If you need to correspond with the CSS, or if you are including additional information on a separate sheet of paper with the PCS, be sure to include the applicant's full name, date of birth, Social Security number, and home address.

Instructions for Completing The Parents' Confidential Statement

Part I: The following instructions are for those PCS items that frequently cause problems. Complete the work sheet first, referring to the instructions. When you have completed the work sheet, transfer the information to the original copy to be submitted to the CSS. Some points to remember:

- *Complete all items legibly. Enter amounts in dollars; omit cents. If no information can be provided for an item, enter "None" in the space. Do not enter "same" or "all" where dollar amounts are requested.*

- *Explain all circled-number items and unusual family circumstances.*

- *Do not write in the gray areas marked for "CSS USE ONLY."*

One out of every three forms is returned to parents because it is incomplete. The principal causes have been failure of parents to explain *all* circled-number items and failure to provide estimates for the next year.

ITEM 1A: If the student applicant does not have a Social Security number, he should secure one through the nearest district Social Security office.

ITEM 2B: If you cannot describe your family situation using the boxes, explain in Part II.

ITEM 3: Enter the name, city, and state of each college and agency to which you want copies sent. If more than six colleges and agencies are to receive copies, list the additional colleges at the top of Part II.

ITEM (5B) : In Part II, indicate the relationship of the other dependent(s) to the student applicant, the total dollar amount of support you provide, and whether you claim the other dependent(s) for federal income tax purposes.

ITEM (7) : Salaries and wages before taxes: Total all income from employers (including bonuses, drawing accounts, and commissions) before payroll deductions for each of the years requested. Do not include reimbursements for business expenses. If the estimated salaries and wages for 1968 are more than $1,000 lower or higher than the salaries and wages for 1967, explain in Part II. If income is from several sources, itemize in Part II. If actual 1967 figures are not yet available, give your best estimate. Be sure to include an estimate of income for 1968 or the form will be returned to you.

ITEM (8) OTHER INCOME: Enter all dividends, interest, and gross income from self-employment or rented property, and so on. (Report in ITEMS 15 and (16) the amount of principal from which interest or dividends are received.) Also include in ITEM (8) payments from Social Security, pensions, child support, state aid, rations and quarters allowances, or aid from friends or relatives. In addition, enter an estimated amount for other nontaxable income such as free housing, food, services, and so on. Itemize or describe the sources of other income in Part II.

ITEM (9) BUSINESS EXPENSES: List only those business expenses that are paid from your salary or other income, *are not reimbursed*, and are allowable as federal income tax deductions. Itemize in Part II. *Business expenses that are not itemized by dollar amounts and those that are not acceptable federal income tax deductions will not be considered.*

ITEM (10) UNINSURED MEDICAL EXPENSES AND COST OF MEDICAL INSURANCE: Enter here the *sum* of all medical and dental expenses *not covered by insurance*. Include psychiatric and orthodontic care plus the cost of annual medical insurance premiums. *If the amount you enter here for 1968 exceeds $400, itemize (giving amounts for each item for both years) in Part II.*

ITEM (11) OTHER EXTRAORDINARY EXPENSES PAID: Enter here emergency or extraordinary family expenses, for example, alimony, child support, natural disaster expenses, termite control, tuition of parent if his course of study is directly connected with work, unreimbursed moving expenses, and so on. Itemize and explain in Part II, giving amounts for each item. (*Do not include payments for home appliances and furnishings, car, commutation expenses, household help, medical insurance, medical or dental expenses, retirement plan, contributions, etc.*)

ITEM 12 FEDERAL INCOME TAX PAID: Enter combined parents' total federal income tax paid for 1966 and parents' total federal income tax paid or estimated to be paid for 1967. Include the amount withheld from your wages. Enter "None" where appropriate. Do not leave blanks.

ITEM 13 HOME (IF OWNED): Enter market value of your home, not the tax-assessed valuation. If your home is part of a business property, enter here only the value of the dwelling. If your home is part of a farm, enter "None" in this item and see the instructions for the Farm Supplement.

ITEM (14) OTHER REAL ESTATE: This may be any real estate or property other than your own residence. Specify in Part II the type of real estate; if it is income-producing, include the total income received in ITEM (8) and tax-deductible business expenses in ITEM (9). Do not include property that is part of your business or farm.

ITEM 15 BANK ACCOUNTS (PERSONAL SAVINGS AND CHECKING): Enter total present personal savings and checking accounts balances. List in ITEM (18) any funds in the name of the student applicant.

ITEM (16) OTHER INVESTMENTS: Include the *present market value* of stocks, bonds, trusts, or other investments. Itemize nature and amount of holdings in Part II. Any *income* from these investments must be included in ITEM (8).

ITEM (17) INDEBTEDNESS: Do not include current bills for normal living expenses, charge accounts (regular or revolving), appliance loans, mortgages, auto indebtedness, insurance loans, or business or farm indebtedness. Do not include in this item expenses already paid or estimated to be incurred such as those listed in ITEMS (10) or (11).

ITEM (18) STUDENT'S OWN ASSETS: Enter the total assets the student has in his own name such as bank accounts, trust funds, inheritances, stocks and bonds, real estate, and current *cash* value (not face value) of annuities or educational insurance policies. Explain any restrictions on the use of these assets and indicate the amount currently available for college expenses in ITEM 20B . Do not include life insurance policies, stamp or coin collections, or the value of personal property.

ITEM 19 : If there are more than six children, list additional children in Part II.

Column 19A : Do not include room, board, fraternity fees, or travel.

Column 19B : List total amount of scholarship or gift aid awarded to each student, even if such aid exceeds entry in Column A.

ITEM 20 TOTAL RESOURCES FOR STUDENT FOR 1968-69: Estimate the maximum amount in dollars you can pay toward the student's total college expenses for one academic year (including tuition, room, board, fees, transportation, clothing, personal expenses, and so on). For ITEMS (20D) and (20E) indicate in Part II the monthly benefits received by or for the applicant from these sources. In addition, estimate and explain fully in Part II any financial aid the student may receive from other sources entered in ITEM (20F) : outside scholarships; gifts or loans from relatives, friends or organizations; government or foundation grants; or family educational insurance policies.

Part II: Explain here other special circumstances, such as divorce, separation, unemployment, illness, widowhood, special housing problems, or any other unusual circumstances that affect your income or standard of living. Note that the financial aspect of these circumstances must be shown in the appropriate items in Part I or they may not be considered. *If the applicant is self-supporting, his income should be entered here.*

COLLEGE SCHOLARSHIP SERVICE
Parents' Confidential Statement
Academic Year 1968–1969

Part I

(Do not send to CSS after September 1, 1968)

Submit this form after transferring information from work sheet

1A STUDENT APPLICANT

LAST NAME   FIRST NAME   MID. INIT.   (1) ☐ M   (2) ☐ F   SEX   MO. DAY YEAR DATE OF BIRTH   SOCIAL SECURITY NUMBER

1B ARE YOU A U.S. CITIZEN?   YES ☐   NO ☐   **1C** WHAT IS YOUR MARITAL STATUS?   SINGLE (1) ☐   MARRIED (2) ☐

2A STUDENT APPLICANT'S HOME ADDRESS

NUMBER AND STREET   CITY   STATE   ZIP CODE

2B APPLICANT NORMALLY LIVES WITH (CHECK ALL THAT APPLY)
(1) ☐ FATHER   (3) ☐ STEPFATHER   OR   (5) ☐ MAINTAINS OWN RESIDENCE
(2) ☐ MOTHER   (4) ☐ STEPMOTHER

CHECK IF ANY APPLY:
(6) ☐ FATHER IS DECEASED   (8) ☐ FATHER IS UNABLE TO WORK   (0) ☐ OTHER SPECIAL CIRCUMSTANCES (EXPLAIN)
(7) ☐ MOTHER IS DECEASED   (9) ☐ PARENTS ARE SEPARATED OR DIVORCED

3 LIST COLLEGES AND AGENCIES TO WHICH COPIES OF THIS FORM ARE TO BE SENT. (CHECK HERE IF YOU LIST MORE THAN FOUR) ☐

NAME	CITY	STATE	CSS USE ONLY	NAME	CITY	STATE	CSS USE ONLY

Father or Male Guardian

4A NAME OF FATHER   AGE

HOME ADDRESS

OCCUPATION AND TITLE

EMPLOYED BY: YEARS WITH FIRM

CHECK IF YOU WILL RECEIVE RETIREMENT BENEFITS FROM: (1) ☐ SOCIAL SECURITY (2) ☐ ANOTHER PLAN (3) ☐ NEITHER

Mother or Female Guardian

4B NAME OF MOTHER   AGE

HOME ADDRESS

OCCUPATION AND TITLE

EMPLOYED BY: YEARS WITH FIRM

CHECK IF YOU WILL RECEIVE RETIREMENT BENEFITS FROM: (1) ☐ SOCIAL SECURITY (2) ☐ ANOTHER PLAN (3) ☐ NEITHER

5A ENTER NUMBER OF CHILDREN YOU WILL CLAIM AS TAX DEPENDENTS ON YOUR FEDERAL INCOME TAX RETURN FOR 1967.....................

5B ENTER NUMBER OF OTHER DEPENDENTS RECEIVING FINANCIAL SUPPORT FROM FAMILY (DO NOT INCLUDE ANYONE ENTERED IN 4A, 4B AND 5A)..................

6 DO YOU OWN A BUSINESS OR ARE YOU A FARM OR RANCH OWNER, OPERATOR OR TENANT? (IF YES, COMPLETE BUSINESS OR FARM SUPPLEMENT)...... NO ☐ YES ☐

Parents' Annual Income and Expenses

	$ TOTAL 1966	$ TOTAL 1967	$ ESTIMATED 1968
7 SALARIES AND WAGES BEFORE TAXES A. FATHER, STEPFATHER, OR MALE GUARDIAN			
B. MOTHER, STEPMOTHER, OR FEMALE GUARDIAN			
8 OTHER INCOME			
9 BUSINESS EXPENSES			
10 UNINSURED MEDICAL EXPENSES (INCLUDE COST OF MEDICAL INSURANCE)			
11 OTHER EXTRAORDINARY EXPENSES PAID			

	FOR 1966	FOR 1967
12 FEDERAL INCOME TAX PAID	$	$

Parents' Assets and Liabilities

	A. PRESENT MARKET VALUE	B. UNPAID MORTGAGE
13 HOME (IF OWNED) YR. PURCHASED 19___ PRICE $___	$	$
14 OTHER REAL ESTATE		
15 BANK ACCOUNTS (PERSONAL SAVINGS AND CHECKING)		
16 OTHER INVESTMENTS (PRESENT MARKET VALUE)		
17 INDEBTEDNESS (DO NOT INCLUDE MORTGAGE, AUTO LOANS, INSURANCE LOANS OR CHARGE ACCOUNTS)		
18 STUDENT'S OWN ASSETS (INCLUDE SAVINGS, ENDOWMENTS, TRUST FUNDS, STOCKS AND BONDS)		

CSS USE ONLY   B/F   A.   B.   C.

19 LIST BELOW ALL CHILDREN, STUDENT APPLICANT FIRST   CHECK HERE IF YOU LIST MORE THAN SIX ☐

FIRST NAME ONLY	AGE	NAME OF PRESENT SCHOOL OR COLLEGE (1967-68)	WILL HE ATTEND SAME SCHOOL IN 1968-69?	YEAR IN SCHOOL 1967-68	TUITION PLUS FEES 1967-68 (DO NOT INCLUDE ROOM AND BOARD)	TOTAL AMOUNT OF SCHOLARSHIP OR GIFT AID, 1967-68
APPLICANT						

ENCLOSE CHECK OR MONEY ORDER PAYABLE TO COLLEGE SCHOLARSHIP SERVICE: $2.50 FOR FIRST COLLEGE OR AGENCY LISTED AND $2.00 FOR EACH ADDITIONAL COLLEGE OR AGENCY.

AMOUNT ENCLOSED $___

20 TOTAL RESOURCES FOR STUDENT FOR ACADEMIC YEAR 1968-1969

A. FROM PARENTS' INCOME AND ASSETS.................... $___
B. FROM STUDENT'S ASSETS....................
C. FROM STUDENT'S SUMMER EARNINGS....................
D. FROM VETERANS BENEFITS....................
E. FROM SOCIAL SECURITY BENEFITS....................
F. FROM OTHER SOURCES....................
TOTAL....................

(DO NOT WRITE IN THIS SPACE)

Part II

In the space below explain all circled items and any special family circumstances the college should know.

Parents' Certification and Authorization

We declare that the information reported on this form, to the best of our knowledge and belief, is true, correct, and complete. We authorize transmittal of this form to the colleges and agencies named in Item 3 and its use by the College Scholarship Service (CSS) as described in the *Instructions*. The CSS or any of the colleges and agencies named to receive copies of this form have our permission to verify the information reported. If requested, we agree to send to the CSS, or to any college or agency named to receive a copy of this form, an official photostatic copy of our latest federal income tax return obtained from the appropriate district office of the United States Internal Revenue Service.

Signatures of both parents (or guardian) {_____

_____   *Date* _____

COLLEGE SCHOLARSHIP SERVICE

Parents' Confidential Statement–Supplement Section
Academic Year 1968-1969
(Do Not Send To CSS After September 1, 1968)

GENERAL INFORMATION

The Supplement Section of the Parents' Confidential Statement (PCS) is to be completed by parents who own a business or who are farm or ranch owners, operators, or tenants. The Supplement (A for business owners, B for farmers or ranchers) must be returned to the College Scholarship Service (CSS). You can avoid delay in complete and accurate reporting to the colleges and agencies by including the Supplement *with* Parts I and II. If you have already submitted Parts I and II, send the Supplement to the CSS office where you filed them. The correct address may be found at the bottom of this page.

◀ **Instructions for Completing PCS Supplement A**

Complete the work sheet of Supplement A before transferring your entries to the copy that is to be submitted to the CSS. It is suggested that you use current and past federal income tax returns for reference in completing the Supplement.

In the case of partnerships or corporations where items are not readily separable as to ownership, indicate the total amounts in the spaces provided, and then report your percentage share and amount of ownership in the appropriate spaces. The expenses listed on this Supplement should not be included in Item ⑨ on Part I of the Parents' Confidential Statement.

Business Assets and Indebtedness

Current Assets: Add the cash in your business account, cash value of inventories, and other current assets. This total is to be entered on Line D.

Subtract any reserve for bad debts from notes and accounts receivable. Enter difference on Line G.

Total current assets are then listed by adding Lines D and G.

Fixed Assets: List all buildings and land associated with this business. If your home is physically a part of the business establishment, do not include the value of the dwelling.

Add present market value of equipment, land and buildings, and other fixed assets. This total is to be entered on Line L. Subtract the listed reserve for depreciation from this total and enter difference on Line N. Add Line H and Line N and enter this figure on Line O.

Indebtedness: Add business accounts and notes payable, accrued business expenses, and any mortgage against the business property. Enter this total on Line S.

Indicate your share of the total net capital value of the business (Line T) on Line U. Express this as your percentage of ownership on Line V.

Operating Income and Expenses

Enter the amounts for the various entries listed, giving specific sources of gross income and business expenses as requested. If parents receive a salary or drawing account from the business, the total amount should be listed on the Supplement and entered in Item ⑦ on Part I in the column headed "Total 1967."

Subtract entry on Line X from that on Line W and indicate this as "Net Income from Business, 1967." Enter your share (the percentage and dollar value) of this amount. Transfer this amount to Item ⑧ on Part I in the column headed "Total 1967."

Using the same procedure as given above for computing "Net Income from Business, 1967," compute "Net Income from Business, 1966" and enter this figure on Line Z.

COLLEGE SCHOLARSHIP SERVICE
Box 176, Princeton, New Jersey 08540
Box 881, Evanston, Illinois 60204 • Box 1025, Berkeley, California 94701

Figure 14

Supplement A

To be completed by owners of businesses

(**Do not send to CSS after September 1, 1968**)

Submit this form after transferring information from work sheet

STUDENT APPLICANT																				(1) ☐ M (2) ☐ F					

LAST NAME — FIRST NAME — MID. INIT. — SEX — MO. DAY YEAR — DATE OF BIRTH — SOCIAL SECURITY NUMBER

LIST COLLEGES AND AGENCIES TO WHICH COPIES OF THIS FORM ARE TO BE SENT. (CHECK HERE IF YOU LIST MORE THAN FOUR) ☐

NAME — CITY — STATE — CSS USE ONLY — NAME — CITY — STATE — CSS USE ONLY

NAME OF PARENT'S BUSINESS _____

BUSINESS PRODUCT OR SERVICE _____

TYPE OF BUSINESS (CHECK ONE)   ☐ CORPORATION   ☐ PARTNERSHIP   ☐ INDIVIDUAL PROPRIETOR

ADDRESS OF BUSINESS _____
STREET — CITY — STATE

STATEMENT OF BUSINESS ASSETS AND INDEBTEDNESS AS OF .... _____ _____
MONTH   YEAR

ENTRIES BELOW SHOULD NOT REPEAT INFORMATION GIVEN IN ITEMS 13 , (14) , 15 , (16) , OR (17) ON PART I OF THE PCS.

CURRENT ASSETS:

A. CASH (BUSINESS ACCOUNT ONLY)...................... $_____

B. INVENTORIES.. _____

C. OTHER CURRENT ASSETS............................ _____

D.   TOTAL (LINES A, B, C)............................ $_____

E. NOTES AND ACCOUNTS RECEIVABLE.................. $_____

F. RESERVE FOR BAD DEBTS............................ _____

G.   SUBTRACT (LINE F) FROM (LINE E)............... _____

H.   TOTAL CURRENT ASSETS (LINE D) PLUS (LINE G)............ $_____

FIXED ASSETS:

I. EQUIPMENT.. $_____

J. LAND AND BUILDINGS.................................. _____

K. OTHER FIXED ASSETS.................................. _____

L.   TOTAL (LINES I, J, K)............................... $_____

M. RESERVE FOR DEPRECIATION.......................... _____

N.   SUBTRACT (LINE M) FROM (LINE L)............... _____

O.   TOTAL VALUE (LINE H) PLUS (LINE N). ENTER THIS FIGURE HERE........ $_____

INDEBTEDNESS:

P. ACCOUNTS AND NOTES PAYABLE...................... $_____

Q. ACCRUED EXPENSES, ETC.............................. _____

R. MORTGAGE (BUSINESS ONLY).......................... _____

S.   TOTAL INDEBTEDNESS (LINES P, Q, R), ENTER THIS FIGURE HERE........... $_____

T.   TOTAL NET CAPITAL VALUE, SUBTRACT (LINE S) FROM (LINE O)............ $_____

U. YOUR SHARE OF THE TOTAL NET CAPITAL VALUE OF BUSINESS AS LISTED ON LINE T.. $_____

V. EXPRESS ENTRY MADE ON LINE U AS A PERCENTAGE OF OWNERSHIP ENTER THIS PERCENTAGE FIGURE HERE.................... _____ %

OPERATING INCOME AND EXPENSES OF BUSINESS FOR CALENDAR YEAR 1967

GROSS INCOME (SPECIFY SOURCES):

.... $_____
.... _____
.... _____
.... _____

W. TOTAL INCOME.................. $_____

EXPENSES (SPECIFY SOURCES):

NUMBER OF NON-FAMILY EMPLOYEES _____

YOUR WAGES OR DRAWING ACCOUNT. $_____

WAGES PAID TO OTHER FAMILY MEMBERS......................... _____

WAGES PAID TO NON-FAMILY EMPLOYEES........................ _____

RENT.................................... _____

OTHER.................................. _____

.... _____

.... _____

.... _____

DEPRECIATION (1967 ONLY).......... _____

X. TOTAL EXPENSES................. $_____

NET INCOME FROM BUSINESS, 1967:

SUBTRACT (LINE X) FROM (LINE W).. $_____

OF WHICH YOUR SHARE IS........... _____ %

Y. OR.................................. $_____

ENTRY ON LINE Y SHOULD BE INCLUDED IN ITEM (8) AND EXPLAINED ON PART II OF THE PCS.

NET INCOME FROM BUSINESS, 1966:

Z. NET INCOME.................... $_____

SIGNATURES OF BOTH PARENTS (OR GUARDIAN) _____

DATE _____

Figure 15

Instructions for Completing PCS Supplement B ▶

Complete the work sheet of Supplement B before transferring your entries to the copy that is to be submitted to the CSS. It is suggested that you use current and past federal income tax returns for reference in completing the Supplement.

In the case of partnerships or corporations where items are not readily separable as to ownership, indicate the total amounts in the spaces provided, and then report your percentage share and amount of ownership in the appropriate spaces.

Section I. *Location and Description of Farm*

Describe the location of your farm in the spaces provided. If you own farms other than the one described in this section, describe the location and acreage of each on a separate sheet. Use the present local market value of your farm acreage to indicate a per-acre value and list the principal income-producing products from your farm enterprise (i.e., dairy, beef, hogs, grain, etc.). If your farm is a partnership or a corporation, indicate this information as well as your percentage of ownership.

Section II. *Farm Value: Inventory of Farm Assets*

Report the number and present market value of all farm assets you own or are purchasing.

If your home is located on your farm, be sure to include it on Line 1 in the value of your land and building.

Report the present market value of your farm machinery and equipment at its purchase price minus the depreciation taken against it. Federal income tax Form 1040-F, Part V, will be helpful in determining this amount.

In listing the numbers of your livestock, grain inventories, and other farm assets, you should estimate as accurately as possible their current market value in the spaces provided.

Section III. *Farm Indebtedness*

The indebtedness items in Section III pertain only to your farm operation, not to personal debts. Enter current total amount owed in the column headed "Current Debts" and then indicate the amount of payment (principal plus interest) which will be made against each item during 1968.

Section IV. *Farm Income*

Report your farm income and expenses for each of the years indicated in the columns in Section IV. This information can be taken from Part IV of your federal income tax form 1040-F. For any of the years for which the federal income tax returns have not been completed, estimate the information as accurately as possible using your farm records.

Note: If farm income is reported on the accrual basis, the required information for this section can be found in Part VII, federal income tax Form 1040-F. In this case, you should disregard Items 1 and 2 in Section IV on Supplement B, and begin your entries by listing Gross Profits.

The net amount of gains and losses from sales or exchanges of livestock and farm machinery (Item 9) can be transferred from the federal income tax Form 1040-D. Report all gains or losses at their full amount. Do not include other property sales or exchanges reported on 1040-D.

Calculate "Estimated 1968 Farm Income" in Item 11 of Section IV by averaging the total farm income entries for 1965, 1966, and 1967. This figure is to be transferred to Item ⑧ on Part I of the PCS under the column headed "Estimated 1968."

Do not include farm expenses as part of business expenses in Item ⑨ on Part I.

Section V. *Farm Benefits*

Describe your family dwelling arrangement by checking one of the three items in Section V.

Check whether or not your family receives from your farm any of the products listed in Item 2.

Supplement B

To be completed by farm or ranch owners, operators, or tenants

(Do not send to CSS after September 1, 1968)

Submit this form after transferring information from work sheet

STUDENT APPLICANT						
LAST NAME	FIRST NAME	MID. INIT.	SEX (1) ☐ M (2) ☐ F	DATE OF BIRTH MO. DAY YEAR	SOCIAL SECURITY NUMBER

LIST COLLEGES AND AGENCIES TO WHICH COPIES OF THIS FORM ARE TO BE SENT. (CHECK HERE IF YOU LIST MORE THAN FOUR) ☐

NAME	CITY	STATE	CSS USE ONLY	NAME	CITY	STATE	CSS USE ONLY

I. LOCATION AND DESCRIPTION OF FARM:

1. LOCATED IN THE TOWNSHIP OF_____IN THE COUNTY OF_____IN THE STATE OF_____
ON_____ROAD_____MILES_____FROM NEAREST CITY OR TOWN, WHICH IS_____
(DIRECTION)

2. TOTAL ACRES OWNED_____PRESENT MARKET VALUE PER ACRE $_____

3. NUMBER OF ACRES:

	OWNED	RENTED FROM OTHERS	RENTED TO OTHERS
TILLABLE........			
NONTILLABLE PASTURE.........			
WOODLAND AND WASTE..........			
TOTAL.........			

4. NUMBER OF ACRES: IN TRUCK CROPS_____ IN PRODUCTIVE ORCHARDS_____ UNDER IRRIGATION_____

5. PRINCIPAL PRODUCTS:
_____
_____
_____

6. YOUR FARM BUSINESS IS (CHECK ONE):
☐ A PARTNERSHIP ☐ A CORPORATION
PERCENT OF YOUR OWNERSHIP_____%

II. FARM VALUE: INVENTORY OF FARM ASSETS AS OF_____

MONTH_____ YEAR_____

	NUMBER	PRESENT MARKET VALUE
1. LAND AND BUILDINGS.........................		$_____
2. FARM MACHINERY AND EQUIPMENT*............		_____
3. BEEF CATTLE............................		_____
4. DAIRY CATTLE............................		_____
5. HOGS..................................		_____
6. SHEEP.................................		_____
7. POULTRY (SIZE OF FLOCK)..................		_____
8. GRAIN (BUSHELS)........................		_____
9. HAY AND STRAW (BALES)..................		_____
10. OTHER FARM PRODUCTS ON HAND:		_____

11. OTHER FARM ASSETS:
_____
_____

12. ACCOUNTS RECEIVABLE................. _____
13. TOTAL FARM VALUE...................... $_____

*COMPUTE AT ORIGINAL COST MINUS DEPRECIATION

III. FARM INDEBTEDNESS AS OF_____

MONTH_____ YEAR_____

	CURRENT DEBTS	PAYMENT DUE IN 1968*
1. MORTGAGES ON FARM..............	$_____	$_____
2. NOTES PAYABLE TO BANKS..............	_____	_____
3. NOTES PAYABLE TO PCA...............	_____	_____
4. NOTES PAYABLE TO INDIVIDUALS.........	_____	_____
5. BALANCES OWED ON FARM MACHINERY AND EQUIPMENT.....	_____	_____
6. FARM CHARGE ACCOUNTS OWED (FEED, FERTILIZER, ETC.)...............	_____	_____

7. OTHER FARM DEBTS (SPECIFY):
_____
_____

8. TOTAL FARM INDEBTEDNESS....... $_____ $_____

*INCLUDE PRINCIPAL AND INTEREST IN ENTRIES

IV. FARM INCOME:

THE ENTRIES BELOW CAN BE TRANSFERRED FROM PART IV, FEDERAL INCOME TAX FORM 1040-F (IF ON THE ACCRUAL BASIS, TAKE FROM PART VII, 1040-F)

	1965	1966	1967
1. SALE OF LIVESTOCK, PRODUCE RAISED, AND OTHER FARM INCOME......................... $	_____	$_____	$_____
2. PROFIT (OR LOSS) ON SALE OF PURCHASED LIVESTOCK AND OTHER PURCHASED ITEMS.....................	_____	_____	_____
3. GROSS PROFITS—ADD (ITEMS 1 AND 2).............	_____	_____	_____
4. FARM EXPENSES.............................	_____	_____	_____
5. DEPRECIATION.............................	_____	_____	_____
6. OTHER FARM DEDUCTIONS........................	_____	_____	_____
7. TOTAL DEDUCTIONS—ADD (ITEMS 4, 5, AND 6)........	_____	_____	_____
8. NET FARM PROFIT—SUBTRACT (ITEM 7) FROM (ITEM 3)	_____	_____	_____
9. NET CAPITAL GAINS OR LOSSES FROM THE SALES OR EXCHANGES OF LIVESTOCK AND FARM MACHINERY (LIVESTOCK AND FARM MACHINERY SHARE OF AMOUNTS ON FEDERAL INCOME TAX FORM 1040-D)...	_____	_____	_____
10. TOTAL FARM INCOME—ADD (ITEMS 8 AND 9)......... $	_____	$_____	$_____

11. ESTIMATED 1968 FARM INCOME $_____ (AVERAGE OF 1965, 1966, AND 1967 TOTALS IN ITEM 10)
NOTE: ENTER ESTIMATED 1968 FARM INCOME IN ITEM ⑧ ON PART I OF THE PCS.

V. FARM BENEFITS:

1. FAMILY DWELLING (CHECK ONE):
☐ OWN HOUSE
☐ CASH-RENT HOUSE
☐ RENT-FREE TENANT HOUSE

2. DOES YOUR FAMILY RECEIVE ANY OF THE FOLLOWING PRODUCTS FROM YOUR FARM?

MILK ☐ YES ☐ NO
BEEF ☐ YES ☐ NO
PORK ☐ YES ☐ NO

SIGNATURES OF BOTH PARENTS (OR GUARDIAN)
_____
_____

DATE_____

In addition to the federal national defense student loan program and several state loan programs, there are loans that are controlled by individual colleges, commercial loans that operate much like loans for an automobile or TV set, and loans from interested groups and agencies. These are discussed in detail in chapter VII. Of more interest to parents than to students is the comparison of fifteen state loan plans found in figure 16.

One loan program deserves special mention because of its acceptance by institutions of higher learning and the lending institutions that participate in the program. It is United Student Aid Funds, Inc., a private, non-profit corporation that has established a nationwide program similar to those sponsored by state governments. United Student Aid Funds, Inc. insures its lenders and borrows from a guarantee fund created originally by contributions from foundations, corporations, and similar sources. With these gifts as a base, colleges are invited to deposit funds with the corporation, which creates a reserve to be used in guaranteeing loans to students attending any of those colleges. As of the beginning of the 1965–66 academic year, more than seven hundred colleges and seven thousand lending institutions participated in the program.

The terms that govern United Student Aid Funds, Inc. loans are comparable to other loans: 6 percent simple interest charged on the amount with the first payment due four months after graduation, and the repayment period extending to fifty-four months.

The application is reviewed by the lending institution for its approval, and then to the corporation for its guarantee. The college may stipulate that the funds be paid directly to the borrower or to the college itself. The college provides periodic reports on the borrower's academic progress, but the collection responsibility is accepted by the bank. In the event of default, the loan is subrogated to the corporation, which attempts to collect on the account.

Insurance Programs. These programs are usually more costly than other means of paying for education. Insurance is first insurance and secondly savings; it is not designed primarily for contributing to the savings of a family.

Savings. Money does not inflate and, therefore, becomes less valuable over the years; money saved for ten years may not purchase as much education as it would have purchased when first saved. Wise investment of money would have purchased more education at a later day than did savings.

Mutual Funds. Mutual funds have established over the years an acceptable record of interest payment and capital investment. There is a risk in this type of program, but, generally, an investor stands to gain as the nation's economy gains. An investor stands to gain or lose depending on the inflationary situation of government. If you expect money to buy less goods at the time your son or daughter is in college, then mutual funds may be worth further consideration. If you feel otherwise, or think that many companies and corporations are going to experience financial difficulty or go bankrupt, then the outlook of mutual funds as a source for guaranteed financial assistance for college is poor. The interest on capital is equal to the interest earned on savings, and it could be more.

Deferred-Payment Plans. Some colleges have deferred plans whereby parents start paying tuition while the child is still in elementary school and pay for a college education like insurance. The advantage to this approach is that parents pay tuition cost at today's "market," and not what tuition will cost ten or twelve years hence.

Parents Beware

Parents want the very best for their children. Educating their children is of prime consideration for most parents. They will leave no stone unturned to help their teen-agers to attend college. Parents want them to make good grades, and they want them to be prepared for the best college they can attend. Indeed, parents should not rest until the talents of their children are fully developed. But parents ask: "Isn't this problem of education too important to leave to the immature judgment of children?" "Who should help set goals?" "Is one parent more effective than another?" "What is the aim of education?" "Are we to equate an 'A' in arithmetic with an 'educated' man?" In short, parents want to know what they can do and what they should not do to help prepare their sons and daughters to achieve academic success in college.

First of all, parents should be aware of actions and attitudes that may be harmful. With the present-day emphasis on going to college, parents should be careful not to place too much pressure on their teen-agers to achieve above their ability in every subject, to join every extracurricular activity, or to plan only for highly selective colleges and universities. One of the more serious ways a parent, with good intentions, can damage the attitudes of their children toward college is to build false hopes about a particular prestige college or the likelihood of receiving a scholarship, or both. Parents who, in a survey, reported their children at the top of their class expected them to attend college. They planned on their obtaining a scholarship and saw little opportunity for failure in college. Only 80 percent of the parents who reported that their children earned average grades expected them to attend college. Grades, as viewed by parents, and expectations concerning college attendance are strongly related, but parents should be realistic in their expectations.

Lofty goals are admirable, but not at the expense of your children's best interests. You can do your teen-agers a grave injustice by expecting too much of them. You can cause them to rebel against the idea of attend-

Comparison of 15 state loan programs

Figure 16

Program	Annual Loan Limits	Minimum Monthly Repayments	Percent of Guaranty	May Loans Be Used *Outside* of State?	May Part-time Students Borrow?
California State Scholarship and Loan Commission	$1,000 year	$30 month	100% principal	Yes	No, full-time only
Connecticut Foundation for Financial Assistance to Higher Education	1,500 year	None	100% principal and interest	Yes	May borrow regardless of credits
College Student Loan Plan Indiana State Scholarship Commission	1,000 (undergraduate) 1,500 (graduate)	None	100% principal	Yes	No, full-time only
Louisiana Higher Education Assistance Commission	1,000 year	None	90% principal and interest	USAF handles out-of-state loans	No, full-time only
Massachusetts Higher Education Assistance Corporation	1,000 (undergraduate) 1,500 (graduate)	None	90% principal and interest	Yes	Must be at least half-time
Michigan Higher Education Assistance Authority	1,000 (undergraduate) 1,500 (graduate)	$30 month	100% principal	Yes	Must be at least half-time
New Hampshire Higher Education Assistance Foundation	1,000 (undergraduate) 1,500 (graduate)	None	80% principal and interest	Yes	Must be at least half-time
New Jersey Higher Education Assistance Authority	1,000 (freshman and sophomore) 1,250 (junior) 1,500 (senior and graduate)	$30 month	100% principal and interest	Yes	No, full-time only
New York Higher Education Assistance Corporation	750 (freshman) 1,000 (sophomore) 1,250 (junior) 1,500 (senior and graduate)	None	100% principal and interest	Yes	Must be at least half-time
North Carolina State Education Assistance Authority	1,000 (undergraduate) 1,500 (graduate)	$30 month	Loans made through state-sponsored nonprofit foundation	Yes	Yes, but priority to full-time students
Ohio Higher Education Assistance Commission	1,000 (undergraduate) 1,500 (graduate)	$30 month	100% principal and interest	Yes	Must be at least half-time
Pennsylvania Higher Education Assistance Agency	1,000 year	$30 month recommended	100% principal and interest	Yes	Must be full-time undergraduate and at least half-time graduate. $500 maximum.
Rhode Island Higher Education Assistance Corporation	1,000 (undergraduate) 1,500 (graduate)	$30 month	80% principal	Yes	Must be at least half-time
Virginia State Education Assistance Authority	1,000 (undergraduate) 1,500 (graduate)	$30 month	90% principal	No, USAF handles out-of-state loans	No, full-time only
Wisconsin Higher Education Aids Commission	1,000 (undergraduate) 1,500 (graduate)	$30 month	None, direct program	Yes	Must be at least half-time

ing college by holding on to unrealistic goals. Some capable students have been known to lose interest in attending college or have developed psychological problems when they felt they did not live up to the expectations of their parents. There is evidence suggesting that mothers, who are not highly achievement motivated, are usually more effective than fathers in helping students prepare for college, because mothers tend to exert less pressure for specific goals.

Parents should also remember that it is the sons and daughters, not the mothers and fathers, who will enter college. Although parents are becoming more informed about college because of the abundance of information on the subject, the college image held by parents is about twenty to twenty-five years out of date. It is sometimes more difficult to change parents' preconceived notions of college procedures and policies than it is to educate their children.

Here are some specific "parent beware" items. Some may apply to your individual situation. They are offered for your consideration and may serve to prevent disappointment. As an interested parent, you should beware of:

Too much concern about a place for your son or daughter in college. There will be a place for your teen-ager if he or she is of college caliber. There is a college program to fit almost every ability level.

Your own personal motives. Attending college should not be only the parents' idea. In general, parents should give their children more freedom in helping make the choices that affect their lives, but parents can provide perspective and mature judgment.

Putting off until tomorrow the planning of your teen-ager's education. To be of maximum assistance to your young man or young lady, you should become informed on the objectives, policies, and practices of colleges that may be selected. Review vocational and career materials and college catalogs with your teen-ager.

Expecting your boy or girl to be academically and emotionally ready for college, unless they have been prepared. Parents have a responsibility in these kinds of development. You should do all that is within reason to prepare your child for college, realizing that you stop at the college door. You can't go to school for them. From this point on they must make the decisions. The best you can do is prepare your teen-ager for making them.

Worrying about what might have been if the decision to go to college had been reached earlier. Concentrate on what can yet be done. Visit the high school counselor and get a realistic look at your child's potential. Ask teachers to suggest activities that will help stimulate interest and develop needed abilities in your son or daughter.

Picking the college for your young man or lady. Parents should not consciously or unconsciously pick the career field to be followed or the college to be attended. Just because Aunt Matilda went to Snider U. is not a good reason for your son to go there. The parent whose college ambitions outrun his child's abilities should seek assistance from the school's guidance office in gaining a realistic picture of the kind of college the student is suited for. Help your teen-ager make a realistic choice.

Expecting too much from a college education. Regardless of how many ivy-covered walls a college has, or how many of its alumni are listed in *Who's Who,* or how many Rhodes Scholars it has graduated, it cannot guarantee your boy or girl academic or career success. However, some colleges have better reputations than others, and this fact most certainly should be considered.

Waiting to arrange the financial program. This is one area of college planning that is clearly within the jurisdiction of parents. Sons and daughters of parents who plan a program to meet rising costs go to college.

What Parents Can Do in the Home

There are many things you can do that will prepare your children for college. You can be understanding of their interests. You can listen to their concerns, be a sounding-board for their ideas, and recognize signs of talent, interest, and ability. You can appreciate their abilities and their limitations. You can attempt to see their problems and concerns through teen-age eyes. You can accept and love your children as individual human beings. You can provide purpose by instilling and nurturing in them the "dream" of going to college. You can encourage good study habits, better grades, and wide interests and participation. You can provide a place for study in the home. You can study college requirements and become informed of admissions requirements and differences in institutions. You can open new horizons of interest and knowledge through travel and by taking them to cultural centers and exhibits. You can gain an understanding of teenagers' characteristics, and probably find your teen-agers to be normal in most respects. You can recognize the importance of "their" group, and realize that social pressures are at their peak during the teen-age years.

Parents can be of most help to their teen-agers by understanding certain factors about college, and encouraging a wise selection of colleges to which to apply. Here are hints to help you help your teen-agers:

1. Develop your child's personality through planned activities including travel, books and other reading materials, and practical experience in potential career fields, art, music, etc. Many colleges say they prefer the "well rounded" student to the "ivory towered, head in the clouds" type. Stimulate interest in, appreciation for, and positive attitudes toward college as a means to a more desirable and productive life.

2. Encourage good study habits. Provide a place and time for study in the home. Don't be lulled

into thinking studying is the school's jurisdiction. This is no place for a hands-off policy. Your child's future is at stake and facilitating good study habits is the very least you can do to start him on the right road.

3. Assist your teen-ager, through frank discussions, to select one or more occupational fields that are suitable and of interest to him. This may be done by reading, working, visiting, and inquiring about fields in which he has some interest. Watch out for the images! Movies, T.V. and newspapers would have all lawyers highly successful, and doctors working with nurses in freshly starched uniforms and never lose a patient. These images are not true-to-life.

4. Help your son or daughter become crystal-clear on the purpose of attending college. Take time to sit down with your college-bound youngster and discuss the values of going to college. The student should be given the opportunity to express his views on the subject; through frank discussion you can help clarify foggy thinking.

5. Keep an open mind on the selection of a college. Consider all the factors with your teen-ager first, then let him make a choice. Don't put the horse before the cart. There is a tendency, particularly for parents who attended college, to say the college they attended is the one their children should attend. Research has shown this is true even when the parents did not attend the college they chose first:

6. Brace yourself: costs are rising and will increase by about 50 percent by the end of the decade. Plan a financial program; start saving early.

7. Although enrollments are rising year by year, don't get too discouraged, and don't let your teen-ager become too discouraged if he is qualified for college and is interested in attending. He can be admitted to an accredited college, and it need not be a prestige college. The prestige colleges will become less influential as more and more students graduate from other colleges and achieve positions of authority in industry, business, and the academic world.

8. Encourage and assist your son or daughter in collecting and reviewing information about colleges, and consider their important differences. More colleges have openings at the junior and senior levels than at the freshman and sophomore levels. This may be reason enough to consider junior colleges. If a junior college is located in your community, it will offer the advantages of convenience and considerable savings.

9. Discuss the problem of college-planning freely with your son or daughter. It is very important that you keep an objective and open line of communication on this subject. It is easy to become too personally involved for objective analysis of your child and sound decision-making.

10. Prepare your teen-ager for the academic and social adjustment that will come when he goes away to college. The college dropout rate is high and is caused by many reasons. Reasons stemming from academic difficulty are given by only one-half of the students who drop out of college.

What Parents Can Do in the School

Schools do for children only what parents have delegated them to do. The home and school are in partnership for the development and welfare of your children. The home has the greatest influence on the development of the child's personality, while the school is charged with the intellectual development of the child. You have a right, as a taxpayer, to be concerned with, and informed about, your school and to see that it is developing the capacities, talents, and interests of your teen-agers.

There are many things you can do to influence the school. Here are a few to serve as guides for interested parents:

1. Take an active interest in the school. Develop an understanding of its philosophy and objectives. Learn what your school offers. Get to know the administrators, counselors, and teachers.

2. Insist on a sound education, rich in the basic foundations needed by students who aspire to attend college. In addition, the schools should have activities for student participation in many fields of interest.

3. Suggest an enrichment program. An enrichment program is one designed for interested, talented students or ones with a particular aptitude that should be developed at a deeper level.

4. Insist on a quality guidance *program,* not just a guidance counselor. The first and foremost consideration for a good guidance program is a director and sufficient number of guidance counselors who are well prepared and competent in the field. Having only a counselor in a school falls far short of having a comprehensive guidance program; facilities, materials, and staff are needed. Staff freedom is needed, too, to do the job of studying students, determining their capabilities, and recommending enrichment and remedial programs on both individual and group bases.

What Parents Can Do in the Community

Local communities have a responsibility to recognize the potential value of their children by providing the necessary financial support and environment for their development.

Most communities have valuable resources that can be used in the further development of college-bound students. The school can point out some of these resources, but, for the most part, leadership will come from interested parents, groups, and organizations concerned about the academic preparation of youth in the community. Even if local groups organize activities for teen-agers, it is still the parents and other interested persons who initiate, plan, and conduct them.

Ideas you may wish to consider when locating community resources are:

1. Look upon the community as an extension of the home and school. The community cannot do for your teen-ager what the home and school can do, but it can provide facilities for developing interests, jobs for gaining experience, and people to serve as representatives of occupational areas.
2. Youth programs of churches, divisions of civic clubs, etc., are of value, and, with the assistance of parents, can make a contribution.
3. The community serves as a testing ground for student interests and capabilities in potential career fields. For example, science fairs have done much to stimulate interest and develop skills in science. Unquestionably, they have been the key that made the difference between going or not going to college for many students planning to study science.
4. Discover agencies and people in the community that can assist in bringing out latent talent. Music, dancing, surveying, and accounting, for example, are all worthy of development. If it appears that your teen-ager has potential in one of these fields, seek out persons, groups, or agencies where he or she can gain experience, participate, and read and learn more about them.
5. Parents can organize new activities in existing organizations. Don't miss an opportunity if it presents itself!

Chapter Eleven

How Can I Adjust to College Life?

Now that you have been admitted to college, it is up to you to stay in. Life on campus is not like life at home. Your success and happiness on campus will be influenced by how easily and how well you adjust to it. Adjusting to college life can be both an academic and a social problem. Your abilities, both intellectual and nonintellectual, will be taxed. For some of you, it will be the first time you will be living and working with others full time. Dormitory life is different from living at home. During your stay on campus you will have a new and different kind of freedom, but you will also have a new and different kind of responsibility. You will be expected to behave as a self-disciplined young man or woman. You very likely will have a stranger for a roommate who will become a close lifelong friend and with whom you will share some of your happiest experiences, as well as your money, clothes, and books. The better you adapt to these new situations, the more you will enjoy college.

To make the transition to college life, you must get acquainted with the college and your fellow students. You will get to know other students during freshman orientation, and by participating in clubs and other organizations. A college or university must have rules to adequately care for the ten thousand or more students on its campus. Deans establish social and academic rules to protect students and to prevent chaos. They want to keep you in college by actively working at what might be termed "freshmen conservation." You must learn the rules about the use of a car on campus, how to register for classes, how to drop and change courses, and how late you may stay out of the dorm without being penalized.

Many students have problems in planning the use of their money and time. You will probably find there is not enough of either. You will need to adjust your spending habits. Learning to plan ahead must come early if you are to remain in college.

What you do on campus will become a part of a very important permanent record. You should strive for above-average work. In a very real sense, college is preparation for life. Four years may seem like a long time, but college records will remain with you much longer. You will want to plan a balanced program while you are in college. A satisfactory academic record without some extracurricular activities to reveal your interests and personality is not too impressive to employers. Make the best of your opportunities while you are on the campus.

You are probably aware that as many as one-half of the students who enter college fail to graduate. A higher percentage of students attending public colleges and universities drop out of college than do students who attend highly selective or private institutions. Insufficient funds, inability to meet academic standards, lack of motivation, poor study habits, unwillingness to spend the necessary effort and time studying, lack of purpose, and change in occupational or professional objectives are common reasons why students quit college. A principal reason for students not completing college is that they are not prepared to adjust to college life. Experience has shown that more freshmen drop out of college than do other students. Younger students discontinue their college studies more frequently than do older students. Students who have skipped grades in elementary and secondary school have more difficulty than those who have not been advanced. The one element in all college dropouts is immaturity. The more mature a person is, the better able he is to adapt to college.

Getting Into the Swing of Things

You will have fun at college! You will be working and studying with people of your own age and ability, with some who have similar interests. Since a college education prepares students for living, as well as for earning a living, you should participate in the social life of the college you attend. This is the purpose of the many valuable activities found on college campuses. The college supplies you with an academic advisor, but you will get no help from him in planning your social life. It is up to you to make the most of your opportunities. Most students who are satisfied with college have made the effort necessary for success.[1] Once you get into the swing of campus activities you will be a happier student, and a better one, too.

If you are like most college students, you may be a little homesick sometime during your first semester in college. The best prevention and antidote for initial loneliness at college is to immerse yourself in campus activities. Get to know your fellow students. Don't be shy. Take the initiative and make the first move. You are all in the same boat and other students are wishing that someone would break the ice. Get to know something about them, where they live, what they do in their spare time, and what their talents are. In this way you will find that you have much in common with many students on campus.

College is an ideal place to alter your social behavior if you have been reluctant to be outgoing in meeting people and participating in social activities. Early in your first semester, the college will hold mixers and socials. Many clubs will have open-house parties and smokers. Fraternities and sororities will hold rushing functions. These activities help you make many new acquaintances.

A technique that will work throughout your campus stay is to attend meetings and join clubs. Pick out the leaders and more capable individuals and get acquainted with them. Participate in groups by making a contribution. Make use of your talents. Others will respect you for your talents if they know about them. If your objective is to get into several campus activities, join more clubs and repeat the process. You will find more in common with members and feel more at home

[1] George Wigand, "Adaptiveness and the Role of Parents in Academic Success," *Personnel and Guidance Journal,* April 1957.

in some organizations than in others. You will meet many students with different experiences and backgrounds, which will broaden your understanding of both the organizations and the student body of the institution.

Some suggestions that will help get you started toward successful adjustment to college are:

Having:
- A cheery personality
- A sense of humor
- A neat appearance
- A liking for people
- The ability to remember names

Being:
- A good conversationalist
- Courteous and tactful
- Considerate of others

Fraternities and Sororities. To pledge or not to pledge will be the question. By joining, you will enjoy the advantages of belonging to a group. If you are elected early to membership in these organizations, the members can help you get into the swing of things. They will help you break the "social ice" by introducing you to members of other organizations. Many fraternities have "sister" sororities that serve as a ready-made source of dates. The disadvantages of joining are cost and time. If you can afford extra expenditures and are interested in joining, do so if you have the opportunity. Should you not get a bid to pledge or not be interested in joining a fraternity or sorority, remember that there is no shortage of good independent organizations on the campus.

Balancing Your Time Budget

"Wow! I am finally free. I am on my own. No one is around to tell me what to do. I can make my own decisions. I can get up when I want to, eat when I want to, and go where I want to. I can do as I please." This is the kind of thinking that has caused many a classroom seat to become prematurely vacant. You are in college because you have demonstrated your academic ability. In college, you will demonstrate your level of maturity by wisely budgeting your time between academic and social activities.

Colleges offer many cultural, recreational, and social activities for development of the students enrolled, but study is the "work" of students. Take an inventory of the items for which you must budget time:

1. Sleeping and eating
2. Studying and attending classes
3. Shopping and personal care
4. Working
5. Attending cultural, social and recreational activities

These activities help you become a more mature person, but they do not contribute equally toward academic success in college. Students don't usually flunk out of college because they budget too much time to organized social and recreational activities, but because they allot too little time to their studies. The wise student uses most of his time for academic purposes, even though cultural, social, and recreational development is important. Because you are in college for academic success, not social success, be selective in your social and recreational activities. If you attend a large university, you won't be able to attend them all, so don't try. Participate in the ones that are of most interest to you, area to which you can make a contribution or in which you need further development.

are associated with your career field, and are in an

The best advice that a college freshman can get for avoiding academic difficulty is not to get behind in course work. The pace set in most college courses is much faster than that in high school. You spend less time in college classes but are expected to spend more time out of class preparing for each course. It is presumed that you are in school to learn, and that you are interested in applying yourself to that end. Also, it is taken for granted that some selectivity in admissions has taken place and that only mature and capable students are enrolled. When a college student starts cutting class and fails to turn in assigned work, he has taken the first steps toward making room for another student. Successful students do the amount of work needed to learn the material, and adjust their schedule to that requirement. Following a time budget is an effective safeguard against getting behind in your studies.

Learn today's lesson today — this is one of the best principles you can follow in college. When students get behind by letting assignments slip by or by not reading the assigned material they compound their problem. In most beginning college courses, learning to understand concepts, facts, terms, and principles is one of the reasons for assignments. Later in the course or in other courses, you will be asked to use these terms by applying what you have learned. Should you not have learned the concepts, terms, facts, and principles well, it will soon be known to both you and the professor. The problem is no different in the sciences than it is in the fine arts. You can't work chemical equations until you have mastered the basic concepts; you can't learn music without learning to read the notes. To get behind in your school work is to cheat yourself.

In planning your time, use common sense. Budgeting time for a balanced program of campus activities means scheduling an adequate amount of time for the more important activities. You may find it helpful to write out a schedule to plan your activities, both academic and nonacademic. Use a typical college schedule, continuing the hours until 10 P.M. Block in your classes and the period you work. Next, schedule regular study periods. It is wise to have some reserve time for work on term papers and difficult assignments. Lastly, schedule other events.

Daily Work and Recreation Schedule

Hours	Monday	Tuesday	Wednesday	Thursday	Friday	Saturday	Sunday
6-7							
7-8	Breakfast	Breakfast	Breakfast	Breakfast	Breakfast		
8-9	English	Speech	English	Speech	English	Breakfast	Breakfast
9-10	Gov't.		Gov't.		Gov't.	Work	
10-11	Botany	Sociology	Botany	Sociology	Botany	Work	Sunday school
11-12							Church
12-1	Lunch	Lunch	Lunch	Lunch	Lunch	Lunch	Lunch
1-2	Phys. Ed.	Botany Lab.		Botany Lab.	Phys. Ed.	Study	Study
2-3		Botany Lab.		Botany Lab.		Shopping	Recreation
3-4	Work	Study	Work	Study	Work		
4-5	Work	and Free	Work	and Free	Work		
5-6	Relax	Relax	Relax	Relax	Relax		
6-7	Dinner	Dinner	Dinner	Dinner	Dinner	Dinner	Dinner
7-8		Study	Study	Library	Basketball		Church group
8-9	Club Meeting	Study	Study		Game	Movies	
9-10	Personal	Personal	Personal	Personal			
10-11							
11-12							
12-1							
1-2							
2-3							
3-4							
4-5							

Learning and Relearning to Study

This is not the opposite of studying to learn, and it is not a play on words. It is a statement that will stand on its own merits. It is possible that you have not learned how to study well enough to succeed in college. This is true of so many students that colleges are offering courses on the subject.

It has never been more important for college students to know how to study than it is today. College work is getting harder, not easier. There is competition among students for college seats, and competition will increase as an increasing number of students apply for college. As college standards rise, the road leading to a college degree will get rougher. You will find good study habits essential to earning high grades in college.

You must learn how to study if you are to keep up with the pace set in most college courses. If you are to learn to work mathematical equations, you must work mathematical problems using these equations. If you are to learn to evaluate chemical processes, you must evaluate chemical processes. If you are to learn to write English themes, you must practice writing English themes. If you are to learn to use principles of economics, you must acquire an understanding of economic principles. If you are to learn to read authoritative opinions and interpret them, you must gain experience in doing so. In short, if you are to learn to study, you must do so by studying.

Efficient use of study time and effective study habits make the difference between academic success and failure. Specific things you can do to improve your chances for success are arranging for and organizing effective study habits and time, being an alert listener, taking adequate and meaningful notes, learning to read with speed and comprehension, and learning to write themes and term papers. Ways to better your ability to take tests are found in "Taking Examinations," p. 147.

Here are some suggestions on how to study:

1. Arrange for a time and place for study. Have a regular place for study—and study. If you study in a dormitory, keep your desk clear of distracting objects. Your desk should be well lighted (you will find that not all dormitory rooms have this characteristic). Your books and study materials should be arranged in an easily accessible location. When studying, it will be best to keep the record player and radio turned off.
2. Be certain of your assignments. You will find it helpful to take assignments down in your notebook. Don't rely on penciled notes in the margin of your texts. Should you be in doubt about an assignment, don't guess; ask the professor. Few things are more discouraging and demoralizing to a student than to spend hours in preparing an assignment, only to find that it was not what the professor wanted. To insure against this, make a list of things that must be done for your courses. During the time set aside for study, check them off as you complete them. In this way, you will be more organized in your studies.
3. Do your own work. No one can learn for you. If you copy an assignment, or have your roommate work a difficult problem for you, it is you, not the professor, who will be cheated. Seek all the advice you want, review all the resources available, make use of dictionaries and encyclopedias, but do your own work.
4. Do your hardest school work first. Hard mental work consumes more energy than easy work, and difficult college study requires that you be mentally alert. Thus, it makes good sense to complete your most difficult assignment first. If necessary, give extra time to difficult assignments by resisting the temptation to go to the student union or other campus "haunts" when there is studying to be done.
5. Budget your study time. It assures that you will have time allotted to all assignments, and that nothing is overlooked. You will become more concerned with some courses and more interested in others. Do not spend all your time on a favorite course, or on the most difficult one either. Budgeting your study time will effectively distribute your study efforts among your assignments.

Most of what you learn in college courses will come through class and laboratory studies and assigned readings. Both of these require an ability to take useful notes to aid retention of subject matter and to recall facts and information. Notes should represent the more important things to be learned in the courses you take.

Most college courses include more information than do high school courses. To discuss the major points of a subject in the allotted time, most professors use the lecture method. The best advice for students in lecture courses is to pay attention, stay alert, and take a set of meaningful notes. Professors give clues to what they feel is most important by saying, "the point to be remembered is," "in the first place," etc. Also, if the professor uses the blackboard, this is your cue that something important is being presented.

Some students do not find lecture courses interesting. A few minutes of review and reflection will increase your interest in the lecture, save hours of study, and increase your understanding. Reviewing the assignments prior to attending class will cause you to be more sensitive to the important points made in the lecture. If you read ahead, and review and raise questions that need answering, you will find that you will be more alert to the principles, facts, and relationships the professor is trying to communicate to you.

Notes taken in a lecture should not be a repetition of what the professor has said. Your notes should include the most important things that are mentioned, but they should be written in your words, not the professor's. This practice will help you recall greater bodies of course content, and will force you to be more alert, thus more interested, in a lecture.

Students have varying degrees of skill in taking notes. What are good notes for you may not be good for your roommate. It will be necessary for you to work out your own personal system. The important thing is that they be useful to you. Usually, the more skillful note-takers write well-organized notes. Most professors lecture from organized notes; therefore, you can follow his organization. A standard form is shown, but you should use one that is suitable to your own needs and habits, and your courses.

I.
  A.
  B.
  C.
    1.
    2.
    3.
      a.
      b.
      c.
        (1)
        (2)
        (3)
          (a)
          (b)
          (c)
II Etc.

Do you like to read? Do you understand what you read? How fast do you read? Much of what you will learn in college will be gained through reading. Not only will you be expected to read textbooks but reference books and other assorted materials. Courses in English, economics, sociology, government, history, are "reading" courses. In these courses you will be assigned large reading assignments and be expected to read rapidly and understand what you read without difficulty. Good students have the ability to organize what they read and what they hear into meaningful knowledge in terms of their experiences.

The way one reads varies according to purpose and subject matter. When you read for enjoyment you read differently than when you are studying a class assignment. You don't read a novel the same way that you read a textbook. When you survey written material to find information for a term paper, you skim it until you find a fruitful area and then slow down and read more carefully. You read easy material faster than you read difficult material. All this is to point out that your reading speed and the degree to which you absorb what you read depends on the nature of the reading material and the purpose you have for reading it.

You can learn to read faster, more accurately, and with greater understanding. Fast readers usually understand and remember what they read. With proper train-

ing, many students can learn to double their reading speed and increase their understanding up to 50 percent. Some colleges have reading and study skills laboratories for the benefit of interested students. Should you take advantage of such an opportunity, the amount of improvement you can expect will depend on your desire to change, your willingness to adopt and practice new techniques, and your persistence in and out of the laboratory.

Reading is both a physical and mental process. You can improve your reading skill, but you must master certain techniques. To increase speed in reading, you must change some of your physical habits associated with reading. Your mind is capable of "reading" faster than your lips and so you should not pronounce words as you read them. When a person's eye span increases from words to phrases and lines, reading speed is usually increased. To understand what you have read, you must look for signals or cues of what the writer is trying to tell you. To do this, you first should understand the total purpose of what you are to read by looking over the general plan of the book in the table of contents, reviewing the subheadings and introductory and summary paragraphs in chapters, and reading topic sentence. You also need to increase your vocabulary to read the material for meaning, with purpose, organization, and complete picture in mind. Look for author's bias, principles, facts, and relationships; for example, price-demand in economics, people-behavior in sociology, and theme-character in literature.

The ability to write well is a skill required of college students. Your writing ability, or lack of it, will be brought into sharp focus in your term papers, themes, and other written assignments. Written work broadens your understanding of a subject area, tests how well you understand reading assignments, applies what you have learned in and out of class, and tests your ability to express yourself precisely, concisely, and logically in acceptable English form and literary style.

Students who were not required to develop these abilities in high school may experience difficulty in college. In fact, poor preparation in grammar and style is one of the greatest stumbling blocks to college success. Should written expression pose a problem for you, ask your English teacher to recommend one or two of the several excellent guides to clear writing.

For written assignments, research the topic well and you should find sufficient material for a paper. Encyclopedias, library card catalogs, *Reader's Guide to Periodical Literature, Educational Index,* and scholarly journals are good places to begin your search for information. The librarian will be of help, too. As you collect your information, record the source, author, publisher's name, and the date of publication, to use in giving credit to original sources in footnotes and bibliographies. After reading your material, outline the major points you wish to present. Then organize your material for the specific purpose of the assignment. Draft your theme or paper, using words you understand. Most students find it desirable to revise themes one or more times to improve organization, sentence structure, and grammar and to correct spelling and other errors. Some students find it a good practice to set the paper aside for a day or so and then reread it. In the rereading, they raise questions such as: "Is the central idea sound?" "Is it well organized?" "Does the paper say what I want it to say?" "Does it have errors in punctuation, spelling, or grammar?" "Is it what the professor wanted?" Is the paper well organized, neat, and acceptable?"

The appearance of a paper can either hurt or help your grades. If you write well and use a typewriter, you may benefit from a "halo" effect. In most colleges, typewritten papers are almost mandatory. Neatness and a smooth writing style are not substitutes for content, but to an overworked professor who grades dozens of papers each week, a neat theme that is easy to read has a good chance of receiving a better mark than one that is in scrawled handwriting, is poorly typed and clipped together and has bad form in the bibliography and footnotes — even if they should say the same thing. If you improve the appearance of your term papers and themes, your grades will improve.

There are very good reasons why you should get to know your professors. Many students, particularly in large universities and colleges, are hesitant to talk with their professors because classes are so large that students may feel the professor does not know them. However, if you should find yourself slowly but surely slipping into academic "hot water," schedule a conference with your professor to give him an opportunity to diagnose the reasons you are having difficulty, and to suggest ways you may improve in his class. Be sincere and discuss your problems frankly. He probably knows more about your problems than you do. Indicate your willingness to improve. Professors like to find students who are willing to exert the necessary energy to overcome initial difficulties and are interested enough to ask intelligent questions about the subject areas they teach. The fact that you have had the initiative to visit him is a mark in your favor. While professors have high standards, they are also human enough to admire, if not pull a little for, persevering students.

There are other values to talking with professors. A conference will allow you to get to know the professor better, and he you. If the class is large, a conference is the only way that you can become Bill Brown instead of student X who sits near the back of the classroom. There is also a psychological advantage for those students who give professors an opportunity to get to know who they are, who ask their assistance in improving, and, perhaps most important, who show that they are willing to exert initiative and show interest by visiting their professors.

Taking Examinations

The best way to pass examinations is to be prepared. Get to know your material well.

Keep up with your daily assignments, review each week's work, and look for the perspective of each course. Fitting the parts into the entire course will help you develop a sense of security and self-confidence that will equalize the inevitable jitters on test day.

Plan your studies; don't rely on cramming for tests. You can't learn during a weekend what you should have learned during a semester. Your brain will not "sponge up" knowledge that fast. Learning is a long-range process, and if you rely on cramming, you may be disappointed on test day.

You recognize that teachers use examinations to evaluate how much students have learned. They have value for students, too. Tests let you know how well you are progressing. More important, however, tests cause you to organize the material presented in class and review it in a new perspective. You are forced to reconstruct what you have learned by rearranging the parts of the course. Basically, tests are of two kinds: objective tests, which require you to write short answers, complete multiple-choice questions and statements, or sentences, declare statements true or false, or match definitions; and essay tests, which will reveal your ability to think logically and critically, analyze situations, and give time sequences as well as to recall factual information.

Plan your strategy for taking examinations by thinking about the kinds of questions that you anticipate will be asked. It will certainly help if you have visited with your professor to discuss the course. He will assist you in learning what he wants on tests and what his personal expectations are. Another way to anticipate test questions is to study with a small group of students by exchanging ideas and asking each other questions about the course material. If you expect an essay question, each student can prepare a few questions to be discussed by the study group. You can prepare for an objective test in the same way, with each student preparing ten to twenty questions. This kind of study will do much to bolster your confidence and, more important, it is a good learning technique and good preparation for taking exams.

Don't build up a mass of unrelated facts, dates, and people. This will only give you a cluttered mind and a poor grade. Research shows that students who prepare for essay questions do better on examinations, even when objective tests are given. Objective examinations test your ability to recall specific facts, but you need to know them to do well on essay questions also. Review your notes and assignments with special emphasis on important facts, concepts, definitions, and relationships. Make all this accumulated knowledge meaningful by looking for patterns of information that reveal principles. Review exercises to learn processes, procedures, and formulas that may be asked or used on test questions. Periodically, practice the type of problems that you anticipate being included.

The only sure way of passing a test is to be certain of the knowledge it will call for. For most students, this means an organized plan of systematic study throughout the semester. Studying should become more intense during the few days prior to a test for the purpose of organizing what you have learned in the course and drilling on what you have not learned. Planned studying will ease your mind about taking tests. During a test, be calm, deliberate, and methodical in completing it. If you feel yourself becoming tense, slow down and keep control. A change in your sitting position helps ease tension. If necessary, stop completely and take a deep breath, close your eyes, and then completely relax for two or three minutes. You may feel a sense of urgency about completing the test, but taking a break during an exam may be time well spent.

When taking objective tests, you may find it helpful to follow this procedure:

1. Read directions carefully. Be sure you understand that instructions are for the total examination or for only parts of it.
2. Go through the test from the beginning, completing those questions you know, skipping those you do not know. Watch carefully for absolute words and statements such as all, never, none, always, etc. Concentrate on one question at a time.
3. Go through the test again, completing the questions that you passed over. In this way, you are assured of answering the questions you know within the time limit. If you are not penalized for guessing, complete all questions as time permits.

The recommended procedure for taking essay examinations is much the same:

1. Read the directions carefully. On essay tests, you will be asked to define, describe, illustrate, compare, explain, interpret, and summarize. Each requires a different answer. Be certain of what is expected.
2. Budget your time. Check the number and point value of questions. Read them. Note if a choice of questions is given. This will give you some idea of how much time you should allow for each. Pace yourself.
3. Think before you write. Concentrate only on one question. This will eliminate jitters and assure speed. Jot down on scratch paper the key points you wish to make. Organize your statements into the best possible sequence. Using precise, concise, and clear terms, write your answer as completely as possible. Leave space for additional statements, and move to the next question.
4. Forget the question you just answered and concentrate on the next one. Follow the same procedure for the rest of the test, answering all the questions you can. You should skip the more difficult questions and come back to them after completing the ones you know. You will save time on the easier questions and allow more time for the harder ones.
5. As time permits, reread the questions and answers. Give consideration to completeness, correctness, wording, spelling, punctuation, and grammar. If there are relationships between questions, or if you have more to add, includes it in the space you provided.

Chapter Twelve

College
With
Open Doors

The following list of colleges with openings for freshmen and transfer students was compiled from a list of more than two thousand four-year accredited colleges and universities. Each college was chosen because it gives consideration to average students, seeks students from other geographic areas, and will increase the number of students to be admitted during the 1966–67 academic year.

There are valid reasons why openings exist at good colleges. For some, it is because geographic location is away from urban centers and main lines of transportation. For many, it is the result of a healthy program of continuing growth and development.

The post-World War II baby boom is still affecting the phenomenon we call the college enrollment explosion. Circumstances and factors at individual schools can bring sudden changes in admissions policies. Remember, too, that this list is by no means complete and that there are many other good colleges and universities for you to consider.

Colleges with Openings

State	Name of college and location

Alabama
  Athens College, Athens
  Jacksonville State College, Jacksonville
  Oakwood College, Huntsville

Alaska
  University of Alaska, College

Arizona
  University of Arizona, Tucson

Arkansas
  Arkansas College, Batesville
  Arkansas Polytechnic College, Russellville
  Southern State College, Magnolia

California
  California State Colleges, at Fullerton and Long Beach
  Chapman College, Orange
  Northrop Institute of Technology, Inglewood
  Pepperdine College, Los Angeles
  University of California: Los Angeles, Riverside, and Santa Barbara (branches)

Colorado
  Adams State College, Alamosa
  Colorado State College, Greeley
  Colorado Woman's College, Denver
  Western State College, Gunnison

Connecticut
  w Annhurst College, Woodstock
  Southern Connecticut State College, New Haven
  m Wesleyan University, Middletown

Delaware
    Delaware State College, Dover

District of Columbia
    Catholic University of America
    District of Columbia Teachers College

Florida
    Florida Memorial College, St. Augustine
    Jacksonville University, Jacksonville
    University of Tampa, Tampa

Georgia
    Berry College, Mt. Berry
    Oglethorpe College, Atlanta
    West Georgia College, Carrollton

Hawaii
    University of Hawaii, Honolulu

Idaho
    College of Idaho, Caldwell

Illinois
    Bradley University, Peoria
    Elmhurst College, Elmhurst
    Illinois Institute of Technology, Chicago
    Millikin University, Decatur
 w Mundelein College, Chicago
    Quincy College, Quincy

Indiana
    Butler University, Indianapolis
    Evansville College, Evansville
    Indiana State University, Terre Haute

Iowa
    Central College, Pella
    Parsons College, Fairfield
    University of Iowa, Iowa City

Kansas
    College of Emporia, Emporia
    Kansas State University, Manhattan
    Ottawa University, Ottawa
    Tabor College, Hillsboro

Kentucky
    Eastern Kentucky State College, Richmond
    Kentucky Wesleyan College, Owensboro
    University of Kentucky, Lexington

Louisiana
    Louisiana College, Pineville
    Louisiana State University and A&M College,
        Baton Rouge
    Northeast Louisiana State College, Monroe

Maine
    Bates College, Lewiston

Maryland
    Maryland State College, Princess Anne
    Western Maryland College, Westminster

Massachusetts
 m Amherst College, Amherst
    Lowell Technological Institute, Lowell
    Northeastern University, Boston
    State Colleges at Boston, Framingham, and Lowell

Michigan
    Eastern Michigan University, Ypsilanti
    Northern Michigan University, Marquette
    University of Detroit, Detroit
    Wayne State University, Detroit
    Western Michigan University, Kalamazoo

Minnesota
    Bemidji State College, Bemidji
    Mankato State College, Mankato
    Moorhead State College, Moorhead
    University of Minnesota, Minneapolis

Mississippi
    Millsaps College, Jackson
    University of Mississippi, University
    University of Southern Mississippi, Hattiesburg

Missouri
    Central Missouri State College, Warrensburg
    Missouri Valley College, Marshall
    St. Louis University, St. Louis
    University of Missouri at Rolla
 m Westminster College, Fulton

Montana
    College of Great Falls, Great Falls
    Eastern Montana College and Rocky Mountain
        College, Billings

Nebraska
    Creighton University, Omaha
    Hastings College, Hastings
    Nebraska Wesleyan University, Lincoln

Nevada
    University of Nevada, Reno

New Hampshire
    Plymouth State College, Plymouth

New Jersey
    Bloomfield College, Bloomfield
    Drew University, Madison
    Monmouth College, West Long Branch
    Upsala College, East Orange

New Mexico
    Eastern New Mexico University, Portales
    University of Albuquerque, Albuquerque

New York
  Alfred University, Alfred
  Fordham University, Bronx
  Hofstra University, Hempstead
  Niagara University, Niagara
  Pace College, Manhattan
  Pratt Institute, Brooklyn
  Syracuse University, Syracuse
  Wagner College, Staten Island

North Carolina
  North Carolina College at Durham
  St. Augustine's College, Raleigh
  Winston-Salem State College, Winston-Salem

North Dakota
  North Dakota State University, Fargo

Ohio
  Bowling Green State University, Bowling Green
  Defiance College, Defiance
  Muskingum College, New Concord
  University of Akron, Akron
  Wilberforce University, Wilberforce

Oklahoma
  Northeastern State College, Tahlequah
  Northwestern State College, Alva
  Oklahoma State University, Stillwater
  University of Tulsa, Tulsa

Oregon
  Cascade College, Portland
  Oregon College of Education, Monmouth
  Southern Oregon College, Ashland

Pennsylvania
  Alliance College, Cambridge Springs
  Lebanon Valley College, Annville
  Lincoln University, Lincoln University
  Lock Haven State College, Lock Haven
  Thiel College, Greenville
  University of Pittsburgh, Pittsburgh

Rhode Island
  Rhode Island University, Kingston

South Carolina
  Furman University, Greenville
  South Carolina State College, Orangeburg
  m Wofford College, Spartanburg

South Dakota
  Black Hills State College, Spearfish
  Northern State College, Aberdeen

South Dakota University, Brookings
Southern State College, Springfield
Yankton College, Yankton

Tennessee
  George Peabody College for Teachers, Nashville
  Lincoln Memorial University, Harrogate
  Milligan College, Milligan College

Texas
  Howard Payne College, Brownwood
  McMurry College, Abilene
  Sam Houston State College, Huntsville
  Texas Southern University, Houston
  University of Dallas, Dallas

Utah
  University of Utah, Salt Lake City
  Utah State University, Logan

Vermont
  m Norwich University, Northfield
  Windham College, Putney

Virginia
  Hampden-Sydney College, Hampden-Sydney
  Old Dominion College, Norfolk
  Roanoke College, Salem
  Virginia State College, Petersburg

Washington
  Central Washington State College, Ellensburg
  Eastern Washington State College, Cheney
  Seattle University, Seattle
  Whitworth College, Spokane

West Virginia
  Davis and Elkins College, Elkins
  Glenville State College, Glenville
  West Virginia State College, Institute

Wisconsin
  Dominican College, Racine
  Lakeland College, Sheboygan
  Marquette University, Milwaukee
  Northland College, Ashland
  Wisconsin State University: Eau Claire,
    La Crosse, and Platteville (branches)

Wyoming
  University of Wyoming, Laramie

Code: *m*—for men only
         w—for women only

Bibliography

American Association of Collegiate Registrars and Admissions Officers. *Credit Given,* 1966 annual ed. Washington, D.C.: American Council on Education.

Bloom, Benjamin S. and Frank R. Peters. *The Use of Academic Prediction Scales for Counseling and Selecting College Entrants.* New York: Glencoe Free Press, Inc., 1961.

Bowles, Frank H., *How to Get Into College.* New York: E. P. Dutton & Co., Inc., 1960.

Brownstein, Samuel C., Weiner, Mitchell, and Kaplan, Stanley. *You Can Win A Scholarship.* New York: Barron's Educational Series, Inc., 1956.

Bulger, Paul G. "Financial Realities and Resources," *Student Personnel Work as Deeper Teaching,* Esther Lloyd-Jones and Margaret Ruth Smith, eds. New York: Harper & Row, 1954.

Burckel, Christian E. *College Blue Book 1959,* 9th ed. Yonkers, New York: Christian E. Burckel.

College Facts Chart. Spartanburg, South Carolina: The National Beta Club, 1959.

College Scholarship Service. *Manual for Financial Aid Officers.* Princeton, New Jersey: College Entrance Examination Board, 1965.

"The Counselor's Handbook—A Guide to the Student Work Program at Southern Illinois University." Carbondale, Illinois: Southern Illinois University, 1960.

Chandler, John R. and others. *Successful Adjustment to College.* New Jersey: Prentice-Hall, Inc., 1958.

Craig, W. Bradford. *How to Finance a College Education.* New York: Holt, Rinehart & Winston, Inc., 1959.

D'Amico, Louis A. *Higher Education: Basic Student Charges, 1963-64.* (U.S. Office of Education, Circular 755.) Washington, D.C.: U.S. Government Printing Office, 1964.

DeYoung, Chris A. and Wynn, Richard. *American Education,* 5th ed. New York: McGraw-Hill, Inc., 1964.

Gardner, K. E. "Too Few Students Finish College." (Illinois Research, III, No. 4, Agricultural Experiment Station.) Urbana: University of Illinois, 1962.

Hawes, Gene R. *The New American Guide to Colleges,* 2nd ed. New York: The New American Library and Columbia University Press, 1962.

Henderson, Algo D. *Policies and Practices in Higher Education.* New York: Harper & Row, 1960.

Hill, W. W. *Credit for College: Student Loan Funds in the United States.* Indiana: The College Life Insurance Company of America, 1959.

Hoffman, Banesh. *The Tyranny of Testing.* New York: Crowell-Collier Press, 1962.

Hollis, Ernest V. and associates. *Cost of Attending College.* (Bulletin 1957, No. 9, U.S. Office of Education.) Washington, D.C.: U.S. Government Printing Office, 1958.

Knoell, Dorothy M. "Focus on the Transfer Program," *Junior College Journal.* May 1965.

Lansing, John B., Lorimer, Thomas, and Moriguchi, Chikashi. *How People Pay for College.* Ann Arbor: University of Michigan Press, 1960.

McKee, Richard C. "College and University Aid for Students," *College Aid for Students.* (U.S. Office of Education.) Washington, D.C.: U.S. Government Printing Office, 1965.

Morgan, Thomas B. "The Class of '68," *Look.* September 22, 1964, pp. 19-33.

National Education Association. "It Pays to Go to School," *Research Bulletin.* Vol. 38, No. 4. Washington, D.C.: National Education Association, 1960.

National Education Association. *Your Child and College.* Washington, D.C.: National Education Association, 1962.

National Vocational Guidance Association. *How to Visit College.* Washington, D.C.: National Vocation Guidance Association, 1960.

"Reports of Temporary Commission on the Need for a State University." Legislative Document No. 33. Albany: New York State Department of Education, 1948.

Sanford, Nevitt, ed. *The American College.* New York: John Wiley & Sons, Inc., 1962.

Smith, George B. "Who Would Be Eliminated? A Study of Selective Admissions to College with an Addendum: The Class of 1958," *Kansas Studies in Education.* December 1956.

Smith, Richard W. and Snethen, Howard P. *Four Big Years.* Indianapolis: The Bobbs-Merrill Co., Inc., 1960.

Sulkin, Sidney. *Complete Planning for College.* New York: McGraw-Hill, Inc., 1962.

U. S. Department of Health, Education, and Welfare. *Education Directory, Part III, Higher Education,* 1964-65 annual ed. Washington, D.C.: Government Printing Office.

Department of Health, Education, and Welfare. *National Defense Student Loan Program; Manual of General Information and Instructions.* Washington, D.C.: Office of Education, 1959-60.

Wigand, George. "Adaptiveness and the Role of Parents in Academic Success," *Personnel and Guidance Journal.* April 1957.

Wolfle, Dael L. *America's Resource of Specialized Talent.* (Commission on Human Resources and Advanced Training.) New York: Harper & Row, 1954.

Wood, Helen. "What's Ahead for College Graduates," *Occupational Outlook Quarterly.* III, No. 4. Washington, D.C.: Department of Labor, December 1959.

Wren, Gilbert C. *The Counselor in a Changing World.* Washington: American Personnel and Guidance Association, 1963.

Wilkins, Theresa B. *Financial Aid for College Students: Undergraduate, 1957-58.* No. 18. (Office of Education.) Washington, D.C.: Department of Health, Education, and Welfare.